W9-CUJ-222

DIRECTING TECHNOLOGY

Directing Technology

POLICIES FOR PROMOTION AND CONTROL

Edited by

RON JOHNSTON and PHILIP GUMMETT

ST. MARTIN'S PRESS   NEW YORK

Copyright © 1979 Ron Johnston and Philip Gummett

All rights reserved. For information write:
St. Martin's Press Inc., 175 Fifth Avenue, New York, N.Y. 10010
Printed in Great Britain
ISBN 0-312-212186
First published in the United States of America in 1979.

Library of Congress Cataloging in Publication Data

Main entry under title:

Directing technology

    Includes index.
    1. Technology and state – Congresses. I. Johnston,
Ron. II. Gummett, Philip.
T6.D57 1979   309.2'12   78-26073
ISBN 0-312-21218-6

78-26073

Printed and bound in Great Britain

CONTENTS

CONTENTS

INTRODUCTION

Philip Gummett and Ron Johnston

There is nothing new about technology itself, nor about the existence of calls that it be directed to what, in various senses, can be regarded as socially useful ends. In the past decade, however, criticism has been growing about the effects which increasingly sophisticated, capital-intensive, resource consumptive and 'less natural' technologies are having, or might conceivably have, on such matters as the quality of human life and the economic or military security of nations. It is the very ubiquity of these kinds of technology that is the basis for society being commonly regarded as more 'technological' today than in the past, and for the urgency of calls for renewed efforts to direct technology to socially useful ends.

'Technology' is a term with many meanings, of which Roy[1] has distinguished three general types: technology as a body of organised knowledge; as the products of organised knowledge; and as the activity of applying organised knowledge. It is distinguished from other forms of knowledge under the first definition, by being 'the science of the industrial arts',[2] and under the second, by its goal as the production of

> any tool or technique, product or process, any physical equipment or method of doing by which human capability is extended.[3]

We will use the term in all these senses, but with some qualifications. First, as Nisbet notes:

> we are prone to think of technology in its physical manifestations — skyscrapers, lawn mowers, nuclear bombs — but technology represents social things as well — organisations and processes concerned with human ends.[4]

Technology is not merely a matter of physical and social hardware, but a force which permeates our political, economic and social systems. Second, although in this book we focus mainly on civilian industrially oriented technologies, we should not forget the tremendous importance of technologies in the military, agricultural and medical spheres. Finally, while we may use the term loosely, we should remember that technology is not a unitary entity, and that different *technologies* may have quite distinct characteristics; they should not be regarded as uniformly creating the same problems and possibilities, nor as responding identically to the same modes of social direction.

The Call for Direction of Technology

With growing awareness of the central role of technology in industrialised societies the acceptability of the proposition that technology implies progress has increasingly been doubted. An unlikely unity of purpose between those concerned to control the harmful effects of technology and those seeking to relate it more efficiently to economic and defence objectives succeeded in propagating the view that technology should emerge from its 'wild west frontier' era and enter a new age of purposive direction.

This emphasis on direction is often a reaction to apparent powerlessness in the face of technology, rooted in an acceptance of technological determinism. But though technology may seem to be the uncontrollable or self-driven motor of social change (witness the current promise and threat of microprocessors), we contend that it does not develop of its own accord, nor does a particular technology impose itself inevitably on society. As Elliott and Elliott argue:

> There are quite clearly social, political and economic pressures which influence technology: it is not the sole determinant of social processes.[5]

Hartland and Gibbons (chapter 5) demonstrate clearly that individual technologies arise neither according to their own ineluctable logic, nor in accordance with the master plan of a single dominant interest. Rather, they emerge from a complex interaction between a variety of political, economic and social needs and constraints, on the one hand, and technical potentials on the other.

In what senses, then, can we speak of the direction of technology? First, we may speak of the direction in which technology is going (direction *of*); this refers to attempts to introduce into the complex process through which new technologies emerge (or fail to emerge) a sense of social purpose, broadly defined. These attempts are concerned to stimulate, or promote, certain kinds of technological development, and to regulate, or control, others.

To speak of social purpose, even broadly defined, is, however, to raise a contentious point: whose social purposes have we in mind? A

second meaning of direction of technology (direction *by*) is concerned
with the processes through which social goals are established and
technological potentials related to them. For some, the market provides
the medium through which those processes may flow. Others argue
that governmental involvement is essential, while still others advocate
a greater role for direct public participation in such forms as industrial
democracy, public hearings about new developments, and public
interest representatives on governmental committees. While the
distinction between 'direction of' and 'direction by' may appear only
of analytical value, one could suggest that much of the heat in some
contemporary debates about the development of technology (such as
nuclear energy) is due to a failure to make that distinction. Thus
proponent institutions may be concerned with establishing the
technological goals towards which they wish to work, whereas objectors
may be more concerned with the way in which social (and
technological) goals are set.

The direction of technology within industry is long established, and
the wealth of literature on the management of research and
development, innovation and the diffusion of technologies indicates
the intensity of efforts being made to improve this process. In the
industrialised countries, however, responsibility for the level and
consequences of technological activity has increasingly been vested in
government. That they have arguably been ill-equipped for this role
may be seen from the fact that most governmental decisions in this
area have been *ad hoc* and reactive. The process of developing a
coherent intellectual framework on which to base policies for the
direction of technology has only recently begun. The object of this
book is to assist this process by analysing the development of
mechanisms for government intervention in issues of technological
importance in various countries and providing detailed case studies
of the operation and effectiveness of those mechanisms in specific
cases.

Is Direction Necessary?

Governments have long accepted a role in the direction of technology
in certain areas. The importance of military technology to national
security has been recognised throughout history. Despite strenuous
opposition to government interference, the British public health
movement's success in passing legislation in the mid-nineteenth century
to improve water supply, sewage disposal and housing and factory
conditions, provided a model for action in many other countries. In

recognition of the importance of food supply, most governments have supported the development and diffusion of improved agricultural methods. Outside these few specific areas, government policy has consisted almost exclusively of what Freeman has labelled *laisser-innover*,[6] i.e. the economist's emphasis on the sovereignty of the market has been accepted as a basis for inaction.

In the past thirty years, however, there has emerged a variety of new forces for increased government involvement. The first of these is the growth in the scale of capital investment required in new and particularly 'high' technology. Galbraith[7] has argued that individual corporations can no longer raise the necessary capital or accept the high risk involved in the development of new technology, and it therefore falls to government to take over this role. This has been contested (Pavitt, chapter 1) but nevertheless it would be difficult to find a single government of an industrialised nation that does not assist industrial development in one way or another.

A second factor has been international and transnational pressure. Many of the actions of government have been induced by increasing international competition, whether it be to support export drives, protect a national industry through tariffs, or ameliorate the effects of the rundown of a traditional industry through retraining grants. The spread of multinational corporations has presented a potential threat to governmental sovereignty in certain areas of policy. Supranational alliances such as the EEC have been responsible for the formulation of new regulations and standards. The fact that pollution does not respect national boundaries and the heightened awareness of interdependence which was created by the 1973 energy crisis have served to emphasise the international context of, and hence the need for, government involvement in many problems with a major technological element.

A third factor has been the growing criticism of technology as a disruptive, alienating and largely anti-human force. It has been seen as responsible for environmental depredation, increasing health and safety hazards, alienation of workers, the growth of barren, materialistic life styles and the reduction of personal freedom. The anti-technology movement has focused particularly on the development of technology for the control of man, whether through the computer's ability to acquire, store and process information about people, the growth of medical knowledge offering potential control not only of the physiological functioning but also of the genetic make-up of individuals, or the development of new techniques of psychological control. Some of these criticisms have taken the form of extremely naïve and even

anti-rational romantic reactions. Nevertheless, they have provided a
highly vocal contribution to the political pressure which led to
increased government involvement in the direction of technology – a
role incidentally which Western governments have been, on the whole,
not loath to accept.

Direction as Promotion and Control

The direction of technology involves two kinds of activity which, in a
sense, act against each other yet are also opposite sides of the same
coin. We refer to the activities of promoting and controlling technology,
the former referring to the encouragement of technology and the latter
to its regulation.

The distinction between these activities is not clear-cut. In practice,
to decide not to promote a technology is to control it; likewise, a
decision to promote one technology, by pre-empting scarce resources,
controls another. But the distinction does have an institutional reality
in the world of practical affairs which justifies its use as the principal
axis of this book. Thus, in the pursuit of greater public accountability,
governments frequently allocate responsibility for the promotion and
control of particular technologies to separate agencies. In the United
States, after some three decades of leaving responsibility for atomic
energy with the Atomic Energy Commission, the federal government
eventually allotted responsibility for promotion to the Energy Research
and Development Administration, and for control to the Nuclear
Regulatory Commission. In Britain, governmental sponsorship of
industrial innovation rests primarily with the Department of Industry,
but the Department of Employment controls the effects of such
innovation on health and safety in the work place; and while the
Department of Energy sponsors nuclear energy, the Department of the
Environment regulates the disposal of nuclear waste.

Promotion

Governments promote technology in large part because they have done
so in the past; all governments find themselves bound by prior
commitments which may be difficult or impossible to undo, and which
may lead to the expectation of further commitments along the same
lines in the future (as in the aircraft and shipbuilding industries of a
number of countries). Beyond this, however, governments promote
technology in particular sectors because this appears to them to be
important for the realisation of various national goals. The goal of
national security is one which, if it is to be met using nationally-

produced technology, requires governmental promotion of technology
since no other promoter is appropriate. Governments may also seek to
support the industrial sector, particularly in areas where the market
mechanism is regarded as working imperfectly. They may wish to
improve the nation's health, its environment, its communications
network or its agriculture so as to achieve various social or economic
goals. In at least some of these sectors, and increasingly in all, the
pressure to act will be international as well as national in origin.

There are two main ways in which governments promote technology.
The first is by performing or directly encouraging research and
development (R & D) and the second is by encouraging the utilisation
of new technology. Governments may arrange for research and
development to be done in their own laboratories or by outside
organisations under contract (as Gummett discusses in chapter 4).
They may also provide research funds for disbursement in the higher
education sector and through such organisations as the National Science
Foundation in the United States, or the research councils in Britain.
Finally, as Chapman shows (chapter 2), they may provide various
incentives to encourage industry to perform more R & D.

The utilisation of new technology may be encouraged by government
information schemes, as occurs in many countries in the agricultural
sector. Another, often underestimated, approach is through the
imposition of performance standards, of which a former permanent
secretary to the British Ministry of Technology has said:

> there is probably no central action which can contribute more to the
> general improvement of technology than the establishment of
> standards, and the reduction of variety and introduction of proper
> arrangements for quality assurance; for where performance standards
> exist, manufacturers must get the technology to enable them to
> meet them.[8]

Hartland and Gibbons (chapter 5) illustrate the importance of standards
and also of another promotional mechanism, that of government
procurement of advanced technological products. Other mechanisms
include governmental action to restructure certain sectors of industry,
and various forms of industrial subsidy, including direct support, tax
allowances on new capital goods and the use of the tariff barrier
(Pavitt, chapter 1, and Chapman, chapter 2).

The promotion of technology is not, however, free from difficulties.
Whatever the mechanisms chosen, there will inevitably be problems in

ensuring that information about them is effectively disseminated so
that it reaches all the potential beneficiaries (and not just the big
corporations which have efficient systems for gathering information of
this sort). Added to this will often be a measure of industrial suspicion
of governmental action: promotional schemes which are here today
may well be gone tomorrow, as the political wind changes, leaving
companies with partly completed investments which, under other
circumstances, might not have been begun.[9] Then there are the
questions of the competence of governmental bodies in selecting
technologies for direct support, the fears that they may ignore the less
glamorous technologies or that they may fail to assist mature industries
to avoid declining under international pressure (Stubbs, chapter 6), and
the worry that support for particular industries (aircraft, nuclear power)
may help to create political lobbies whose programmes may acquire
considerable momentum (Williams, chapter 3, and Pavitt, chapter 1)
and thereby remove themselves to some extent from public
accountability.

The record of direct intervention has not been marked by a high
level of success (Pavitt, chapter 1, and Stubbs, chapter 6) and it may
be that governments are limited to, and can act most effectively by,
indirect forms of intervention (Hartland and Gibbons, chapter 5;
Stubbs, chapter 6).

Control

In certain cases, an economic justification has been made for the
control of technology (Reppy, chapter 7). However, more commonly,
the argument for control has derived from public, professional and
governmental concern for the safety, wellbeing and rights of individuals.
These concerns, as we have already indicated, have arisen over such
issues as environmental pollution, health and safety at work, the use
of science and technology for the actual or potential curtailment of
civil liberties and the need to safeguard societies from domination by
experts. The mechanisms chosen for the control of technology reflect,
as Price argues (chapter 13) the political styles of particular societies.
They can be classified in terms of Nelkin's categories of participatory,
reactive and anticipatory controls,[10] noting of course that always
there are budgetary controls.

Participatory controls, according to Nelkin, involve the attempt by
citizen groups or so-called public interest scientists to influence
technological decisions and to do this in terms of community values.
Airport planning, aircraft noise, location of anti-ballistic missile sites,

and location of nuclear facilities are among the most notable types of issue on which such groups have acted. Interest is increasingly being shown nowadays in moving beyond piecemeal, *ad hoc* participation to the regular and continuing involvement of public interest or community representatives in decision-making in such fields as pesticide control (Gillespie, chapter 11) and pollution (Eva and Rothman, chapter 8). The more technically-minded trade unions may also have a growing role to play in the control of particular technologies, as Yoxen argues (chapter 12) in relation to recombinant genetics.

Reactive controls are generally those imposed by regulatory agencies and the courts, and represent the most traditional of Nelkin's three modes of control, while anticipatory controls, at least as represented by the more formal methods of technology assessment and technological forecasting, are perhaps the most novel. Hartland (chapter 10) discusses three approaches to the enhanced accountability of governments to legislatures which could well fall within the anticipatory mode, while Gibbons (chapter 9) links the anticipatory mode with the participatory through his concept of the technology assessment system, according to which serious attempts should be made to identify and involve all interested parties before beginning to evaluate a new technological development

As with promotion, so also with the control of technology there are many problems. Difficult judgements abound on, for instance, the acceptability of various kinds of risk. The participatory mode carries with it the fear of demagogy, the prospect of indefinite debate with no resultant decisions, and the problem of ensuring that potential participants have adequate access to information. The reactive mode, by definition, is often too late to prevent disasters (thalidomide; Seveso; various aircraft accidents) and involves difficult questions over the appropriate composition of regulatory boards, and over intragovernmental opposition between regulatory and promotional activities. The anticipatory mode raises the problem of *ex ante* analysis, of who should do the analysis, and of the political nature of technology assessment (Gibbons, chapter 9).

Finally, beyond all these considerations of institutions and techniques for the promotion and control of technology, lies the possibility that in themselves they may be insufficient to the problems faced by advanced industrial societies. Price (chapter 13) argues that what is also needed is a renewal of the meaning of 'politics', coupled with a conscious drive to develop the quality of human judgement. But whether in this wider sense of politics, or in the narrower sense in

which the term is more commonly used, this volume will have failed
in its intentions if it does not clearly demonstrate that the direction of
technology is, necessarily, a political process.

Notes

1. R. Roy, 'Social Control of Technology', *Control of Technology*, Unit 1
(Milton Keynes, Open University Press, 1978), p.14.

2. *Concise Oxford English Dictionary*; John Bigelow, a Harvard Professor who
coined the term in 1816, defined it as 'the application of science to the useful
arts'.

3. D. Schon, *Technology and Change* (London, Pergamon, 1967).

4. R. Nisbet, 'The Impact of Technology on Ethical Decision Making', in
J. Douglas (ed.), *The Technological Threat* (Englewood Cliffs, N.J, Prentice-Hall,
1971).

5. D. Elliott and R. Elliott, *The Control of Technology* (London, Wykeham
Publications, 1976), p.7.

6. C. Freeman, *The Economics of Industrial Innovation* (Harmondsworth,
Penguin, 1974), p.21.

7. J.K. Galbraith, *The New Industrial State* (Harmondsworth, Penguin, 1969).

8. Sir Richard Clarke, 'Mintech in Retrospect – II', *Omega*, vol.1 (2, 1973),
p.147.

9. A.H. Rubenstein, *et al.*, 'Management Perceptions of Government Incentives
to Technological Innovation in England, France, West Germany and Japan',
Research Policy, vol.6 (1977), pp.324-57.

10. Dorothy Nelkin, 'Technology and Public Policy', in Ina Spiegel-Rösing,
and Derek de Solla Price, (eds.), *Science, Technology and Society* (London, Sage,
1977), pp.393-431.

Part One

THE PROMOTION OF TECHNOLOGY

1 GOVERNMENTAL SUPPORT FOR INDUSTRIAL INNOVATION: THE WESTERN EUROPEAN EXPERIENCE

Keith Pavitt

Similarities and Differences

Industrial innovation is of common and high importance to Western European countries. All countries have relatively high wage economies, most of whose exports are in manufactured goods. Competitiveness therefore depends heavily on the ability to incorporate new technology into products and production methods. Similarly, most countries are relatively densely populated and significantly dependent on external sources of certain raw materials, energy sources and foodstuffs. This has stimulated extensive technical change in Western Europe to develop substitute sources (e.g. synthetic materials and nuclear energy), more efficient intensive methods of agricultural production, and more economic methods of using intermediate inputs.

Since the Second World War, all Western European countries have been part of the same economic and political system. They are all heavily dependent on US military protection, even if France and the UK have developed and now maintain their own nuclear strike forces, and even if Sweden and Switzerland take a neutral stance outside military alliances. They all took part in the rapid economic recovery from the consequences of the Second World War, and had rates of economic growth that — until 1973 — were well above those of preceding historical periods. This rapid economic growth went hand in hand with the even more rapid increases in international trade and international investment that followed the reductions in tariff protection and foreign investment controls in the 1950s and 1960s. Rapid economic growth in the 1950s and 1960s was also accompanied in all countries by increases in the training and employment of qualified scientists and engineers, and in expenditures by industry and government on research and development activities (R & D).

In spite of these important similarities, there remain significant differences in the patterns of innovative activities within the region, and related to countries' size and to their recent economic and political histories. Many aspects of these differences can be seen in Tables 1.1 and 1.2. The heavier emphasis on government support for big

Table 1.1: Some Comparisons of R & D Activities in Ten OECD
Countries

	1	2		3 1967	4 1975	5 1967	6 1975
Belgium	0.3	17.5	(30.8)	1.0	1.1	n.a.	2.1 (1973)
France	0.7	43.8	(58.1)	5.9	6.0	n.a.	2.0
F.R. Germany	0.9	26.0	(33.4)	11.4	12.6	2.2	2.7
Netherlands	0.8	8.7	(14.0)	2.4	2.1	3.5 (1969)	3.6
Italy	n.a.	29.5	(39.8)	2.4	2.8	n.a.	n.a.
United Kingdom	1.0	56.0	(68.4)	10.4	7.4	3.3	2.7
EEC Total	n.a.	n.a.	(n.a.)	33.5	40.0	n.a.	n.a.
Sweden	0.7	32.1	(39.9)	1.2	1.7	2.7	3.2
Switzerland	n.a.	30.9	(37.6)	2.3	1.7	n.a.	n.a.
Japan	0.6	16.1	(22.3)	11.7	17.8	2.4	3.0 (1973)
USA	1.3	70.4	(70.9)	49.6	42.6	3.5	4.2
Total	n.a.	n.a.	(n.a.)	100	100	n.a.	n.a.

Column 1: *Government R & D expenditures as a percentage of GDP, 1973.*
Source: OECD document DSTI/SPR/76.29 (Paris, September 1976).
Column 2: *Percentage of Government R & D expenditures on big technology, 1975.* First number comprises defence, space and energy (mainly nuclear) R & D. Second number in brackets also includes R & D specifically for industrial development, most of which is in fact spent on civil aviation and advanced electronics. Source: OECD document DSTI/SPR/77.8 (Paris, March 1977).
Columns 3 and 4: *Percentage of ten countries' industry-financed R & D, 1967 and 1975.* Source: OECD.
Columns 5 and 6: *Industry-financed R & D activities as a percentage of domestic product of manufacturing industry.* Source: Information supplied by the Science and Technology Indicators Unit, OECD, Paris.

technologies in France, F.R. Germany and the UK reflects their size and their geopolitical ambitions. Amongst these three, Britain has declined in relative importance in these technologies since the Second World War as France and Germany have grown in relative economic strength and political assertiveness. This British decline extends beyond the big technologies to all industrial R & D activities. In part, it reflects the decline of industrial productivity, industrial exports and industrial employment relative to other Western European countries; and in part it reflects a diminishing willingness of British industrialists to spend

Table 1.2: Some Comparisons of Industrial Performance in Eight
  OECD Countries

	1	2	3 1967	4 1976	5
Belgium	6.2	177	n.a.	n.a.	116
France	5.4	168	8.5	9.8	132
F.R. Germany	5.5	160	19.5	20.6	125
Netherlands	6.7	202	n.a.	n.a.	107
Italy	5.6	102	7.0	7.1	161
United Kingdom	3.5	100	12.3	8.7	92
Japan	9.5	n.a.	9.8	14.6	n.a.
USA	2.7	n.a.	20.4	17.3	n.a.

Column 1: *Annual rates of increase in labour productivity in manufacturing industry: for EEC countries, value added per man-hour, 1955-1974.* Source: D.T. Jones, 'Output, Employment and Labour Productivity in Europe since 1955', *National Institute Economic Review*, no.77, pp.72-85 (August 1976). For Japan and the USA, output per man-hour, 1960-74. Source: National Science Board.
Column 2: *Gross value added per man-hour in manufacturing industry, in 1974.* UK = 100. Source: D.T. Jones, 'Output, Employment and Labour Productivity'.
Columns 3 and 4: *Percentage shares of manufacturing exports of 12 major OECD countries, 1967-1976.* Source: *National Institute Economic Review.*
Column 5: *Employment in manufacturing industry in 1973, 1955 = 100.* Source: D.T. Jones, 'Output, Employment and Labour Productivity'.

their money on R & D activities.

Smaller countries like the Netherlands, Sweden and Switzerland have had lesser ambitions in the big technologies, although Sweden has until now maintained a successful military aircraft industry.[1] They have each maintained highly developed and specialised capacities for industrial innovation in a few large industrial firms: electronics and chemicals in the Netherlands; fine chemicals and machinery in Switzerland; metals, metal products and machinery in Sweden. Rapidly industrialising Mediterranean countries like Italy and — more recently — Spain have developed indigenous capabilities for innovation in certain industrial sectors, while both the system of government support and university education have lagged behind.

These differences have influenced the scale, the balance, the purpose and the justificatory rhetoric surrounding government programmes to promote industrial innovation. However, this writer believes that innovation policies, narrowly defined, as well as economic and political relations amongst the Western European states, will come in future to be dominated by two factors differentiating one part of Europe from another.

The first is the very different endowments of indigenous energy resources in northern and in southern Europe. Broadly speaking the countries in the north are well endowed with coal, oil, gas or uranium, while those in the south have very little beyond a little coal and uranium, some hydroelectricity, and a great deal of sunshine. The split runs more or less between Nordics and Latins, Protestants and Catholics, liberals/social democrats and potential Eurocommunists.

For those who believe that the pattern of international politics can be discerned by looking at a map, such a situation clearly invites speculation about the political and economic future of Europe. For the more prosaic purposes of this chapter, it helps explain the differing emphases now being placed on the development of nuclear energy amongst European countries. Compare, in particular, France, the UK and Germany. France has little coal, little natural gas and no oil. It is therefore heavily dependent both economically and politically on what happens in the Middle East and in the USA, and has therefore embarked on an ambitious programme of building thermal nuclear reactors and is developing a full-scale, sodium-cooled fast nuclear reactor. The UK, on the other hand, is very well endowed with coal, oil and gas, so that — in spite of the pressure of a powerful nuclear lobby — its plans for the expansion of thermal reactor capacity are far more modest, and no decision has yet been taken to build a full-scale, sodium-cooled fast breeder reactor. Germany sits somewhere in the middle, with no oil or gas, but plenty of coal. Immediately after the 1973 oil crisis, it embarked on ambitious plans to expand thermal nuclear capacity. Since then, however, there has been a renewed interest in indigenous coal as a source of electrical energy, and the degree of commitment to the breeder reactor is not as intense and immediate as in France.

The second major factor differentiating Western European countries is their ability to compete on international markets in a world where certain less developed countries are increasingly competitive in standard consumer goods, where energy and a clean environment are increasingly at a premium, and where very rapid strides are being made in the technologies of micro-electronics. Under such circumstances, the capacity to design, build and sell specialised consumer goods, intermediate products, process equipment and other capital goods — together with the ability to integrate electronic advances in a wide

variety of products — will be of prime importance in maintaining
manufacturing competitiveness and manufacturing employment.[2]

One rough indicator of this capacity in a country is its indsutry-
financed R & D expenditures as a percentage of manufacturing output
(or, more strictly, Domestic Product of Manufacturing Industry).
Table 1.1 shows that, measured in these terms, Japan and the USA
have a strong capacity to adapt, as do the Netherlands and Sweden in
Western Europe; and, although strictly comparable data are not
available, Switzerland falls into the same category. On the other hand,
Belgium, Italy and France have a relatively weak capacity. That
Germany and the UK find themselves at the same level as the UK in
1975 is misleading. As Table 1.2 shows, the German trend since 1967
has been upwards, whereas the British trend has been downwards. The
considerable German technological strength in machine-building is
inadequately reflected in R & D statistics, whereas the British
concentration on aerospace tends to inflate the R & D figure. In
addition, the status and quality of German engineers are considerably
higher than those of their British counterparts,[3] and this may influence
the effectiveness with which new technology is put into practice.

These differences amongst Western European countries in energy
endowment and in technological capability in manufacturing industry
must be kept in mind throughout this chapter. In the next two sections,
we shall discuss in more detail the nature of government policies to
promote industrial innovation, and then attempt to assess their
effectiveness. And in the fourth and final section, we shall identify
some of the problems of government policy that remain unanswered, or
that will grow in future.

What Government Policies Promote Industrial Innovation?

Innovation and Economic Activity

There is reasonably strong evidence that the government policy that
influences industrial innovation most significantly is not a policy
specifically to promote industrial innovation. The maintenance of high
levels of demand, and buoyant expectations about future demand, have
a strong influence on industrialists' propensities to commit resources to
innovative activities. This is what European industrialists say
themselves,[4] and empirical study shows very clearly innovative firms'
sensitivity to demand conditions.[5] Both before the First World War
and after the Second World War, the expansion of innovative activities
in European industry was closely associated with expanding production

and trade. Between the Wars, slower growth and eventual stagnation dampened innovative activity considerably.[6]

Since 1973, and much slower growth in the OECD area, there is not yet any evidence that industry-financed R & D activities are declining. However, there is some evidence for the USA that they are becoming more defensive in nature, concentrating increasingly on the improvement and modification of existing products and processes (often in response to higher energy prices or more stringent environmental and safety standards), and spending less on longer-term and more radical projects and programmes.[7] Although no similar enquiry has been made into the trends in the objectives of industrial R & D in Western Europe, it is highly probable that the same trends exist. If they persist, they could have a significant influence on Europe's longer-term prospects for economic growth.

However, it would be a mistake to conclude that the chain of causality runs only from good Keynesian demand management to more innovative activities. At the national level, a strong capacity for technical innovation may be an essential condition, in an internationally open and competitive world, for the freedom to practise Keynesian demand policies. A high level of innovation — reflected in cost-reducing investment, and in international competitive advantages in capital and consumer durable goods — is likely to keep exports high, the balance of payments healthy, and thereby leave room for Keynesian policies. Germany has been such a case. A low level of innovation is likely to be associated with low export competitiveness, high import penetration, and a consequent need for reflation without the possibility of practising it: the UK has been such a case, in spite of the cushioning effect on the balance of payments of North Sea oil.

The Growth of Industrial Subsidies

This same international perspective offers probably what is the most useful framework for understanding the roots of government policies to promote industrial innovation since the Second World War. This period has been one of rapid change, and uneven change, both amongst sectors and amongst countries. It has also seen the diminution in Western Europe of the traditional tools of national industrial policy: control over the level of the external tariff and over incoming foreign investment.

Rapid and uneven development has meant that national firms have sometimes found themselves to be uncompetitive, while the elimination of protection has meant that insufficient time has been available for both management and labour to make the necessary adaptations and changes. It has also meant that Keynesian reflation has not worked, because it has simply sucked in imports.[8]

Under such circumstances, there has emerged an 'active and selective industrial policy' composed of a combination of government activities, involving subsidies of various kinds, the promotion of mergers, and preferential procurement policies, the purpose of which has been either to assist the process of transformation, or to shield management and workers in the industrial firms concerned from the consequences of not making it.

In Western Europe, these interventions have been concentrated at the two ends of the technological spectrum in manufacturing industry. At the lower end, textiles, iron and steel and shipbuilding have been subject to intensive competition from Japan and from amongst the more dynamic of the less developed countries. At the upper end, aircraft, space applications, nuclear energy and advanced electronics have been under competitive attack from the USA.

Unfortunately, it is not possible to obtain precise and comparable statistical and other information on the nature and scope of all these interventions. Often the subsidies are disguised as cheap loans or tax rebates, and strenuous efforts are nearly always made to keep them secret both from the electorate and from the international organisations that preside over, or purport to enforce, the international non-interventionist order. Suffice to say that general rhetoric is no sure guide to practice: as far as can be gathered, apparently non-interventionist Germany has subsidised both its coal and its nuclear energy industry, just as has been done in apparently interventionist France.[9]

Government subsidies to R & D activities, and their growth over the past fifteen years, have been a substantial element of 'active industrial policy' in Western European countries. Thorough and internationally comparable statistics on them are published, thanks largely to the efforts of the Secretariats of the OECD and the EEC. Respectable economic cases can be made for a number of forms of government subsidy to R & D; for basic research and training, given that the benefits resulting from them can rarely be fully captured by those who pay for them; for applied research, development and training in sectors where, like agriculture, firms have neither the scale of resources necessary to undertake R & D activities nor the level of skills necessary to be able to benefit from them.

These are the traditional and widely accepted functions of

government in relation to industrial innovation. Since the Second World War, all Western European governments have also established powerful networks of support for R & D activities (civil or military) in the big technologies. They have also established more general programmes of financial support for the development of inventions, or for projects of full-scale commercial development, in industrial firms.

For the remainder of this chapter, I shall concentrate on this range of traditional and more recent R & D subsidies in Western Europe: first to describe them, then to assess their effectiveness, and then to relate them to the wider questions discussed earlier.

Government Policies for R & D and Training

There is not much point in describing in great detail and for each country the institutions and procedures related to these government policies. These tend to be changed quite frequently. As in all government (or other) institutions, formal descriptions give little indication of their functions and objectives, the resources at their disposal, or the impact that they have. In fact, the functions and objectives of the government institutions supporting R & D and training are similar in most Western European countries.

First, there are the traditionally accepted functions of government, namely the support of basic research, education and training. In most countries, basic research and higher education are supported through similar dual mechanisms: bloc grants to institutions of higher education, coupled with grants and contracts awarded specifically for research in these same or related institutions. Both sources of funds in general come from the Ministry of Education.

Beyond these general similarities, there are also some major differences. Perhaps the most important for this book concern the selection, training and status of engineers, where the British tradition (reproduced in Ireland), is very different from either the German tradition (reproduced in Netherlands, Sweden and Switzerland), or the French tradition (reproduced in Italy, Spain and Belgium). In Britain, engineers are trained in the universities, and they have relatively low intellectual, social and financial status. In France and Germany, they are trained in separate and distinct institutions, and they have high intellectual, social and financial status.[10]

There are also some important differences amongst countries, at the level of post-secondary vocational education for technicians and skilled workers. Particularly in the engineering industries, these differences can have a big influence on national capabilities for industrial innovation.

However, on the extent and the nature of these differences, very little comprehensive information is available. Partial evidence suggests that vocational education is much more generously provided for in Germany than in Britain. So far, however, we have far less reliable and internationally comparable statistics on how well most of the industrial work force in Western Europe are trained, than on graduates in theology and sociology.

In addition to providing financial support for basic research and training, most Western European governments – in contrast with those in North America – have supported industry-wide research laboratories and related services: for example, the *centres techniques industriels* in France, the *AIF* in Germany, the TNO in the Netherlands, and the research associations in the UK.[11] The total funds available to these institutions are small: in most cases less than 5 per cent of all industrial R & D. Their impact is relatively much greater in traditional industries (like textiles), where they often make up a significant proportion of total technical effort related to the sectors, and where they have made substantial contributions to improvements in technical and management skills, in process technology and in instrumentation. They have not, however, been provided with sufficient resources to ensure that extension services reach the smallest firms that need them most. In France and Britain, far greater financial rigour has been applied to the funding of these services than to the provision of much larger funds to large and technically sophisticated firms involved in government-funded programmes in the big technologies.[12] In Germany, however, very extensive managerial and technical advice is made available to small firms through the government-financed RKW.[13]

Since the Second World War, all Western European governments have established powerful networks of support for R & D activities in both the civilian and the military big technologies. These networks normally are made up of government or quasi-government laboratories, and of government-financed R & D contracts with industrial firms. Government agencies tend to play a relatively greater role in the nuclear and space sectors. They are in general known widely by their initials and tend to be strong and somewhat autonomous sources of expertise and of political pressure within, or close to, the government bureaucracy: for example, CEA (nuclear energy, France), CNES (space, France), GFK and KFA (nuclear energy, Germany), RCN (nuclear energy, Netherlands), AEA (nuclear energy, UK).

In the aeronautics and advanced electronics sectors, government R & D contracts with industrial firms – whether private or nationalised –

play a relatively greater role. In all the big technology sectors, government policies have also involved industrial mergers, active procurement policies and international (and often European) co-operation.

Finally, since the Second World War, most Western European governments have also established government-financed programmes or agencies outside the high technologies to support either the development of inventions or full-scale projects for commercial development in industry. In France, they are ANVAR, *actions concertées industrielles* and *aide au développement*; in Germany, the new technology programme; in Netherlands, the system of development credits; and in the UK, the NRDC.

Although the *scale* of government support for all these programmes varies considerably amongst countries (higher in France, F.R. Germany and the UK than elsewhere), there are very similar priorities and trends within them. The 'new' innovation policies, concentrating on high technologies and on government funding of R & D in industry, have until recently got progressively more of the money. Nuclear energy, civil aviation, space and advanced electronics take at least three quarters of the government money set aside for civilian, industry-related R & D in the EEC countries. The lion's share goes to nuclear energy, except in the UK, where civil aviation gets most. At the same time, progressively more money has been channelled into full-scale commercial development activities in R & D intensive industries, by comparison with traditional government support for basic research and technology, and for traditional industries.

The organisational arrangements for these various elements of government policy follow a similar pattern. The traditional elements of government policies for innovation have generally been the responsibility of the Ministries of Education (basic research) and the Ministries of Industry (co-operative research and standards). These traditional elements have been subjected to thorough, and sometimes very short-sighted scrutiny, concerning their relevance. Basic research has sometimes been assumed to be a 'free good' from which anyone can benefit, or of economic value only when it contributes directly and obviously to an eventually adopted technology; its importance as a means of identifying, interpreting and transmitting relevant information is neglected. Similarly, the value of applied research in government laboratories has sometimes been measured simply through the amount of contract income it can generate (chapter 4), when much of its value lies in the transmission of information by means that are inevitably informal and unaccountable.[14]

The newer elements of government policies — those concerned with big technologies and with financial support for industrial R & D — have been generated outside these institutions, and embodied in new programmes and agencies, often by politicians, entrepreneural scientists or central bodies concerned with science policy. The accountability of the new programmes and agencies has often been minimal. As time has gone on, both Ministries of Industry and Ministries of Finance have tried — with greater or lesser success — to reduce their autonomy, and to make them part of the normal government structure. This trend reflects not only normal bureaucratic behaviour, but also the increasing criticism to which many of the elements of the new policies for innovation have been subjected. It is to these that we shall now turn.

Government Policies for Industrial Innovation: Assessment

Both analysis and events have led to growing doubts about the economic and social utility of the present patterns of government support for the civilian big technologies. The countries with the biggest such programmes — the USA and the UK — have had, in the OECD area, the worst industrial record as measured by trends in manufacturing productivity and world export shares. Their general level of industrial technology as measured through industry-financed R & D has also declined relative to countries like Japan, the Netherlands, Switzerland and F.R. Germany (see Tables 1.1 and 1.2). Some analysts have argued that government-financed programmes in the big technologies in the UK and the USA have drained qualified scientists and engineers of high quality away from the capital and durable consumer goods industries; the same thing has not happened in Germany and Japan, which is one reason why these countries are increasingly competitive in these sectors.

Some Failures

In addition, with the passage of time, there have been some often spectacular changes in policy, cancellations of programmes and outright admissions of failure. In France, the Government recently reversed an ambitious and costly policy to support the development of an indigenous computer industry.[15] In an earlier analysis of this policy, Zysman argued that its main effect had been to reduce considerably any incentive that the French industry had to change towards more efficient management, more flexible organisation and more profitable and promising products and markets. The prime (and, for Zysman, legitimate) objective of French government policy, to maintain a certain degree of technological independence in a strategically sensitive area, could have been reached much more cheaply and expeditiously through a subsidy to R & D activities, rather than through a policy to maintain in existence an inefficient firm.[16]

In Britain, considerable funds have been committed by the government to the development of civil aircraft and aero engines. A member of the government's economic service, N. Gardner, recently succeeded in publishing a financial assessment of the British government's programme of 'launching aid' for the aviation industry since the Second World War.[17] It showed that, between 1945 and 1974, the government had spent more than £1,500 million (1974 prices), and received back less than one tenth of this amount in commercial royalties. Only one aircraft and engine made a profit for the government: the Viscount and its Dart engine. The largest items of expenditure so far have been the supersonic airliner, Concorde, and the advanced technology engine, the RB 211. Even if these are excluded, the balance sheet is still not flattering: expenditures of £577 million and receipts of £126 million. As Walker has pointed out, a comparison of receipts to expenditures shows that short-haul aircraft have been more successful than long-haul aircraft, and aero engines more successful than aircraft.[18] Little similar information has been published for France or Germany, where the record is probably very similar. The Dutch, however, have done somewhat better by concentrating on short-haul aircraft, of modest technological ambition, but sound commercial prospects.[19]

In the nuclear energy sector, there have also been problems (chapter 3). After building a first generation of gas-cooled, graphite-moderated reactors (Magnox) that had few technical difficulties, and that turned out to be reliable and economic, the UKAEA pressed for the development of a technically more advanced gas-cooled reactor (AGR), the construction programme of which has been disastrous: long time delays, huge cost overruns and still no firm assurance that the design will work reliably. These difficulties stem in large part from neglect or ignorance of elementary engineering principles: the difficulties and dangers of making large jumps in scale and performance characteristics; the problems of on-site construction and of maintenance requirements, and the need to conserve and to concentrate scarce engineering skills into viable design teams.[20]

While it is widely accepted that the British nuclear industry is in a weak condition, quite the opposite is true of F.R. Germany. However, as Keck has argued, this strength derives more from the existence of financially strong, technically competent and independent equipment suppliers and electrical utilities than from any government policy for nuclear energy.[21] The eventually successful designs were developed with the supply industry's own money, and were chosen by the electrical utilities against the advice of government scientists. Furthermore, the main financial thrust of the government's nuclear energy policy has been the sodium-cooled fast breeder reactor. As Keck shows, the German equipment suppliers have refused to commit any of their own money to this programme, although it would be financially and technically feasible for them to do so if they thought it commercially worthwhile.

Finally, it should be noted briefly that European co-operative programmes have often not done much better than national ones. The Europa rocket never worked before it was abandoned after considerable expenditures.[22] Euratom never achieved its promise of developing a European nuclear industry, before it was dissolved.[23] The attempt to conceive a European computer industry based on Dutch, French and German firms quickly aborted.[24] And, of course, there is still Concorde.

Some Explanations

In the light of this evidence of failure, some economists and political scientists have tried to develop an analytical framework to explain it.[25] They dismiss the Galbraithian argument that it is the growing scale imperatives of modern technology that dictate the need for government financial support.[26] On the contrary, they argue that industrialists will commit very large sums of their own money to R & D activities, provided they see the possibility of a satisfactory rate of return. Governments are generally left to finance commercially second-best projects, where technological prowess often takes unjustified precedence over the price and performance characteristics that potential users would like to have; where subsidies are often a means of stopping the managerial and marketing transformations necessary to make the industry efficient; where all the financial eggs are put too early into one technological basket; and where — as a consequence — there builds up a secretive and intervention-breeding system. For this reason, governments should not behave as risk-capitalists, they should concentrate on generous support of background research and skills which help commercial organisations to make commercial decisions with commercial money.

Similar criticisms have been levelled against the much smaller programmes of government financial support for full-scale commercial developments outside the big technologies.[27] In many countries, the distribution of government R & D funds in these programmes reflects almost exactly the distribution of industry's own R & D funds, being concentrated in large firms in the research-intensive industries. Given that the amount of funds distributed by government is very small relative to the funds available to the firms themselves, the effects of government programmes can be no more than marginal, and they often serve simply to keep in existence projects of questionable merit.

Government programmes rarely have access to the competence and information necessary to assess market prospects; they do little to remedy deficiencies in managerial competence; they cannot easily support programmes of incremental improvement innovations; they are too small to bring about any fundamental changes in industrial structure; and they are often not flexible enough in their financial arrangements to reflect the varying needs of different industrial sectors.

Some Future Requirements

These criticisms are powerful and compelling, and must be taken seriously by any practitioner or analyst of government policies for industrial innovation. However, they must not be taken necessarily as a blanket justification for a complete 'hands-off' policy to industrial technology. Not only does such a policy neglect the social and environmental costs, which will be discussed in greater length in Part 2 of this book, it neglects the experience of those government projects and programmes that have been successful. It also neglects three important and related reasons why some government intervention in industrial innovation beyond support of skills and of basic research can be justified. These are market imperfections, long-run international competitiveness and the costs of adjustment.

Market imperfections can be of many sorts. First, international monopoly power in strategic resources and technologies, justifying strong government support for certain technologies: for example, full-scale demonstration plant for coal gasification or liquefaction, in case the OPEC countries suddenly put up the price of oil beyond $25 a barrel. Until 1973, the combination of the price mechanism and of government policies for R & D support did not produce the diversity and the flexibility of energy sources necessary for the diminution of monopoly power. On the contrary, the price mechanism led to heavy dependence on oil, and governments put all their R & D eggs in the nuclear basket.[28]

Another market imperfection is the imperfect access that small firms often have to finance and skills. This justifies government support for research and extension services, and for finance for small and medium-sized firms of the kind provided in the Netherlands through their programme of Development Credits.[29]

Industrial firms also tend to have relatively short-term time horizons (especially when expectations about future growth are pessimistic), and therefore to commit insufficient resources to longer-term developments in fundamental technology. A strong case can therefore be made for government support of R & D work related to fundamental technology. In this context, it is interesting to note that, as Walker has shown, the successful activities of the NRDC in the UK have been the development and licensing of *inventions*, and not the financial support of full-scale commercial development.[30]

Another inevitable government concern is long-term industrial competitiveness in a rapidly changing world. As noted in the opening section of this chapter, Western European countries will be increasingly constrained to compete in international markets on the basis of skill and technology. However, they have been at a comparative disadvantage in some big technologies, given the US government's stimulus through huge military and space programmes. Some European experiences show how such disadvantages can be redressed, or, at least, lived with. In F.R. Germany, the combination of a strong electrical engineering firm (Siemens/Kraftwerkunion) and an independent electrical utility (RWE) has led to the emergence of a competitive nuclear industry. In the UK, new and more professional management in ICL has specialised its product range and improved its market position; and the European Airbus appears to have found a profitable niche in the aircraft market. In all these successful cases, technology policy has been closely interwoven with production and marketing policy, and an essential ingredient has been competent management in the industrial firms involved.

In some countries, the concern about innovation and international competitiveness goes beyond the big technologies, because industrialists exercising their commercial judgement do *not* support commercially promising innovations, with a consequent loss of international competitiveness.[31] This is the case for the UK. It has inevitably led to growing government intervention, the efficacy of much of which can be doubted.

Finally, in all countries, there remains the problem of adjustment of firms and individuals in a world of rapid technical, competitive and poltical change. The social costs of such adjustment are considerable and — given the time that it takes to develop new skills, new products and new markets — it will often be a lengthy process. Under such circumstances, some form of government intervention or help is politically inevitable. But what form should it take? R & D or other subsidies? Training? Management changes? The development of long-term market strategies? Unfortunately, no clear answer can be given to this question, because there has not yet been any systematic study of past successes and failures.[32] Suffice to say that it will often be a mix of inputs, that will vary from case to case, and from sector to sector. Will governments be able to develop the competence and the flexibility to meet such requirements?

Conclusions and Speculations

What problems remain, or are emerging, in relation to innovation policies in Western Europe? To some extent, there has been a significant shift since the early 1960s. There is less of a fatal fascination with the big technologies because they are big. In particular, there is much less talk about the imperative need for Europe to combine and compete comprehensively with the USA in space applications and big jet aircraft. The policy problems now being faced are more prosaic: How many cheap and simple rockets should Europe build? Where and how should Europe co-operate in US space programmes? Where and how should Europe co-operate to exploit further the niche found by the Airbus, or co-operate with the dominant US competitor, Boeing?

In electronics, the problems posed by microprocessors are more severe and more important. Beyond the concerns about their effects in displacing jobs in assembly and in precision engineering, it is recognised that they will increasingly permeate a wide range of capital and consumer goods, and often have a profound influence on their design and performance. Under such circumstances, what must Europe have? A full-scale design and production capability in all areas? Specialised design and production? Design teams? And where should Europe get the capability? Through government subsidy in Europe? Or through buying a US company? The same questions are being asked in all Western European countries.

In energy, as we have already stressed in the introduction, fundamental problems remain. In all Western European countries there is increasing recognition of the past and present neglect of the technologies of energy conservation, and of energy sources other than nuclear. Government R & D programmes are diversifying into coal, solar, district heating, etc., but it is too early to be able to assess budgetary trends. It is not too early, on the other hand, to criticise the continuing official belief that energy demand will continue to increase in future in Europe, and that large programmes of nucelar energy will in consequence be needed in all countries.

The United Kingdom's strategy for energy R & D should be evident to all, except perhaps the ardent nuclear advocates in the Atomic Energy Authority: wait, see and go slowly with thermal and breeder reactors, while developing technologies related to coal and undersea oil. In France, the commitment to nuclear energy is bound to be strong, unless abundant oil is found in French waters.

However, it is the Federal Republic of Germany that will have the greatest long-term influence on Europe's energy problems. Its industry and utilities have direct access to coal and related chemical technology, and to both water-cooled and gas-cooled thermal nuclear reactors. Given the competence and financial independence of the electrical utilities, it is in Germany that the relative merits of coal and nuclear energy in generating electricity should first become apparent, and, within nuclear energy, between water- and gas-cooled reactors. Furthermore, F.R. Germany will play a major role in the future of the sodium-cooled fast breeder reactor. At present, the Federal German government is committed financially to a 300 MW reactor of its own, while being a minor partner to the French government in the building of the full-scale Super-Phoenix. In the next five to ten years, it will have to decide whether to go ahead with a full-scale German equivalent of Super-Phoenix (the SNR-2). If it should decide not to, on either economic or safety grounds, the ramifications in France, Europe and elsewhere in the world would be enormous.

While governments are becoming more differentiated and discriminating in relation to the big technologies, similar trends can be detected in other aspects of innovation policy. In a number of countries, government funding of industrial R & D is being shifted out of small and short-term projects in big firms, towards longer-term and more speculative projects or towards medium and small-sized firms. And greater interest is being shown in the potential role of research associations in easing the conversion of the traditional industries towards the better product design and process technology that will be necessary if they are to survive increasing competition from the less developed countries. Finally, it is being recognised that the value of basic and applied research programmes in universities and government laboratories cannot be assessed by cost/benefit analysis, which concentrates on the short-term and the specific, when the very value of these programmes is that they are long-term or diffuse in impact. Government support of long-term research will become more important and necessary, as industrial research becomes shorter-term.

However, other problems remain. The growing concern for environment, amenity and safety over the past ten years has had a major impact on the rate and direction of innovation in the automobile, drugs, chemicals and other intermediate products industries. The controversy surrounding this impact to some extent reflects political problems in designing and monitoring public regulations.

There is also the problem of technical change and international competitiveness among the weaker, peripheral countries of Western Europe. It is becoming increasingly recognised in all countries how much competitiveness depends on good R & D and design, allied to good engineering and good marketing. Yet there remain significant differences among countries in their apparent willingness and ability to act on this fact. Recent research into the impact of government policies for innovation, which stresses the influence of the general economic climate on the propensity to innovate, offers little guidance to policy makers, except to suggest indirectly that the attitudes and skills of management may be a major determining factor.

Finally, it should be noted that beyond the specific problems and possibilities of government policies to promote industrial innovation in Europe, bigger things are at stake. Differences of national interest because of differing energy endowments could be exacerbated or reduced as a result of policies for technical change. For example, one of the problems of European Common Energy Policy is a mirror image of that related to the Common Agricultural Policy: how to persuade the French to buy expensive British or German coal, instead of cheap Australian coal. Technical progress making Northern European coal more attractive technically and commercially would increase the possibility of a political agreement.

Even more important for the future of Europe are differences among countries in the technical quality, adaptiveness and efficiency of their manufacturing industry. Unless these differences are reduced in future, it is unlikely that the EEC would survive economically or politically. Continuing differences would mean that the German centre would be richer than the northern and southern periphery. The centre would not be willing to subsidise inefficient industry at the periphery, and the periphery would not be able to pay subsidies to inefficient farmers at the centre. Beyond government policies to promote innovation, the name of the game is the long-term future of Europe.

Notes

1. Ingemar Dorfer, 'Science and Technology in Sweden: the Fabians versus Europe', *Research Policy*, vol.3 (1974), pp.134-55.

2. Keith Pavitt, 'Technical Change in the OECD Area: Prospects and Problems', *Futures* (to be published).

3. Peter Lawrence *et al.*, 'Engineers in Germany', *The Chartered Mechanical Engineer* (September 1977).

4. Al Rubenstein *et al.*, 'Management Perceptions of Government Incentives to Technological Innovation in England, France, West Germany and Japan', *Research Policy*, vol.6 (1977), pp.324-57.

5. Christopher Freeman, *The Economics of Industrial Innovation* (London, Penguin, 1974).

6. Keith Pavitt and Luc Soete, 'Technical Effort and Economic Performance: Some International Comparisons', mimeo. (Science Policy Research Unit, University of Sussex, 1978).

7. McGraw-Hill, *Surveys of Business' Plans for Research and Development Expenditures* (published annually, New York).

8. See Claude-Albert Michalet, 'France', in Raymond Vernon (ed.), *Big Business and the State* (London, Macmillan, 1974); Harry Johnson, 'Foreword', in Geoffrey Denton *et al.*, *Trade Effects of Public Subsidies in Private Enterprise* (London, Macmillan, 1974); W. Corden and G. Fels (eds), *Public Assistance to Industry: Protection and Subsidisation in Britain and Germany* (London, Trade Policy Research Centre, 1975).

9. Ibid.

10. Lawrence, 'Engineers in Germany'.

11. Keith Pavitt and William Walker, 'Government Policies towards Industrial Innovation: A Review', *Research Policy*, vol.5 (1976), pp.14-97.

12. Keith Pavitt, 'The Choice of Targets and Instruments for Government Support of Scientific Research', in Alan Whiting (ed.), *The Economics of Industrial Subsidies* (London, HMSO, 1978); and 'Governmental Support for Industrial Research and Development in France: Theory and Practice', *Minerva*, vol.14 (1976), pp.330-54.

13. Erik Rupp, 'The RKW: A New Approach towards Technology Transfer: Methods for the Promotion of Innovation in Small and Medium Sized Companies', *Research Policy*, vol.5 (1976), pp.398-412.

14. Michael Gibbons and Ron Johnston, 'The Roles of Science in Technological Innovation', *Research Policy*, vol.3 (1974), pp.220-42.

15. J. Jublin and J.M. Quatrepoint, *French Ordinateurs* (Paris, Editions Alain Moreau, 1976).

16. John Zysman, 'Between the Market and the State: Dilemmas of French Policy for the Electronics Industry', *Research Policy*, vol.3 (1974), pp.312-36.

17. Nick Gardner, 'Economics of Launching Aid', in Whiting, *Economics of Industrial Subsidies.*

18. William Walker, *Direct Government Aid for Industrial Innovation in the UK*, Report to TNO, Holland, mimeo. (Science Policy Research Unit, University of Sussex, undated).

19. *Country Report: The Netherlands*, mimeo., TNO (Netherlands, August 1976).

20. Howard J. Rush, Gordon MacKerron and John Surrey, 'The Advanced Gas-Cooled Reactor: A Case Study in Reactor Choice', *Energy Policy*, vol.5 (2, 1977), pp.95-105.

21. Otto Keck, *Fast Breeder Reactor Development in West Germany: An Analysis of Government Policy*, Doctoral Dissertation (University of Sussex,

June 1977).

22. Michael Schwartz, 'European Policies on Space Science and Technology, 1960-1975', mimeo. (Science Policy Research Unit, University of Sussex, 1978).

23. Lawrence Scheinmann, 'Euratom: Nuclear Integration in Europe', *International Conciliation*, no.563, Carnegie Endowment for International Peace.

24. Jublin and Quatrepoint, *French Ordinateurs.*

25. See, in particular, George Eads and Richard Nelson, 'Government Support of Advanced Civilian Technology', *Public Policy*, vol.19, pp.405-27; and John Jewkes, *Government and High Technology*, Occasional Paper No.137 (London, Institute of Economic Affairs, 1972).

26. John K. Galbraith, *The New Industrial State* (London, Hamish Hamilton, 1967).

27. Science Policy Research Unit, *The Current International Economic Climate and Policies for Technical Innovation*, mimeo. (Staff group Strategic Surveys, TNO, Netherlands, November 1977).

28. John Surrey and William Walker, 'Energy R & D: A UK Perspective', *Energy Policy*, vol.3 (2, 1975), pp.90-115.

29. *Country Report: The Netherlands* (August 1976).

30. Walker, *Aid for Industrial Innovation.*

31. Pavitt and Soete, 'Technical Effort and Economic Performance'.

32. Such work has now begun at the Centre for Contemporary European Studies, University of Sussex.

2 FEDERAL INITIATIVES IN CANADA'S TECHNOLOGICAL DEVELOPMENT

Ian Chapman

The factors which have influenced Canada's technological development are individually not unusual and indeed some are shared by other industrial nations, but in combination they have created a situation which has no exact parallel. Like the US, Canada is a large country well endowed with natural resources. Canada's population, however, is only one tenth that of the US, and it is upon this small population that it must rely to amortise the cost of developing new manufactured products and putting them on the world market. This factor is shared with a number of the smaller industrial countries, Sweden for example, but Canada has had no free access to large markets since the days of the British Empire. In all of the above, there is a strong similarity with Australia's situation, but to a much larger extent than Australia, Canada's industry is foreign owned. In its technological development over the past hundred years, Canada has had to face the problems which today face some underdeveloped countries in much more dramatic form. Indeed, many would contend that Canada has yet to come to grips with the vital question of technological sovereignty.

One can discern two phases of government involvement in support of technological development.[1] The first was in the late nineteenth century when the government provided the necessary infrastructure for resource development — railways, geological surveys, experimental farms, etc. In this period, secondary manufacturing industry was allowed to develop behind tariff barriers which encouraged foreign ownership. This policy led to problems which the government has attempted to overcome in the past thirty years — the second period — by promoting an indigenous industrial technological capability. This chapter will concentrate upon this latter period and upon the federal government's support for industrial technological development. This is not to suggest that support for technological education or the work carried out in the government's own laboratories are unimportant, but the lessons to be learnt from the successes and failures of government initiatives to promote industrial development justify this emphasis.

41

Characterisation of Canadian Industry

An appreciation of Canada's industrial strengths and weaknesses can
be gained from export and import trade statistics. While overall there
is only a small trade imbalance, exports are concentrated in natural
resources and resource-based goods with little value added, while
imports are of high value-added manufactures.[2] Thus in 1976, Canada
experienced a $10 billion deficit in manufactured goods — a deficit
made up by net exports in resource-based products, primarily in metals,
wood, wheat and fuel. The deficit has grown rapidly recently — $6.3
billion in 1973 and a reported $12 billion in 1977. The deficit illustrates
the basic problem of a resource-based economy whose products are
subject to fluctuation in world prices and demand, but whose imports
of finished goods reflect the ever-increasing costs of inflation and
energy. Moreover in Canada's case, much of her resource industry is
controlled by multinational corporations who can switch production
from one country to another as demand and production costs dictate.[3]
The trade imbalance in end products is even more revealing if it is
examined in detail. The fastest growing industries in the past decade
or so have been in the 'high' technology sector. Of these, electronics,
computers, pharmaceuticals and plastics are considered key indicators
of a country's strength in science and technology, and the imbalance is
substantial in each of them.[4]

The weakness exhibited by some high technology industries has
received a great deal of attention. Much of the comment has focused
upon the relatively low level of industrial R & D, as Canada devotes
less of its GNP to R & D than most other countries, and of that a much
lower proportion is spent in the industrial sector.[5] It is difficult to
overemphasise just how important this finding has been in influencing
government policy towards technological development. The level of
funding for industrial R & D, and how it related to economic growth,
were major preoccupations of the influential Special Senate Committee
on Science Policy (the Lamontagne Committee)[6] and that
preoccupation has been reflected in the paramount importance the
government has accorded incentive schemes for industrial R & D to the
virtual exclusion of other aspects of the innovation process. Only very
recently has this tendency been reduced (but not abandoned) with the
introduction in 1977 of the Enterprise Development Programme which
has subsumed the industrial R & D incentive schemes into a larger
scheme in which all aspects of the innovation process including
marketing have been included.

Many people lay the blame for these weaknesses on a further important characteristic, namely the degree of foreign control over much of Canada's industrial sector. The majority of Canadian industries contain a significant foreign-controlled element, usually of branch plants based upon US parent companies. Economic nationalists are highly critical of this phenomenon which they believe gives Canada a 'branch plant economy' controlled from abroad.[7] They point to the relatively low level of R & D which subsidiaries perform – often one third of what their parent firms spend in the US, per $1,000 of sales.[8] Canadian-owned companies generally do no better.[9]

Government Agencies for Technological Support

There are two types of government agency involved in promoting Canada's technological development. First, those concerned with developing appropriate overall strategies and policies, including advisory councils, and second, the departments and agencies which administer the programmes. On paper, the organisation looks tidy and clear-cut. The Ministry of State for Science and Technology (MOSST) is a horizontal 'policy ministry', that is it administers no programmes itself but attempts to co-ordinate and review the whole spectrum of scientific and technological activities of the government. It provides advice and comment to the cabinet and is uniquely placed to advance broad policies on technological matters. Through this ministry, the cabinet also receives independent advice from the Science Council of Canada (SCC), a body made up of representatives from industry and the universities. From time to time, the Economic Council of Canada (ECC), also an independent advisory body, comments upon technological matters with economic implications.

There are five government departments or agencies which together administer most of the programmes for direct technological aid to industry – the Department of Industry, Trade and Commerce, the National Research Council (NRC), Atomic Energy of Canada Ltd (AECL), the Department of Communications and the Department of National Defense.

MOSST has had a troubled career in the seven years it has existed. The ministry came into existence as part of Canada's search for a science policy in the 1960s and early 1970s. Prior to that time, the NRC was the effective voice for science and technology, building up its own laboratories and operating as a wide-ranging agency, but avoiding confrontation with the established mission-oriented agencies in its activities.[10] The Royal Commission on Government Organisation marked the first effective challenge to this informal advisory structure, pointing out that the government seemed hardly to be aware of how policies for science and technology developed and certainly had no means to develop new ones which, the Commission claimed, were badly needed in the industrial sector.[11] As a result of the Commission's recommendations, the SCC and its secretariat were established, the latter being the forerunner of MOSST. The Senate committee on Science Policy picked up these themes, first using the lack of industrial research to finally dispose of the NRC's power,[12] and then arguing for a strong co-ordinative ministry. However, it has not been particularly effective, and it has been suggested that in its early years the ministry promised too much too publicly.[13] Following a reorganisation under its most powerful minister to date it now keeps a low profile and seems to be fulfilling its advisory and co-ordination role much better. The establishment and enhancement of its 'Make-or-Buy' policy is one concrete example of the kind of role the ministry can play, but it has little ability to move policies in opposition to the wishes of the large mission-oriented departments.

Of these departments, that of Industry, Trade and Commerce is the most important in terms of aid to industry — the NRC now reports through this department. Thus, together with AECL, these two agencies control the major government expenditures in the aerospace, nuclear and electronics industries, the industrial sectors most favoured by government support.

Methods of Technological Promotion

There are five principal ways in which the Canadian government has intervened to promote technological development.

A. Regulatory

(1) Through negotiations with other nations on tariff levels and by trade agreements which create opportunities for export trade.
(2) By creating the legal and regulatory framework which may modify industrial practice towards desired ends.

B. Non-Regulatory

(3) By incentive programmes which stimulate innovation.
(4) As a procurer of goods and services of a technological nature.
(5) By direct subsidy or purchase of nationally sensitive industries such as energy.

The balance of the chapter will be devoted to an examination of each of these activities.

Tariff Policy

In the late nineteenth century, Canada as a new country was preoccupied with developing its natural resources. In terms of secondary manufacturing industry, Canada had a choice: it could adopt a continental policy and confine itself to trading natural resources for finished goods with the US, or it could adopt a nationalist tariff policy and encourage the development of manufacturing industry. Political judgement and sentiment in favour of Britain and the Empire favoured the latter policy and a national tariff policy was established — a policy which has survived until today, and has profoundly influenced technological development. However, there was insufficient capital to finance both resource and industrial development and moreover, the necessary technical skills were lacking. It was inevitable, therefore, that those needs should be met by the financially and technologically powerful neighbour. Encouraged by the tariff policy, help usually took the form of branch plants of the parent company which competed for the small Canadian market, and also gained market access to Commonwealth preference. The plants typically produced the entire line of goods manufactured by the parent company, in small production runs. As Eastman and Stykolt point out:

> The size of the market in which a plant operates is an important determinant of the size of the plant and its average costs relative to the lowest costs that could be achieved by a plant of optimal size.[14]

These general observations can be supplemented by more specific research carried out by Daly and Globerman in a study examining the relationship between tariff and science policies.[15] One conclusion from their study was that the tariff was a major factor retarding more rapid rates of technological change (i.e. rates of innovation and diffusion) in Canadian manufacturing industry. They advanced three ways in which this result might come about.

(1) By raising the cost of capital relative to labour in tariff-protected industries. Salter has shown that this tendency will defer the date of obsolescence and result in a larger proportion of an industry's capital equipment being outmoded.[16]

(2) Tariff levels foster an industrial structure characterised by inefficient

small plants producing a wide range of output in short production runs. Development and/or adoption of new technology is characterised by significant fixed costs and innovation/adoption can be profitable only if these costs are spread over a large output.

(3) Protective policies can create monopolistic market conditions which weaken the incentive for improved efficiency. Again, this conclusion is supported by research which suggests that high levels of industrial concentration along with other barriers to effective competition seriously reduce rates of adoption of new technologies.

They also reported on adoption patterns of Canadian manufacturers for several specific innovations — numerical control machines, paper-making processes and tufting equipment in carpet making. Their studies confirmed, at least in these industries, that there was a slower adoption of capital-embodied innovation in Canada than in other developed countries, confirming (1) and (2) above. The slower adoption of the less capital-intensive carpet machinery suggested that the anti-competitive effects of the tariff can indeed retard the adoption of new techniques. Finally, in a more comprehensive trade flow study, they concluded that industries in which Canada enjoys a relative trade surplus are characterised by lower domestic US tariff levels, less processing for final use as a percentage of total output and greater levels of concentration.

The evidence suggests that the tariff plays an important role in Canada's technological development. What have been recent government initiatives in this area? The federal government has been trying to meet in part the first of Daly and Globerman's points by extending help to industries which need to import machinery to be used to generate export sales. The programme administered by the Department of Industry, Trade and Commerce remits import duty and according to a SCC study, 16,000 applications were being processed annually by 1970-71, with remissions amounting to $7.5 million.[17] Canadian manufacturers of the machinery are protected once they are in a position to supply.

The Canadian government has been a wary participant in the General Agreement on Tariffs and Trade (GATT), as it has always rejected total free trade with the US because of fears about the consequences for domestic industry. The Canada-US bilateral agreement on automotive products (the Auto Pact), under which the US allows the free entry of new cars, buses and trucks and original replacement parts substantially made in Canada and in return Canada allows US automotive products to enter duty free if imported by a manufacturer, is therefore a significant departure. Since the introduction of the Auto Pact in 1965, Canada's exports of automotive products have risen in value from $350 million to $6,427 million in 1975, and are now the single largest item in manufactured export goods.[18] Product specialisation has occurred involving longer production runs and so the agreement has been heralded as an example of the benefits Canada could expect from joining the US trade area. However, some caution must be exercised in assuming first that the Auto Pact is and always will be to Canada's benefit, and second, that similar advantages would apply across the whole of domestic industry.

The Canadian auto industry is almost completely owned by US parent companies. There is always a tendency for US firms to view their Canadian subsidiaries as just another plant like the ones in the US. The removal of the tariff on automotive goods simply allowed the US auto companies to at last rationalise production for the whole of the North American market, and to treat the Canadian plants *exactly* like the ones in Michigan and Ohio. The benefits in trade and jobs for Canada are obvious and increased profitability arising from product specialisation was sufficient incentive for the US companies to invest the necessary capital. The problems with the Pact, however, are that Canada is a net importer from the US, and furthermore, the low level of R & D has been reduced still further, so that it is still importing its technology as finished machines and plants. If a significant part of the industry had been controlled by Canadians, it would have been forced to seek a specific part of the market and invest the necessary capital or be overwhelmed by the technical superiority of the US manufacturers. It is this necessity to be innovative or disappear which appeals to the advocates of free trade, but it is precisely the previously noted lack of innovation in Canadian industry as a whole which makes others fearful. However, it is significant that free trade has been largely achieved throughout the European Communities with few reports of firms failing as a consequence. Negotiations in the Canada-US context for free trade would have to take into account the degree of US control of Canadian industry, and the transition would have to include possible job retraining and moving expenses for workers.

Taxation

All governments of industrial nations raise revenue through the medium of taxation, and most governments today are conscious of the effects taxes can have on the climate for business investment, jobs and economic growth in general. Thus the reduction of corporate income tax from 47 per cent to 40 per cent in the 1972 Canadian budget was intended to stimulate investment and provide new jobs. The elimination of sales tax on research equipment for industry and more rapid depreciation allowances for capital goods needed for manufacturing and processing might all be said to encourage the manufacturing sector to invest in new technology. The Canadian government has tended to favour and establish various R & D incentive schemes aimed at stimulating technological innovation. Some of these incentive schemes have been based upon remission of taxes. The grant-based schemes for industrial R & D will be discussed in the next section.

In 1961, the government amended the Income Tax Act to allow companies to deduct 100 per cent of their allowed expenses for R & D, both capital and operating.[19] But by the end of the decade, the government had switched the emphasis of incentive schemes for industrial R & D to grants. The percentage of the whole assistance package that was made up of tax rebates dropped to 50 per cent in 1970-71, having been as high as 64 per cent five years earlier. A special study of the tax incentive scheme made for the ECC recognised the advantages of such schemes. Companies were free to decide what projects to pursue and how much to spend on them, and were encouraged to start R & D activities, even if at a low level. Furthermore, they were encouraged to carry on with R & D after work sponsored by a contract or grant had stopped. Disadvantages were that the five-year experimental period of the scheme was too short, and companies with large base-year expenditures were discriminated against. The Economic Council recommended to the government that a new tax-based incentive scheme should be instituted.[20] The scheme should be for a ten-year period, with a credit, against tax payable, of 25 per cent of all R & D expenses allowed in the programme. Companies with insufficient taxes payable in a given year would be allowed to 'bank' their credit against future taxes.

At the time the government declined to follow the Council's recommendation, believing that a grant-based system was more easily controlled, less discriminatory and would reach a larger number of companies. However, in 1977, a modified form of the recommendation was introduced. A 5 per cent tax credit for R & D expenses for a three-year period was implemented. Predictably, industry spokesmen have pointed out that the credit is too small and for too short a period, given that R & D lead times are often 5-10 years before any sales can be expected.[21] In a recent speech, the Minister of State for Science and

Technology indicated that he accepted these arguments,[22] and indeed,
the government as a whole now favours tax-based schemes over grant-
based schemes for R & D.

Non-Regulatory Grant-based R & D Incentive Schemes

These schemes had their origin in the US-Canada defence production
agreements. In 1958, a joint committee on behalf of Canada and the
US approved a set of immediate and long-term objectives for production
sharing.[23] The integration of the respective defence production
capabilities was seen to be beneficial to both partners, supporting the
defence of North America and increasing the participation of Canadian
industry in the production of defence weapons and equipment.

By 1962, it was generally recognised that, while advances in defence-
oriented industry had spin-off effects for the rest of the economy,
non-military segments of industry also needed support in the area of
R & D if Canada was to remain internationally competitive. The civil-
oriented Industrial Research Assistance Programme (IRAP),
administered by the NRC, was initiated in 1962 to provide financial
assistance for the establishment of new industrial research teams or for
the expansion of existing research groups. Concentrating on long-term
research within smaller companies, costs were to be shared equally by
the NRC and industry, the government paying salaries and the firm
paying for equipment and overhead costs.[24]

IRAP provided financial assistance for 400 projects undertaken
between 1962 and October 1971, for a total expenditure of $30
million.[25] Although the programme was designed for small companies,
only about 20 per cent of the beneficiaries were companies with fewer
than 100 employees.[26] The chemical and chemical products and
electrical products industries received most assistance; the paper, food
and beverages, rubber, primary metals, machinery and non-metallic
minerals industries received less; and wood, metal fabrication,
petroleum and coal products and transportation equipment industries
were the least supported.[27]

The establishment of a federal Department of Industry in 1963 was
indicative of the government's recognition of the economic importance
of industrial development. Previously a branch of the Department of
Defence Production, industry became a department in its own right,
concerned with the advancement of R & D, particularly within the
non-military industrial sector of the economy. Its first major venture
in 1965 took the form of the Programme for the Advancement of
Industrial Technology (PAIT), which marked a departure from the only

other civil-oriented programme, IRAP in its emphasis on product development.[28] PAIT provided a form of 'development insurance' whereby firms would pay back a government contribution of up to 50 per cent of the costs incurred in the development or improvement of a product or process only if successful. Repayment with interest could be made over a period of ten years.[29] In 1970, repayment for assistance received under PAIT was discontinued. Up until that time, the government had contributed approximately $34 million towards industrial development.[30] The sales potential of the first dozen projects selling was estimated at $52 million over a period of five years, export sales accounting for 60 per cent of the total.[31]

Another programme, initiated in 1967, was to assist Canadian universities in establishing and administering industrial research institutes which would provide services to industry. In this way industry would be able to make use of valuable personnel and equipment provided by the university for the specific purpose of research and development. In this same year the Industrial Research and Development Incentives Act (IRDIA), perhaps the most ambitious industrial R & D policy of the Federal government, was introduced. Under IRDIA, firms were given cash grants, not subject to income tax, or credits against federal income tax, equal to 25 per cent of all capital expenditures (excluding land) incurred in the past fiscal year on R & D, and 25 per cent of the increase in current expenditures in Canada for R & D over the average of such expenditures in the preceding five years. IRDIA was seen by the government to be more effective and less discriminatory than the tax incentive it replaced.

Under the Industrial Research and Development Incentives Act, 1,937 grants were issued between 1967 and 1971 for a total value of $70 million.[32] The larger, more technologically sophisticated industries proved to be the chief benefactors. The electronics and electronic products sector had received 249 grants worth a total of $14.7 million by the end of 1971, while the aircraft and aircraft parts sector had received 210 grants for a total of $8.3 million. In 1972 the number of companies receiving IRDIA grants under $5,000 was increasing at a rate of 29 per cent annually, between $5,000 and $10,000 at a rate of 17 per cent annually, and between $10,000 and $15,000 at a rate of 43 per cent annually.[33]

By any overall measure of success one must conclude that Canada's piecemeal approach to increasing industrial R & D through incentive schemes failed despite some individual success stories. The number of firms conducting substantial R & D was not significantly increased, foreign-owned firms were, if anything, reducing their R & D commitment, and the country was still largely reliant on imported technology. There are three reasons for this failure: the federal government has proved very reluctant to encourage industrial R & D at the expense of intramural R & D; the incentive schemes have consistently helped large-scale R & D, particularly in the electronics and aeronautical industries, but often in amounts that were small in comparison with the firm's own resources; industry, particularly foreign-owned, has failed to respond to incentives and expend its own resources on scientific research.

Reluctance on the part of the federal government to part with its firmly entrenched R & D establishment is understandable. The NRC and the departmental laboratories have evolved over the past fifty years and cannot be suddenly terminated; nor should they be. As the Science Council noted, there are important and legitimate areas for government involvement in research: where industries are traditionally fragmented, where regulation or standardisation is required, where facilities are very expensive, and where either long-term survey-type research or basic research divorced from the teaching function is needed.[34] Nevertheless much of the research conducted by government agencies for the use of industry would be more effectively performed within the industrial sector. The recent contracting-out policy recognises that fact (see later).

Most industrialised nations support industrial R & D and, like Canada, they have tended to concentrate their aid in high-technology industries such as aerospace and electronics;[35] industries which Maddock points out in the context of the UK contribute only a small proportion to export sales (chapter 1).[36] The low level of R & D performance by Canadian industry relative to the US and the UK has often been defended in terms of the large degree of industrial research devoted in these two countries to defence and to large-scale national projects such as space exploration. This is a weak argument, however, since Canada has heavily supported R & D projects related to defence in the electronics and aerospace industries since 1959. (This argument has become even less true as the US now spends less than one third of its R & D budget on space and defence.)[37]

Government policy has shifted its emphasis from R & D incentive schemes to schemes with wider relevance to the whole innovation process. In 1977 the Department of Industry, Trade and Commerce replaced all its incentive and aid programmes with one Enterprise Development Programme. Industry had been critical of the multitude of programmes each of limited scope and with its own administrative and approval procedures based in Ottawa which had tended to neglect the management and marketing strength of the companies which were necessary for commercial success. The new programme is designed to overcome these weaknesses both administratively and by focusing upon promising smaller and medium-sized firms prepared to undertake relatively high-risk projects in relation to their resources which promise good rates of return on the total investment.[38] The government now supports industrial R & D indirectly through tax concessions (which have the added advantage of not appearing in departmental estimates in a period of financial stringency!), and aids all aspects of innovation. To these has been added a new policy — the contracting-out policy.

Procurement and Contracting-out

One of the major ways a government can influence national technological development is to use its considerable buying power to purchase technological services and goods from its own industries and universities.[39] The Canadian government has been criticised because it has tended to support 'in-house' scientific activities even when they could have been obtained outside the public sector. Government intramural R & D expenditures have consistently been about 40 per cent of the GERD and have grown steadily during the past three years, as has government support for university research. In the most recently reported year support for industry has actually fallen, due to replacement of IRDIA by tax-based schemes.

The one form of government support which has increased steadily has been contract research. This fact must be recognised as being a result of one of the Ministry of State for Science and Technology's few successful policies. The so-called 'make-or-buy' policy was announced in 1973.[40] Under the policy, government departments were required to contract-out their technological requirements for new programmes to industry. In 1974, the policy was extended so that firms could submit unsolicited proposals to the government which the appropriate department might support. Finally in 1976, all departments were required to review their programmes with a view to transferring the technological requirements of as many as possible to the industrial sector.[41] In the past three years, total contracts awarded have almost doubled in value, and by 1978-9 amount to $149 million or 55 per cent of federal science expenditures in industry.[42] An evaluation of the make-or-buy policy revealed that the contract mechanism has favoured small and medium-sized high-technology companies in three specific industry sectors — electronics, transportation and service.[43] It was judged that continuing technological benefits were probable or possible in 65 per cent of the contracts. For reasons of competitiveness, financial stability and international credibility, individual companies consider research contracts as a strong mechanism to encourage and favour industrial innovation. Contracts resulting from unsolicited proposals were thought to be particularly useful in this regard.[44] However, it was obvious that large parts of industry were not reached by the policy under the old guidelines. The extension of the policy guidelines to include current in-house work will mean that departments such as Agriculture, which hitherto have not participated in significant contract research, will now involve industries in different sectors, for example, food and energy.

Direct Government Intervention

In Canada, this has taken two forms: direct purchase of ailing but technologically important firms (what in other countries would be called nationalisation!), and the total development of an industry by government agencies. The first is very unusual and will be examined here for the case of the aircraft industry. The second has become a fairly common practice since 1945, following the worldwide model provided by the nuclear industry (chapter 3). The aircraft industry is interesting on two counts. It provides an excellent example of the good and bad effects of foreign ownership, and also of government intervention in a high-technology industry where the concern is much broader than with technology alone.

The Canadian government learned early on that it alone could not afford to fund expensive aircraft. In 1959, the newly-elected government under John Diefenbaker refused further support for the development of a totally Canadian designed and built fighter plane, the Avro Arrow. Costs had more than tripled and in the absence of any prospective sales abroad, the project was cancelled.[45] The project's demise was instantaneous. Within days all but the few workers required to dismantle the existing airframes had been dismissed, and Canada lost an aeronautical design team which had taken years to build. Canada now buys its military aircraft from the US, but negotiates substantial sub-contracts for Canadian firms. Typical of this kind of agreement was the awarding of a $32 million sub-contract to Canadair for parts of the 18 P3 Lockheed Orion long-range patrol aircraft bought for its NATO role of ocean and submarine surveillance.

However, the government was well aware that it could afford to lose

neither the expertise nor the jobs involved in Canada's remaining
airframe industry, particularly in a time of economic depression. Since
1975, Canada has bought de Havilland of Canada Ltd. and Canadair on
precisely these grounds. In both cases the companies were foreign-
owned, and the parent company was unwilling to finance extensive
development of new aircraft in Canada. Besides the $40 million
purchase price for each firm, the government has committed $89
million to develop and build the de Havilland DHC-7 STOL aircraft
and $50 million to carry on design and development work for contracts
which Canadair had been awarded. Speaking about these purchases, the
Minister said:

> Plans to purchase two aerospace firms are two major steps towards
> implementing a strategy for restructuring Canada's aerospace
> industry. In the past the growth and further development of those
> airframe manufacturers has been impaired by the fact that they are
> foreign-owned and controlled. These companies have had little
> independent authority to make decisions.[46]

He could have been speaking of nearly all of Canada's manufacturing
industry. In fact, repatriation of control and the accompanying
improvement in the balance of payments were probably not as
important as other factors, such as the jobs which would have been
lost. Moreover, as has been shown already, the government had already
substantially aided the industry through its grant incentive scheme.
Nor could it ignore the export sales of this industry, which if small,
amounted to $453 million in 1976, balancing imports of $410 million.[47]
Ironically about half of these export sales come from a highly successful
company in the aircraft industry which is foreign owned.

Pratt-Whitney Aircraft of Canada Ltd. is a subsidiary of the US
United Technical Corporation. The Canadian subsidiary has been given
the corporate responsibility for worldwide manufacturing and marketing
of small gas turbines for aviation, exports more than 95 per cent of its
turbine line, amounting to export sales of $200 million in 1976,[48] and
spends 12 per cent of its sales on R & D. It received its early start in
this line with the help of United Aircraft but has built its own team of
managers and market specialists. In every way, Pratt-Whitney is
precisely the kind of example the government seeks to encourage; a
company which specialises in one line, for which it is totally responsible
from R & D to marketing, manufacturing a product using few resources
and adding high value in the manufacturing process, and which finally is

an aggressive exporter.

Conclusion

This chapter has demonstrated that Canada is to some extent an unusual industrial nation because of a combination of geography, population, access to markets, its resource-based economy and the degree of foreign control of its manufacturing industry. But it has also shown that the government has adopted means to create new technological development which are by no means unique. Canada's AECL hardly differs from France's Commissariat à l'energie atomique, and Canada's response to an ailing airframe industry was to nationalise it, exactly as the shipbuilding and aircraft industries were nationalised in the UK. The Canadian government provides a substantial proportion of industrial R & D expenditures, again like France.

Canada is unusual in the degree to which it has identified technological innovation with industrial R & D. Much of the government's support has gone, in one form or another, to increase the funds devoted to industrial R & D. But despite every conceivable incentive scheme, the level of R & D funding remains at 1 per cent, where it was fifteen years ago, and industry's contribution remains very low. Therefore, the kind of massive increase in R & D funding implied by a goal of 2.5 per cent is simply unrealistic. Government can hardly afford it and industry has shown no interest. And why should it? Firms only undertake commitments to R & D when they believe it is commercially wise to do so. But the structure of Canadian industry scarcely demands it. The fruits of R & D are generally available at lower cost from abroad, often from a parent company. Also, whereas Japan has chosen to purchase licences which can lead to further development, Canada, because so much of its industry is of the branch plant kind, has accepted technology embodied in machinery usually requiring little further development.

The Science Council has called for the government to help develop a new industrial strategy which would allow Canada to exercise technological sovereignty, which in turn would encourage the development of original technology.[49] As part of that strategy, it suggests Canada must shift from what Gilpin has called an importation strategy to scientific and technological specialisation,[50] thus becoming like Sweden and the Netherlands. The government's policies should support the development of indigenous technological capabilities in selected areas. In fact the government has been doing that in its emphasis upon support for the aerospace, nuclear and electronics industries. These high-technology industries are also favoured by other nations, most notably the US, the UK, France and West Germany. This is not surprising since these have been fast-growing areas since 1945. Canada has avoided trying to compete across the whole spectrum of these industries, and has concentrated instead on developing the kind of indigenous technological capability called for by the Science Council. The airframe industry produces rugged bush and passenger planes, the satellites are for communications and remote sensing, the computer industry is beginning to sell 'software' abroad, and even the nuclear industry is based on indigenous technology and resources. But despite technological success in all these areas, they do not contribute much to Canada's economy — less than 10 per cent of all goods shipped. The government has announced that its priorities now lie in developing technology in areas broadly defined as oceans, food, energy, space and transportation. Some of these continue existing policies, and there is no reason to believe that any more substantial benefit to the economy will result than in the past.

The aim of the Enterprise Development Programme to help small to medium companies, and the extension of the contracting-out principle to all existing government programmes, are likely to help those companies in the less glamorous but economically important industries who wish to keep abreast of new technology, and it is in this way that the government will have the greatest direct impact upon future technological developments. The Canadian government is not alone in its uncertainty as to how to influence technology in the industrial sector.[51] However without massive, politically unpopular intervention in the economy, it is unlikely that the government can radically alter the technological course of the nation.

Notes

1. This chapter refers only to activities of the federal government, and all references to 'government' imply this. The chapter therefore neglects the influence of the provincial governments.
2. *Statistics Canada*, Merchandise Trade (1974-6).
3. Recent closing of nickel ore mines in Ontario by a multinational corporation illustrates this point. The company can obtain ores more cheaply in Indonesia.
4. *Statistics Canada*, Canada Year Book (1975).
5. OECD, *Gaps in Technology Between Member Countries: Analytical Report* (Paris, OECD, 1969).
6. Senate of Canada, *A Science Policy for Canada*, vols.1-3 (Ottawa, Special Committee on Science Policy, 1970-3).

7. K. Levitt, *Silent Surrender* (London, Macmillan, 1970), pp.130-5.

8. Science Council of Canada, *Innovation and the Structure of Canadian Industry* (Ottawa, SCC Special Study No.23, 1972), p.65.

9. A.E. Safarian, *Foreign Ownership of Canadian Industry* (New York, McGraw-Hill, 1966).

10. G. Bruce Doern, *Science and Politics in Canada* (Montreal, McGill-Queens University Press, 1972), p.22.

11. *Royal Commission on Government Organisation*, vol.4 (Ottawa, 1964).

12. Ian Chapman and Michael Gibbons, 'Innovation and the Senate Report on Science Policy', *Journal of Canadian Studies* (Spring 1978), pp.30-7.

13. P. Aucoin and R. French, 'The Ministry of State for Science and Technology', *Canadian Public Administration* (Fall 1974), pp.461-81.

14. H.C. Eastman and S. Stykolt, *The Tariff and Competition in Canada* (Toronto, Macmillan, 1967), p.102.

15. D.J. Daly and S. Globerman, *Tariff and Science Policies* (Toronto, University of Toronto Press, 1976).

16. W.E.G. Salter, *Productivity and Technical Changes* (London, Cambridge University Press, 1966).

17. Science Council of Canada, *Governments and Innovation* (Ottawa, SCC Special Study, No.26, 1973), p.199.

18. *Statistics Canada*, Merchandise Trade Exports, Imports.

19. G. Paquet, 'Taxation and Science Policy', *Canadian Tax Journal* (September-October 1971).

20. Economic Council of Canada, Second Annual Review (Ottawa, ECC, 1965), p.175.

21. *Financial Post Conferences*, Research and Development: Strategy for Success, Ottawa (25 January 1978).

22. Hon.J. Buchanan, 'Industrial Research and Development: Will Canada Meet the Challenge?' (MOSST Press Release, 3 April 1978).

23. Department of Defence Production, *Annual Report*, 1958, p.26.

24. Department of Industry, Trade and Commerce, *Doing Business in Canada: Federal Incentives to Industry* (1972).

25. Science Council of Canada, *Governments and Innovation*, p.63.

26. *Financial Post* (12 June 1965), p.66.

27. Science Council of Canada, *Governments and Innovation*, p.63.

28. *Financial Post* (19 September 1964), p.6.

29. Debates, House of Commons, 20 May 1966, Drury.

30. Science Council of Canada, *Governments and Innovation*, p.65.

31. *Financial Post* (10 August 1968), p.11.

32. Science Council of Canada, *Governments and Innovation*, p.63.

33. R. McDougall, 'IRDIA Celebrates a Birthday', *Canada Commerce* (April 1972).

34. Science Council of Canada (*Annual Report* (1971-2), pp.45-6.

35. For example see, K. Pavitt, 'Governmental Support for Industrial Research and Development in France: Theory and Practice', *Minerva*, XIV (3, 1976), pp.330-54.

36. I. Maddock, 'End of the glamorous adventure?', *New Scientist* (13 February 1975), pp.375-8.

37. *Financial Post* (5 July 1975), p.3.

38. D.G. Boxall, 'The Enterprise Development Programme', *Department of Industry, Trade and Commerce* (Ottawa, August 1977).

39. C. Freeman, *The Economics of Industrial Innovation* (Harmondsworth, Penguin, 1974), p.305.

40. MOSST, *The Make-or-Buy-Policy* (Ottawa, 1975).

41. Treasury Board, *Policy and Guidelines for contracting-out the government's requirements in Science and Technology* (Ottawa, 1977).

42. MOSST, *Federal Science Expenditures, 1975-6 – 1977-8* (March 1977), p.64.

43. MOSST, *The Make-or-Buy Policy* (1975), p.17.

44. Ibid., p.22.

45. Debates, House of Commons (20 February 1959), J.G. Diefenbaker.

46. *Canada News Facts*, 1211 (1974), Gillespie.

47. *Statistics Canada*, Exports and Imports, 1974-5 (July 1977).

48. *Financial Post Conferences*, Research and Development.

49. Science Council of Canada, *Annual Report, No.11* (Ottawa, 1977).

50. R. Gilpin, 'Technological Strategies and National Purpose', *Science* (31 July 1970), pp.441-8.

51. K. Pavitt and W. Walker, 'Government Policies Towards Industrial Innovation: A Review', *Research Policy*, vol.1 (1976), pp.11-97.

3 THE DEVELOPMENT OF NUCLEAR TECHNOLOGY

Roger Williams

Technology and politics are both in different senses the arts of the possible and, increasingly, out of their interaction has been born the actual. This is strikingly true of the development of civil nuclear energy. For the first fifteen years in the development of nuclear technology the dynamic link between technical potential and political will was provided mainly by military considerations, specifically weapons and submarine propulsion. In the following decade economic possibilities began to provide a second connection, and for about the last fifteen years there have been both civil and military nuclear drives. These have been, and are, interconnected, but their overlap is not complete nor is its extent generally agreed.

The exploitation of civil nuclear power has given rise to many different kinds of political question. Broadly they can be divided into the organisational, technical and economic on the one hand, and the environmental and ethical on the other. This essay briefly reviews each of these two categories of question in turn and then addresses itself to the future, specifically to the proper location of nuclear energy in overall energy policy, and to the public policy aspects of nuclear decision-making. A difficulty fundamental to the essay and not satisfactorily resolved within it is that different states have had different experiences with the development of nuclear energy, and yet one wants sometimes, as here, to reflect on the process from a broader perspective than is afforded by a single national viewpoint.

Institutionally the development of nuclear energy has been handled in a variety of ways but all countries appear to have treated it as something of a special case.[1] The intent has normally been to facilitate the exploitation of the new technology while retaining, as it has been thought, an unusually high degree of political control.

The first of these objectives has commonly been realised, but enhanced political oversight has proved in the event a much less straightforward goal. This is principally because when orthodox political arrangements are suspended, those which replace them usually turn out to have their own shortcomings. In the US for instance, in an unprecedented departure, executive and legislative monopolies were

59

created in the form of the US Atomic Energy Commission (USAEC) and the Joint Committee on Atomic Energy. Many of the problems characteristic of monopolies then followed. In Britain too an executive monopoly was created, the legislature in this case lacking the will to assert itself. The particular organisational form chosen for the UK Atomic Energy Authority (UKAEA) thereafter gave that institution many of the worst features of each of the two types of public body on which it was based: government departments and nationalised industries. The result in both the US and the UK was that civil nuclear politics became a category apart, certainly to the disadvantage of public accountability, and frequently to that of good decision making as well.

One definite advantage did ensue from the fact that nuclear energy was everywhere treated politically and administratively as a case apart. The occupational and environmental health and safety standards of this industry were from the outset made uniquely high. The knowledge that these standards had to be especially stringent was in fact among the considerations which had ensured a special status for nuclear energy in the first place. It does not follow that the nuclear standards which have been adopted and evolved are right in any absolute sense, or for all time, or for example, that the assumptions regarding accident probabilities are unchallengeable. What can be asserted is only that no other industry has ever been established to the standards of this one. It should also be said here that the soundness of nuclear energy policies and standards quite apart, it is highly desirable that the hazard philosophy of this industry be applied more widely. In Britain it seems clear that this was one of the objectives the 1975 absorption of the Nuclear Installations Inspectorate (NII) into the Health and Safety Executive was meant to accomplish.

In setting up institutions and giving them remits, policy makers both create a lobby and structure the subsequent range of policy options. In the nuclear case the resulting lobby also had some special characteristics. First among these was the tradition of secrecy inherited from military nuclear programmes, and second was the arcane nature of the nuclear establishment's pursuits. There was as well from the beginning a sense of romance and an ill-defined but seductive promise. Politicians and officials, capable of being the most sceptical of beings, were in this case generally very uncritical.

It was also not always realised in the early years that in this technology, more perhaps than in any other, the functions of sponsorship and regulation had to be clearly separated. This had formally occurred in the UK by the late 1950s and led to the establishment of the NII, but it took another decade and a half to be accepted in the US for example, and only in 1975 did the Nuclear Regulatory Commission (NRC) emerge there as an independent agency. In both cases many of the regulatory personnel had necessarily in their earlier careers been inculcated in the philosophies of the sponsorship agencies. It therefore took some time for the NII in Britain to acquire a confident approach of its own, and the same transitional period had to be expected in the US in the case of the NRC.

Excluding the 'ethical-environmental' issues, the principal policy questions raised by civil nuclear energy can all be traced back to the decisions and circumstances of the technology's early years.[2] The US, Britain and Canada, and to a lesser extent France, all enjoyed some direct inheritance from their wartime efforts. The Canadians have since found it possible to persist with the heavy water reactor (HWR) line they initially adopted. The US settled on the pressurised light water reactor (PWR) as a direct consequence of the decision to initiate a submarine propulsion programme, added the boiling water reactor (BWR), and later found no serious technical constraint in the way of light water reactor (LWR) development for civil purposes. Britain and France, much more limited at the outset in the coolant/moderator/fuel possibilities open to them, opted instead for gas-graphite natural uranium reactors. Britain later moved from these to the gas-graphite enriched uranium reactor, while France switched to American LWRs. West Germany, coming in later, faced fewer constraints and in particular met with no hindrance to the adoption of the LWR. Japan and Italy elected to begin with both gas-graphite and light water stations, but eventually consolidated on the latter.

The philosophy of a reactor development programme with two main stages, thermal and fast reactors, had taken early root in Britain, was soon accepted also in France and later in West Germany, but was never thought urgent in the US, or even necessary in Canada. In the US this was because there was felt to be no pressure to hasten civil nuclear development, but even when that pressure did begin to emerge the US could comfort itself with the size of its uranium reserves. In Canada the HWR was viewed as capable of performing the function of thermal and fast reactors combined. On the fuel side, Britain, France and West Germany having each arrived by different routes at enriched uranium reactors, all three then came to think it essential to have a source of enriched uranium independent of the US. France eventually had to settle for a wholly independent enrichment programme, West Germany given the sensitivity of the issue never had any real choice but to join in an international collaborative programme, and only Britain found it possible to follow a mixed strategy, converting the Capenhurst diffusion enrichment plant from military to civil use and co-operating in a tripartite centrifuge project with West Germany and the Netherlands. Britain, France and West Germany also had a common interest in fuel reprocessing and were able to concert their arrangements in respect of this.

Within reactor programmes fast breeder reactor (FBR) development in particular has often been spoken of as offering a classic opportunity for international collaboration, yet the three major European FBR projects have been pursued virtually independently of each other, and only one of them has involved collaboration. The nuclear field as a whole on the other hand has shown that collaboration can work, the Dragon High Temperature Reactor (HTR) and tripartite enrichment projects standing out in the research and development and commercial categories respectively. The contrast between the development of the light water and gas-graphite reactors is also instructive in this connection. In the first case, American companies having established themselves in the technology, firms elsewhere, and notably in West Germany, then obtained the basic technology under licence. By contrast, although Britain and France both chose to give the highest priority to the gas-graphite line, they never managed to pool their efforts, and France switched to LWRs as soon as political circumstances there permitted this shift to a foreign technology.

Of the three main types of thermal reactor, light and heavy water and gas-graphite, despite the almost complete international dominance the former have achieved, it is not certain that they are better in any really fundamental techno-economic sense. It is clear that they have had substantially more resources expended on them than have either of the other types, that they have been sold exceptionally hard, and that choosing them has come to be the only commercially orthodox policy for a country free of all prior attachment. It is also apparent that LWR operators stand to benefit from the sheer number of these reactors now working or under construction. What it is impossible to know is what the relative status of the three main thermal reactor types would now look like had the US not opted for LWRs. Such an observation may be thought of academic interest only, in that we are where we are no matter how we arrived there. Britain's confirmation in 1978 of her commitment to the Advanced Gas Cooled Reactor (AGR) and Canada's continuing confidence in the HWR show, however, that these countries are not wholly convinced of the advantages of the LWRs, and where the

HWR at least is concerned it seems unlikely that the last word has as yet been written.

It is of interest that it was usually described as both a necessity and a virtue of the British approach that it was a 'narrow front' one by comparison with that of the US. The greater resources of the latter were supposed to have allowed a much wider coverage of the multiplicity of reactor types originally thought to be feasible. Closer inspection, however, suggests that Britain's approach was not really all that much of a 'narrow front' one after all. This description might perhaps have been accurately applied to the succession Magnox-AGR-HTR (Marks I-III, as they became known, of the gas-graphite reactor). But even here there were three distinct reactors and several different commercial designs of both Magnox and the AGR rather than a steady improvement of one basic reactor. In addition, there was the Steam Generating Heavy Water Reactor as a deliberate break with the narrow front, and the FBR as a long-term option. At the same time, if the American approach is to be regarded as 'broad front', then it must be said that this narrowed sharply to a commercial attack based on two versions of the LWR, the PWR and the BWR, plus a flirtation with the HTR.

The US and West Germany found it easier to establish strong nuclear construction industries than did either Britain or France. One important reason for this was that the US and West Germany left the industrial initiative to existing strong firms, whereas Britain and France initially decided in favour of encouraging consortia arrangements, several independent firms being involved in each consortium. As a result, the General Electric Company and Westinghouse led the way in the US, AEG and Siemens in West Germany. In Britain, by contrast, no less than five consortia were originally established, each having a turnkey construction capability but each having weaknesses derived from its mixed membership. When the workload proved inadequate the British consortia were forced to amalgamate, their number first falling to three. Further rationalisation reduced them to two and then to one, their character having meanwhile changed and there being also by now a public shareholding. This was a long drawn-out and debilitating process.[3] At the time of writing the structure of this one remaining organisation is being yet again amended. Industrial weakness of the kind implied by the consortia arrangement could not but undermine the prospect of commercial success, even had the reactor position been satisfactory. Since this was also confused in both Britain and France, these countries gave themselves two problems both of which the US and West Germany mostly avoided.

The questions of industrial structure and reactor choice which dominated civil nuclear power policies in the 1950s and early 1960s were essentially technocratic concerns. They involved what Galbraith has called the technostructure and, intermittently and mostly for ratification, the polity. In their resolution the wider public enjoyed at best only an observer status. In the late 1960s this began to change and what has become known as 'the nuclear debate' has since then steadily widened. Perhaps more surprising than the rise of the anti-nuclear lobby which subsequently occurred in the late 1960s was the time it had taken for this opposition to manifest itself. It is also material that when the opposition did begin to crystallise nuclear power was to begin with only an important target of opportunity within a wider environmental movement.

There were no doubt many reasons why the opposition had not appeared earlier. One reason was probably the fact that the military dimension of nuclear technology had for two decades drawn the sting of criticism and protest, while simultaneously allowing the infant civil nuclear industry to appear by comparison a bounteous relief. Another reason may have been that the visibility of civil nuclear power in the US was not great until the upsurge in nuclear ordering there following the proclaimed breakthrough in 1963 to economic nuclear power.

That the opposition to nuclear power should first have become focused in the US was chiefly a matter of cultural resonance. But when this movement began to coalesce in the US it was assisted by a technical factor. The LWRs which by then had come to dominate the American commercial scene were reactor types which from the beginning had been recognised as posing particularly taxing safety problems. When the same reactors began to capture the international market as well, this allowed the opposition to be exported with the reactors, and the phenomenon quickly found fair sustenance in the liberal democracies of continental Western Europe.[4]

Once the nuclear debate did get under way, just as the complex nature of nuclear technology had earlier allowed the engineers somewhat to mystify, so in due turn it now allowed their opponents to obfuscate. If engineers could talk of using FBRs to burn the rocks and thus solve the world's energy problems, then opponents could speak of a grapefruit-sized plutonium lump as being capable of bringing an end to civilisation. Truth however is rarely so simple as to be clarified by such metaphors, or yet so complicated as to require them.

A number of organisations were formed or reoriented to represent the various groups opposed to nuclear power, Friends of the Earth (FoE) being the most internationally prominent amongst them. A substantial opposition literature naturally followed, some of it thorough and technical, some simply standard lobby copy.[5] Unhappily, one of the least satisfactory features of the consequent debate, at least in its early stages, was the difficulty neutrals had in winning recognition. By 1976 there was no shortage of literature critical of nuclear power, and there then appeared several official or semi-official reports which lent a new tone to the opposition. The Flowers, Fox and Ford reports, in particular, though far from anti-nuclear, provided much grist for the mill of bodies like FoE.

It can be seen that the opposition to nuclear power has had a number of distinct themes. Reactor safety has been a central one of these and has had two major sub-themes, relating respectively to the LWR and the FBR. Concern about the LWR has also centred on its ecological impact in normal operation. Another important opposition theme has been the implications of the controlled, that is deliberate, release of radioactivity from nuclear installations. Then there have been the fears about nuclear wastes, how and especially where to store them. Yet another issue, plutonium recycling, has given rise to several separate objections. First among these has been that even in the best of worlds this material is inherently too dangerous to be allowed to become the basis of an energy economy. Second, this not being the best of worlds, the possibility of terrorism in the context of plutonium has been held to be a real one. And third, the security arrangements made to counter this second problem could well, it has been argued, introduce a third grave problem, basic infringement of civil liberties. The spectre of nuclear weapon proliferation, it has also been suggested, while closely linked to all civil nuclear activities, is especially closely related to plutonium recycling.

In addition to these concerns having their origin squarely in the technology of nuclear power there have also been broader objections, to the central-station generation of electricity for instance, and indeed to the imposition of technology and of technical fixes quite generally. In some cases the nuclear opposition movement has also certainly been used as a vehicle by individuals and groups having political aims unconnected with nuclear energy, or even with technology as a whole.

The exponents of nuclear power have answered these various objections, though rarely to the satisfaction of their critics, as follows. They have argued that reactors, including the FBR, can be engineered to be as safe as is thought necessary, so that the probability of a given reactor accident is made as small as is judged appropriate in proportion to its potential consequences, the whole being subject to independent regulation. They have produced figures to show that controlled releases of radioactive material are well in line with natural radiation. They have also pointed to the excellent occupational health record of the nuclear industry, to demonstrate that nuclear accidents in practice are of negligible significance, and also to indicate that the existing radiation standards are fully adequate. Plutonium recycling they have dealt with either by suggesting that it is unnecessary — essentially the Canadian position and also the interim American one under President Carter — or else by showing that if it is economically justified, then it can be made technically and socially safe through a variety of technical arrangements and without undermining the freedom of a society. Nuclear waste they have insisted is only a technical problem, and one which could already have been solved had the engineers thought it urgent, but which certainly can be solved, and sooner rather than later, if nuclear expansion is made conditional upon the establishment of an acceptable solution. To the opponents of large-scale electricity generation and advanced technology in general they have essentially said: 'Show us first that the public really wants your ideal society with all its consequences, for until you do we must be the servants of the existing economic, and therefore, energy order.'

The one point which the nuclear advocates have conceded is that there exists a military danger intrinsic to nuclear energy, but this they have maintained is a danger whether or not civil nuclear power is exploited. Opponents of nuclear energy have not accepted this latter distinction. All the criticisms of nuclear power if valid are clearly of political and economic significance, but this one perhaps more than any other. Since nuclear advocates and critics can both agree that it is the military aspect of the technology which remains most disturbing, who is right as to the contribution of civil nuclear energy, advocates or objectors? Probably to some extent both sides are. The construction of a nuclear weapon requires a certain basic industrial capability. The number of countries possessing this is steadily increasing and this is a situation which may be expected to continue. For these countries the constraints in the way of nuclear weapons are therefore political and not technical or economic. In that sense supporters of civil nuclear power are correct. This problem will not disappear, whatever happens to civil nuclear energy, for as has been said, all future ages of man are inescapably nuclear ones. It should also be noted that for the existing nuclear weapons states the civil aspect played no part in their decisions to develop nuclear weapons, nor did it significantly facilitate the execution of those decisions once taken. The same factors might not obtain in the future as did in the past, but it still seems highly probable that it is the political and not the technological parameters which in any given case would be decisive. That said, it must be admitted that one of the determinants historically of nuclear weapon *potential* among states has been the growing world familiarity with civil nuclear technology, as promoted by governmental initiatives such as the Atoms for Peace programme, and also as increasingly fostered by commercial activity.

We have now outlined both the 'technocratic' and the 'ethical' issues attached to nuclear energy and it is time to put them into some comprehensive policy perspective. One can think of any decision as being at the apex of two event cones. Converging upon the decision there is then a process of policy deliberation, a process which will include feedback from previous decisions. Diverging from it is a process of policy execution. Of any decision one can proceed to ask questions about both of these processes and also about the locus and immediate characteristics of the decision itself. Whether or not a given decision is to be described as a good one must obviously depend upon value judgements, though rarely completely so if the analytical criteria are specified. In any case, thinking about decisions in the way suggested here forces one to consider alternative deliberation-decision-execution processes. It also implies that one element of an effective decision-making system would be a facility to benefit from previous decision cycles. Only a few of the ideas which arise from such a model as this can be pursued here.

In the terms of the model it is readily apparent that where nuclear energy is concerned all states have experienced considerable difficulty in accommodating their deliberative processes to the wide public interest. As with other technologies, for the first two decades of civil nuclear development the same general assumption was made practically everywhere: it was the function of government to take decisions in the public interest. By contrast, it has now been recognised in some quarters that the process of deliberation can properly include as well some non-governmental definition or definitions of the public interest. Here one can only point out that the resulting device of 'opening up' government can itself easily become in insincere hands an instrument of manipulation exactly as is the more traditional technique of invoking confidentiality.

We cannot alter the fact that present options are the heirs to past decisions, but at the same time using hindsight to improve foresight is a basic principle of wisdom. Bearing in mind Britain's inflexible, largely because programmatic, development of nuclear energy, it would appear that she at least could with advantage have proceeded more slowly, allowing more time and a wider debate at each point of decision.

Though Britain's experience could not strictly be described as typical, one lesson from the civil nuclear past still seems plain enough, though in practice it remains controversial. This is that all relevant information needs to be made publicly available so that the rightness of particular decisions may be judged at the time they are taken by the widest possible audience, and so that these decisions may be kept under general review as the assumptions on which they were based become modified by new developments. Only on clear grounds of national or commercial necessity does it seem persuasive that information should not be made public, and in these cases the decision to withhold information would ideally itself be a fully explained one. Had such practices been adhered to in the past it is difficult to believe either that nuclear decision making would have been as inadequate as it frequently was — and this not only in Britain — or that the nuclear industry would suddenly have found its motives questioned in the way which has occurred in recent years. National and commercial security apart, the only other grounds for withholding information from the public are, after all, that one fears their response, or else that one has something to hide. But as the AEA chairman for instance has said, the British public has 'far more intelligence than it is usually credited with' — and we have no right to assume less of other equally mature publics.[6] With openness and a healthy debate the public can be relied upon not necessarily to understand the technical ramifications of any argument, but certainly in time to know which institutions — and even which individuals — it can best trust. Public debate about principles has now won a reluctant acceptance, but it is still widely assumed that the responsible authorities should not engage in public discussion of their technical problems.

On the other hand, it needs to be acknowledged that the nuclear debate has brought out some of the shortcomings of participation as a political ideal. The call for enhanced participation is so often at root a demand only for a different decision. If then the call leads to a more open decision-making process, but still to the same basic decisions, then there is commonly a sense of anti-climax, frustration or downright bitterness and alienation.[7]

The nuclear debate has also underlined the unequal resources in time, expertise and money of the participants. In part this is inevitable and, some would also say, as it should be. Public bodies are after all charged to define and uphold the public interest as it appears to them or as they are directed, and to suggest that they cannot to some degree be trusted to do this is to undermine an essential plank of public administration. Yet it is difficult to be entirely comfortable with this situation, and a sine qua non would appear to be the regular *and full* ex post facto calling to account of public bodies. A body which has done its homework thoroughly has little to fear from the cold light of public scrutiny, and one which has not does not deserve confidentiality. Debate, it will be said, takes time and costs money. So it does, but there is no need for great concern on that score unless the costs are completely disproportionate in comparison with the project at issue. Even then, the value of liberal democracy does not lie in its capacity to take quick and cheap decisions. Put another way, project autocracy is one thing, but policy autocracy, which all too often has been the nuclear norm, is quite another.[8]

But how to ensure a rigorous yet balanced debate? Here there seems no alternative in the long run, and looking beyond the nuclear field, to the conscious encouragement through public funding of alternative policy proposals. It is not enough to rely on individuals, pressure groups and university departments to generate such proposals. In a field as technical as nuclear energy especially much more is required. We can be confident we have taken the best decision only if all reasonable alternatives have been properly delineated and assessed. That is rarely the case in contemporary public policy. If this is still a counsel of perfection in 1978 it will not seem so for much longer. Policy monopolies will surely be seen in the long run to be as unattractive as commercial ones.

There is, despite the criticisms entered here, one important sense in which nuclear energy has already suffered to no advantage from the new public response. As was observed above, the standards to which this industry has worked have been high, even if their enforcement has not always been equally thorough in all countries. Furthermore, as also has been suggested, responsible public reviews of one or another aspect of the industry have a vital part to play in furthering these standards. Studies such as the Royal Commission report and the Windscale Inquiry in Britain, the Rasmussen and Ford Studies in the US, and the Fox report in Australia for example, force the nuclear establishment to look again at their assumptions and practices.[9] Some of the questions raised by the nuclear opposition have also been constructive in this sense.

Unfortunately, the hard umbra of critical challenge becomes surrounded by a large penumbra of misleading, mischievous and ill-informed comment. The nuclear establishment could either simply ignore or else carefully dismiss this soft surround, but its very existence serves to prevent the better education of the public. The problem is not peculiar to nuclear energy. Quite generally, the media tend to oversimplify or trivialise. For two decades civil nuclear scientists and engineers could do little wrong: in recent years they have in many quarters been allowed as doing little right. One could say that the public has not been well served by much of the reporting and commenting by newspapers, radio and TV. But the fault does not lie wholly with the media. The public at large tends to want simple black and white statements. It does not normally want to invest substantial amounts of time in specialised matters. It also much prefers to have an authority-figure it can trust. There is no obvious way out of this dilemma, though as was said above in a slightly different connection, if the full facts are invariably tabled, misinterpretation and misunderstandings are likely to be minimised.

After thirty years of headlong development in nuclear and other technologies, some lessons in regard to the policy execution process have been painfully learned. Keep options open to the maximum extent; conversely, minimise inflexible commitments; recognise that decisions are embedded in an international context and wherever possible spread the risks; take note that technological problems are not the only kind of difficulty and operate through an efficient structure with clear lines of authority and control; provide in advance for periodic review; try to learn from experience. Unhappily the British civil nuclear record in particular, examined against these criteria, is hardly satisfactory.[10] Other countries appear to have done better, and some, like the US, very much better. It is, however, impossible in these other cases to eliminate the consequences of the concentration on LWRs. These reactors demonstrably work and it has not yet mattered, and may never matter, that other options have not been pursued. The risks in effect have been spread in that there was a military origin, and even more in that the LWRs now constitute an international technology. The different managerial arrangements in the various countries have resulted in differential achievements, but in that the LWRs as they now stand are a success, all LWR countries have something they can point to with satisfaction.

The nuclear industry is still relatively new. In addition, construction of nuclear stations is commonly a very lengthy process.

Operating experience, though now considerable and growing rapidly, is also limited in regard to the most advanced types and larger sizes of reactor. This makes it extremely difficult to arrive at definitive projections of nuclear economics, and also means that there is effectively no actuarial base for calculations relating to nuclear safety. The Americans were much more cautious about nuclear economics in the 1950s than was Britain, but by the mid 1960s both countries were quoting generating costs in three places of decimals. LWR vendors have remained confident about their economic estimates ever since, but by the mid 1970s Britain was virtually back to a 'build it and see' outlook. In respect of nuclear safety meanwhile, in the absence of adequate statistical information, recourse has been necessary to risk analysis backed up by computer, and where possible physical tests, but the premises and methods involved in such analyses remain a matter of debate. The continuing uncertainties regarding nuclear economics and nuclear safety should not really be seen as surprising in view of the rapid and often non-incremental development of this technology and its military origins and connections. Eventually both economic and safety expectations may be expected to settle down – some would say they had already done so – but until the matter is beyond argument common sense would suggest a policy of caution commensurate with energy need rather than, as has so often been the case, one of optimism fired by commercial opportunity or bureaucratic necessity.

Reflections on the last quarter century certainly make very clear the hazards in forecasting energy. This can be seen for instance in the creation of Euratom and in the major British commitment to nuclear power in 1955-7. These initiatives were both largely responses to non-existent crises. As a result of this early commitment on Britain's part, in the 1960s, no energy shortage having arisen, the country found itself with excess nuclear capacity. The US, better provided with fossil fuels, had been able to indulge a more relaxed approach, yet still allowed itself to claim a nuclear breakthrough in 1963. The battle between coal and nuclear power was thereafter joined in both Britain and the US, and with a vengeance. However, in the 1970s, with a new, more general and, it is supposed, more persistent energy gap in prospect, both coal and nuclear power are held to be necessary. No longer, one is told, are they to be seen as competitors, the question is said to be whether even with the best efforts of both an energy shortfall can be avoided.

Reflection on Britain's nuclear experience also shows the long-term effect of policy decisions meant primarily to cope with an immediate problem. The point is that if a country equips itself with a substantial capacity in, as in this case, nuclear technology, it will be inclined to take advantage of this, or at least rescue what it can from the situation, even if the future turns out to require a radically different approach from that foreseen. The policy slate in other words can never really be wiped clean.

Consideration of the past also shows that in their energy and nuclear energy decisions countries are predominantly influenced by their own perceptions of their energy circumstances. Currently the attitudes of countries such as France, Sweden and Japan demonstrate that politically little has changed and that states still feel that ultimately they must look to their own efforts for their energy security. Here also one sees one paradox of President Carter's nuclear policy of 1977. Intent on avoiding fuel reprocessing, the plutonium economy and the fast reactor, the US has shown in this policy, not for the first time, that it cannot be counted upon as a complacent supplier. Concerned to prevent the widespread adoption of one particular set of nuclear technologies the US initiative of 1977 may actually have accelerated in a number of states the independent national development of all types of nuclear technology, this set included.

One might say that hitherto the development of nuclear energy was an independent variable when it ought to have been a dependent one. Even the US, with a seemingly highly successful record of civil nuclear development, belatedly recognised with the conversion of the USAEC into an Energy Research and Development Agency in 1975 that it was more desirable to have an energy policy than a narrowly nuclear one. Adjustments elsewhere have been less abrupt but the implication may be regarded as quite general. The range of energy options in the 1970s might look very different had the balance of energy R & D funding in the 1950s and 1960s not been tilted so completely to the nuclear option. And it is probably not only the energy picture which has been distorted by the concentration on nuclear R & D. This sector has also undoubtedly attracted funds and highly qualified personnel to the disadvantage of other non-energy R & D fields.

We also understand a little better than we mostly did until the energy crisis of 1973 that we can operate on both sides of the energy equation. We have come to appreciate that some demand mixes make more sense than others, that total demand can be influenced by various conservation techniques, and that it is the function of policy to devise the appropriate inducements to these ends. On the supply side we have realised not only that we must secure as broad as possible a technology mix, but also that we must provide for the mix we want tomorrow by the research we stimulate today.

A persuasive case can certainly be made that a serious energy shortage or major energy imbalances are among the most threatening international possibilities we have to fear. It is only intelligent also to reckon on our having little margin for error in the steps we take to prevent such outcomes, though in the event we may be more generously provided for than we have assumed. If these arguments are accepted then no possible energy source should be neglected without very strong reasons. This in turn means that globally both fusion and fast breeder reactors, and any other nuclear system of comparable promise, must if possible be brought to the point of commercial viability. It does not mean that there need be any kind of programmatic commitment to such technologies, or any commitment at all beyond that necessary to meet the minimum goal.

Whatever one's views on nuclear power programmes based on thermal reactors, there are evidently important extra doubts about the desirability, or at least the timing, of fast reactor development.[11] It is equally apparent that the doubts in this case are not confined to the professional critics of nuclear power. Unfortunately, there is also a tendency for the doubts to be expressed in terms only of safety and security and for the technical and economic aspects to be overlooked. Yet if the general public has learned anything about technology it is surely that the more complex the artefact, then normally the less reliable the initial time and cost estimates for its development. In the case of the fast reactor there is also need to keep in mind the energy situation in which commercial exploitation might eventually take place. The greater and the more inflexible the investment in a technological development the more positive the discounted value of the net advantage clearly needs to be to justify proceeding.

Even if the most cautious position to take is that fast reactor development is on balance necessary lest the eventual energy situation worldwide becomes intolerable without it, this still begs the question of who should do the requisite development work. The most attractive proposition would be a fully collaborative international venture. But failing that, any given country has a strong incentive to pitch its effort at as low a level as is compatible with a later rapid acceleration if this becomes indicated. The strategy would thus be to let others bear the main risk in the confident expectation that if the development is finally successful and fast reactor technology and economics consequently come to be more attractive than alternatives, then licences will quickly allow lost ground to be made up.[12]

In summary, in promoting the development of nuclear energy governments have sponsored a civil technology of unprecedented consequence and major, if uncertain, military significance.[13] There should surely have been more circumspection. On the other hand, given the shortcomings in the 1950s and 1960s, and for that matter still, in the socio-political assessment of technological development, it would have been very surprising if there had been deliberation even roughly proportional to nuclear energy's potential impact. Instead, governments in the most industrialised countries proceeded on the tacit assumption that nuclear technology was, in effect, just another technology, albeit a somewhat special one, and in addition during these years technology as a whole went mostly unquestioned. Further, these governments communicated their nuclear values to the less developed countries, both deliberately and indirectly.[14] At the same time they failed to a greater or lesser degree to address many of the tactical and strategical problems which proved to be associated with the introduction of the new technology — controlling the momentum of development and winning public acceptance for it stand out. On the other hand, and especially if past costs are not examined too closely, there have been successes. In particular, nuclear energy does now provide a significant and growing proportion of electrical generating capacity, and the technology is also unique in not having had to learn from its mistakes.

The early nuclear decisions everywhere pre-empted so much and their effects will indefinitely continue. To return to where this essay began, if technology and politics are arts of the possible, it is now appreciated, as it was not in the beginning, that amongst possibilities there are probabilities, but no certainties.

Notes

1. See for example, Margaret Gowing, *Britain and Atomic Energy 1939-1945* (London, Macmillan, 1964) and *Independence and Deterrence*, 2 vols. (London, Macmillan, 1974); R.G. Hewlett and O.E. Anderson, *The New World 1939-45* (Pennsylvania State University Press, 1962), and R.G. Hewlett and F. Duncan, *Atomic Shield 1947-52* (Pennsylvania State University Press, 1969); C. Allardice and E. Trapnell, *The Atomic Energy Commission* (New York, Praeger, 1974); J.E. Hodgetts, *Administering the Atom for Peace*; Harold Orlans, *Contracting for Atoms* (Washington, DC, Brookings Institution, 1967).

2. Philip Mullenback, *Civilian Nuclear Power* (New York, Twentieth Century Fund, 1963) is a useful early view.

3. See E.F. Wonder, 'Decision Making and the Reorganisation of the British Nuclear Power Industry', *Research Policy*, vol.5 (1976), pp.240-68.

4. See for example, J. Surrey and C. Pluslett, 'Opposition to Nuclear Power: A Review of International Experience', *Energy Policy*, vol.5 (December 1976).

5. From an enormous field: Amory B. Lovins, *Soft Energy Paths* (Harmondsworth, Penguin, 1977); Walter C. Patterson, *The Fissile Society* (London, Earth Resources Research Ltd., 1977); Sheldon Novick, *The Careless Atom* (New York, Delta, 1970).

6. Sir John Hill, 'Nuclear Power in the Public Eye', *Atom* (March 1978).

7. See for example, the reaction to *The Windscale Inquiry* (London, HMSO, 1978).

8. Cf. Lord Hinton, 'Two Decades of Nuclear Confusion', *New Scientist* (28 October 1976).

9. Royal Commission on Environmental Pollution, 6th Report, *Nuclear Power and the Environment*, Cmnd.6618; *The Windscale Inquiry*; *Reactor Safety Study*, NRC WASH-1400, 1975; *Nuclear Power Issues and Choices* (Cambridge, Mass., Ballinger Publishing Co., 1977); First Report of the Ranger Environmental Inquiry, chairman Mr Justice Russell Fox (Australian Government Publishing Service, 1976).

10. For one view see Duncan Burn, *Nuclear Power and the Energy Crisis* (London, Macmillan, 1978). See also David Henderson, 'Two British Errors', *Oxford Economic Papers* (July 1977).

11. See for example, J.S. Forrest (ed.), *The Breeder Reactor* (Scottish Academic Press, 1968); J. Rotblat (ed.), *Nuclear Reactors* (London, Taylor and Francis Ltd, 1977); H. Montefiore and D. Gosling, *Nuclear Crisis* (Dorchester, Prism Press, 1977).

12. Cf. Sir Christopher Hinton, 'Nuclear Power', *Three Banks Review*, LII (December 1961).

13. See for example, Mason Willrich (ed.), *International Safeguards and Nuclear Industry* (Baltimore, Johns Hopkins University Press, 1973); Mason Willrich (ed.), *Civil Nuclear Power and International Security* (New York, Praeger, 1971); Mason Willrich, *Global Politics of Nuclear Energy* (New York, Praeger, 1971); Mason Willrich and Theodore B. Taylor, *Nuclear Theft: Risks and Safeguards* (Cambridge, Mass., Ballinger, 1974).

14. Lee C. Nehrt, *International Marketing of Nuclear Power Plants* (Bloomington, Indiana, Indiana University Press, 1966) for an early view.

4 THE CONTRACT MECHANISM AND THE PROMOTION OF BRITISH TECHNOLOGY

Philip Gummett

The interpenetration of the public and private sectors, particularly in the United States and Britain, has attracted considerable attention during the 1970s. One focus of the discussion has been the need to understand the 'new political economy' in which, amongst other characteristics, 'new sectors of the economy have grown up with government as the market', and a new type of relationship has developed between government and interest groups which is

> distinct from traditional lobbying since the private interests have been delegated public responsibilities and the government has assumed an enlarged role for preserving the health and vitality of society's important 'estates'.[1]

These characteristics of the new political economy are well illustrated by the activity of promoting technology, even at the level of research and development.

In seeking to promote technology through the performance of research and development, governments may set up their own research establishments or may finance work to be carried out in industrial, educational or other institutions. In the United States, the country with the largest research and development effort in the world, the government is the major source of funds for research and development, but most of that money goes to non-governmental organisations, working on federal contracts. In this chapter I shall review some features of the research and development contract mechanism in the United States before showing how attempts to apply contract-oriented thinking in Britain have led to a novel twist in its use. Some observations will also be made about the problems of using government laboratories to promote industrial technology.

The Contract Mechanism in the United States

The contract mechanism developed as a result of the policy choice made in the United States in the 1940s to maintain and expand the nation's research and development resources through contracting, rather than through the establishment of intramural government laboratories. The advantages sought by this approach were considerable. Government would have access to the whole range of scientific and technological expertise available in the country, including those individuals who would be loath to leave the private sector to work in government research establishments. Consequently, there would be access to a wide range of approaches to problem solving, and cross-fertilisation between competing institutions could be enhanced. Furthermore, flexible use of scientific resources would be possible, since the responsibility for responding to programme changes would fall on non-governmental institutions.

There was, of course, nothing new about governments placing contracts for goods and services.[2] But the effects of the application of the contract mechanism to research and development in the United States in the 1940s were sufficient for Price, in the early 1950s, to be writing of 'Federalism by Contract', an early version of the 'Contract State' thesis.[3]

Price identified five types of relationship between government agencies and the private institutions which were undertaking contract research and development.[4] First was the fairly straightforward case where contracts were placed for research leading to equipment improvement or some similar specific objective. Second, 'master contracts' were being placed with some organisations, allowing a continuing relationship between agency and contractor to be maintained with the minimum of formality. Third, there were cases where special tactical and strategic studies, traditionally the exclusive province of the military, were being performed by private contractors. Fourth, to meet certain military requirements which entailed the establishment of new, large-scale laboratories, together with the associated scientific *and* managerial competence, some universities were proving willing to take on such assignments in special, off-campus laboratories. Finally, new private bodies, such as the Rand Corporation, were being established specifically to undertake Federal contracts. In total these developments constituted 'a new and rather unsystematic system of improvised federalism, the significance of which it will take years to appraise'.[5]

At least two new industries grew to maturity, sustained by federal contracts for research and development. In the case of one of these, nuclear power, Orlans has noted that the Atomic Energy Commission operated almost entirely by contract, partly because most of the key industrialists and scientists opposed governmental operation of major installations, but also so as to strengthen the industrial sector and keep non-governmental groups well-informed about the evolving technology.[6] In the other case, electronic components, Freeman has shown the importance of federal contracts in establishing the US industry as a world leader.[7] Many other industries have benefited significantly from the contract mechanism, and recent work by Reppy has shown that the benefit has been even greater than had been commonly realised, large sums of Department of Defense money ($1 billion in 1975) having been registered in the national statistics of research and development as deriving from companies, not government.[8]

The contract mechanism is not without its difficulties. Glenn Seaborg, then chairman of the Atomic Energy Commission, has observed:

> Labour management problems can be more acute in cost-type contractor operations; the timely flow of information between Government top management and the performers of the work may be more difficult; highly qualified contractors usually have their own organizational policies and practices which they prefer to follow and may resist some of the controls and procedural requirements which the Government deems necessary; valuable experience and technological advances may be initially in the hands of a few contractors. . .[9]

Despite these problems, however, successive US governments have preferred the contract mechanism to alternative approaches to government-sponsored research and development. From its origins the mechanism quickly evolved into an extremely flexible policy instrument, although one capable of generating mutual dependence between an agency and its contractors. By the mid-1960s Price was writing of the 'fusion of public and private power',[10] a theme which has since often been explored with reference to military contracts.[11] The general position as regards science and technology was summarised as follows by Danhof in 1968:

> The contractual system is. . .more than a device to get work done for a government agency. An agency's program is built upon contributions from many sources, public and private. There are numerous channels through which interested and knowledgeable groups may suggest courses of action. . .A formal contract is merely a step in a process of interaction between private and public groups

with an interest in a scientific or technical area. . .In both the
formulation and the execution of its program the agency is heavily,
and sometimes wholly, dependent upon the initiative of outside
institutions in developing the expertise necessary to prepare the
proposals and do the work.[12]

Had the objectives sought through the contract mechanism been sought
by traditional methods, Danhof concludes, there would inevitably have
occurred in the United States, despite strong ideological objections, a
vast expansion of governmental establishments. Such a form of
organisation, he argues, 'would have isolated in some large degree the
government's operations from those of private institutions'.
Administrative tidiness would have been a poor substitute for the
'greater stimulus' provided by an 'open competitive system'.[13]

Technology Policy in Britain

It is in terms of arguments such as these that the view began to be
advanced in Britain in the 1960s that a mistake had been made in the
1940s and 1950s in concentrating so much research and development
into the government's own research establishments. The contrast
between British and United States practice can easily be overdrawn,
and Table 4.1 may put the position into perspective, but undoubtedly
there has been a greater relative emphasis in Britain than in the United
States on the use of intramural government research establishments.

The reasons for this difference cannot be properly examined, because
the history of early postwar British science policy has still largely to be
written. One important factor may, however, have been the industrial

Table 4.1: Main Sources of Funds (S) and Sectors of Performance (P)
for Research and Development, 1969. (Percentages of total national
expenditure.)

	Business		Government		Higher Education	
	S	P	S	P	S	P
USA	38	70	58	14	3.4	13
UK	44	65	51	25	0.6	8

Source: *Science Policy*, September-October 1972, cited in Keith Pavitt and
Michael Worboys, *Science, Technology and the Modern Industrial State*
(Leeds, Siscon, 1975), p.11.

structures of the two countries, which certainly helped shape their atomic energy programmes. Unlike the United States, Britain did not, in the late 1940s, have sufficient large companies capable of undertaking major contracts in the atomic energy programme; it was for this pragmatic reason, and not on ideological grounds, that the British government itself undertook so much of the necessary work.[14]

Government support for research and development, both extra- and intra-mural, grew throughout the 1950s. The number of government research establishments reached a peak of about sixty. Doubts, however, began to be expressed in the late 1950s and early 1960s about the role of the more industrially oriented of these establishments, particularly the so-called Industrial Research Establishments of the Department of Scientific and Industrial Research.[15] These doubts arose in the context of more general questions about the organisation and value of government civil research, it having been widely observed that despite a relatively high level of expenditure on R & D, the economy in general, and the state of manufacturing industry in particular, left much to be desired.[16]

A report in 1963 proposed the transfer of the industrial research establishments to a new organisation operating with the autonomy of a research council,[17] but this proposal was overtaken by the Labour victory at the general election in 1964. For several years previously an influential group of scientists and Labour politicians had been developing plans to make more purposive use of science and technology in the service of economic development. It was in this context that Mr Wilson, the leader of the Labour Party, made his well-known reference to harnessing 'Socialism to science, and science to Socialism', and to the new Britain that was to be 'forged in the white heat of the scientific revolution'.[18]

After the Labour victory, a Ministry of Technology was set up with responsibility for the industrial research establishments,[19] the Atomic Energy Authority, the National Research Development Corporation (a government agency which provides assistance in the development of inventions), and with sponsorship responsibilities for the machine tools, computers, electronics and telecommunications industries. The ministry was given the general responsibility of guiding and stimulating a major national effort to bring advanced technology and new processes into British industry,[20] and it soon became clear that this objective could not be achieved by the ministry in its original form. The takeover of the Ministry of Aviation in 1967, with its massive procurement programme in the advanced technology sectors (especially aerospace and electronics), greatly strengthened the capacity of the Ministry of Technology to raise the technological standards of manufacturing industry.

The question of how to relate the work of the industrial research establishments to the overall purpose of the ministry continued, however, to prove extremely difficult. As Sir Richard Clarke, the permanent secretary, observed: 'It was reasonable enough to believe that a relationship existed between R & D, innovation and industrial performance; but this did not tell the Ministry where it should push.'[21] By 1967, however, the idea had entered the ministry that the contract mechanism might offer at least a partial solution. But the way in which that mechanism was to be used differed markedly from practice in the United States and requires careful examination.

Government Laboratories as Contractors

It is not fully clear how this idea gained currency within the ministry, but one important source was Professor Patrick Blackett, later Lord Blackett, one of Britain's leading physicists.[22] Blackett had been closely involved in the Labour Party's science policy discussions prior to the 1964 election, and became a senior adviser to the Minister of Technology. In February 1967, Blackett was to argue that Britain might have 'taken the wrong road' immediately after the war by putting too high a proportion of her research and development into government research establishments, and not involving industry more intimately.[23]

By late 1967 this argument had taken root, but with an unexpected outcome: the Minister of Technology stated that he wished to break down the barriers between research and industrial production; he therefore announced, not that he would be curtailing his own research establishments and putting research programmes out into industry, but that his establishments would be encouraged to undertake confidential contract research for industrial firms.[24]

It is plausible to suggest that the ministry may have been encouraged in this line of thought by developments taking place at the Atomic Energy Research Establishment, Harwell. By 1965, soon after Harwell came under the ministry's wing, it had become clear that the laboratory faced an uncertain future. A watershed had been reached in Britain's civil nuclear power programme: nuclear power was now well established as a source of electricity, and although more research would be needed at Harwell, its scale would only be about one third of the then current level. It was thought within Harwell that to reduce the staff by two thirds would destroy the viability of the laboratory, and so moves began to find an additional new mission which would allow the laboratory to remain viable though at lower strength.[25]

This strategy of diversification has not been unique to Harwell. In describing the comparable case of the Oak Ridge National Laboratory in the United States, Teich and Lambright observed that multiplication of sponsors has become a well-established practice for government research establishments on both sides of the Atlantic. It has been thought of as 'a way to achieve stability or growth; if one sponsor withdraws, the laboratory would still have some important tasks and a degree of financial support would still be available.'[26]

The new mission which was chosen by Harwell was to help British industry with research and innovation. This 'industrial programme', as it came to be called, was to be financed partly from governmental and partly from industrial sources. The latter has taken several forms, ranging from projects fully paid for by an industrial firm to joint developments with both sides committing money and effort (both in variable amounts) under an agreement to share any benefits. By 1974-5, 50 per cent of Harwell's staff were employed on the industrial programme, and about 40 per cent of the income from the industrial programme came from industrial sources, 80 per cent of that being for research and development and 20 per cent for routine services. In other words, since the mid-1960s, Harwell had become a laboratory which not only continued to work on its original atomic energy mission, but also acted as a contractor to government departments and industrial firms for research and development.[27]

Here was a new twist in the use of the contract mechanism. That Harwell should undertake contract work for government departments could be seen simply as a formalising modification of existing arrangements for interdepartmental co-operation. But its performance of research under contract to industrial firms reversed the traditional relationship which the contract mechanism had mediated between the public and private sectors. In contrast, the United States analogue, Oak Ridge, did not seek work from industry, contenting itself with multiplying its governmental sponsors. Teich and Lambright suggest three reasons for the difference. First, Harwell's director doubted whether adequate funds would be forthcoming from governmental sources for Harwell to maintain its viability from those sources alone. Second, there was a clear need for improved productivity and competitiveness in British industry. Third, there was more opportunity in Britain than in the United States for government research establishments to undertake research and development for industrial firms; in the United States many more firms would be capable of doing their own research and development.[28]

By 1970 the weight attached to the modified contract mechanism had increased. In January 1970 the ministry issued a discussion document outlining a proposal that a British Research and Development Corporation be set up, outside the civil service, to run the civil laboratories of the Atomic Energy Authority and of the ministry itself.[29] The proposed Corporation was to be financed partly by a general grant from the government, partly by specific government contracts, and the rest (about one third of its income) from the sale of services, royalty income, joint ventures and other contract work from industry.

> The size and health of the organization was intended to depend upon its ability to provide economically and commercially for industry's needs; and it (the proposal) was an attempt to introduce a market test into predominantly government-financed research establishments. . .if BRDC could not sell its services, its scale of operation would have to be cut down.[30]

The idea of a 'market test' for civilian industrially-related research (at least, for that which fell outside the aerospace and nuclear sectors) became central to thinking about research policy within the Ministry of Technology and its successors, the Department of Trade and Industry (1970-4) and the Department of Industry. It was further expounded in the 1970 document, in words which presaged the Rothschild Report of 1971 (see below):

> no Government department can decide centrally what research programmes are best designed to serve the needs of industry. As a general rule, only the 'customer' knows what he wants, and by his readiness to pay for it, makes the 'supplier' aware of his requirements.[31]

The proposal was, however, lost amidst the changes introduced by the Conservative victors in the election of October 1970. The Ministry of Technology was transformed into the Department of Trade and Industry and, as part of a wide-ranging review of the work of government departments, a review began of the work of the department's research establishments.[32] The review focused on programmes, projects and strategic aims, rather than on institutional reorganisation,[33] and was able to build on similar work begun in 1969 within the Ministry of Technology. As a result of this review, it was possible by early 1972 for Dr (later Sir) Ieuan Maddock, the Chief Scientist, to claim that the department was moving 'to a different concept of determining the programme and monitoring it. We have, indeed, moved quite a long way toward the customer-contractor relationship.'[34]

The language, by this stage, was that of the Rothschild Report of November 1971, which had advocated wider application of the 'customer-contractor principle', to government sponsored applied research and development. Lord Rothschild took this principle to mean that 'applied R & D. . .must be done on a customer-contractor basis. The customer says what he wants; the contractor does it (if he can); and the customer pays.'[35]

Other recommendations of the report were that, within each department, scientific advice to 'customers' (ministers and senior officials) should be provided by a high-ranking 'Chief Scientist', while the supervision of contracts and the overall administration of research establishments should be undertaken by a 'Controller R & D'. The essential objectives of the proposals were to clarify lines of accountability within departments (distinguishing, in particular, responsibility for the formulation of research policy from that for its execution), and to strengthen the hands of ministers and, by implication, their officials, in the formulation of policy for research and development. As regards government research establishments, therefore, the thrust of the proposals was to reduce somewhat their control over their own programmes. For, as Dr Maddock put it, up until this time the research programmes were 'more or less invented' within the industrial research establishments and then 'endorsed by a process of advisory committees and ultimately by myself'.[36] Now, however, government laboratories were going to have to apply to their ministers for funds for programmes in areas that the minister (or his officials) had defined. It was only in this sense that the laboratories would 'tender for contracts'.

In accordance with the Rothschild proposals, but owing more to the way the department's own thinking had been developing than to Rothschild, a new structure for the formulation of research policy was established. This structure, the department claimed, was 'aimed at identifying and involving all the end users'.[37]

What was to be that structure, and how were the end users to be involved in it? As laid out in March 1972 (and as subsequently implemented) the structure was to involve

> a series of broadly based (Research) Requirements Boards which. . .
> would be given. . .direct 'customer' responsibility for commissioning
> work within the R & D fields allotted to them, and which would be
> expected to play the leading role in determining the balance of
> R & D programmes within those fields.[38]

In other words, committees called requirements boards were to be
established with responsibility for fields such as standards and
metrology, chemical and mineral processes, and engineering materials.
These boards were to be responsible for deciding what work in their
respective areas should be financed by the department, and the terms
on which it should be financed.

As for the 'end users', the department argued that it itself had very
little direct use for R & D. Its function was to assist the development
of British industry, and it was industry which should be the end user
of government-sponsored industrially-oriented research. The department
could act only as a 'proxy customer' for research, thus putting it in a
different position from, say, the Department of the Environment or
the Ministry of Agriculture, Fisheries and Food, which regarded
themselves as the direct users of much of the research which they
financed. Hence, whereas the post-Rothschild executive (but not
advisory) machinery for formulating research and development policy
within those latter two ministries comprises only government officials,
about half the members of each requirements board in the Department
of Industry are industrialists, the remainder being academics and
officials.[39]

The identification and involvement of end users has not, however,
stopped with the composition of the requirements boards. Indeed, the
industrialists on the boards would be unlikely themselves to be the
direct beneficiaries of governmentally sponsored research which they
had approved; one could confidently expect questions in Parliament
were this not so. The argument for their inclusion on the boards is,
however, that they will have a better appreciation of industrial
requirements than civil servants could be expected to have.

Among the measures taken to try to improve that appreciation have
been the publicising of the work of the boards, visits by their members
to companies, and requests to companies to comment on the boards'
programmes. In addition, research into the diffusion of innovations
has been supported and, in one case, a proposal has been supported to

allow several factories within one industrial sector to act as 'shop windows', demonstrating the productivity levels that could be achieved with up-to-date technology.

Perhaps the most important of these measures, however, has been the frequent imposition, as a condition of governmental finance, of the requirement that the project in question should be partly supported by an industrial customer. In other words, a government laboratory will often be told by a requirements board that it will get support for a particular project only if, say, 30 per cent of the necessary funds can be obtained from industry. This condition is said not only to serve as a guarantee that a genuine industrial demand for the project exists, but also to foster a new kind of relationship between government laboratories and private firms (one which, at Harwell, pre-dated the requirements boards). Previously, the results of work done at government laboratories, if published at all, were published freely in the technical press. Realising that this practice would be unlikely to appeal to companies which were paying for research and development, the laboratories have begun to apply what, at Harwell, is called the 'Principle of Maximum Unfairness'. According to this principle, the government laboratory co-operates with the industrial firm without publishing the results of the work, at least until the firm has had an opportunity to establish a market lead. This change in practice epitomises the developing commercial-mindedness which has been the most striking feature of the bid by the industrial research establishments, over the past decade, to serve more directly the needs of industry.

Conclusions

Since the Second World War, the operation of the contract mechanism with respect to science and technology has been aimed principally at the procurement of goods and research which were wanted by governments for their own use. The relationships which have ensued between government agencies and private contractors have played their part in the much-remarked fusion of the public and private sectors, particularly in the defence field, but also in high technology more generally, where long lead times, high capital expenditure, the perceived need to maintain a national capacity to produce 'strategic' goods and the uncertainties of the technology itself have been among the factors educing this interdependence.

Contracting for goods has probably been as common a practice of British as of American government, but the application of the contract mechanism to scientific R & D has, in the main, been more highly developed in the United States. The Rothschild Report introduced the language of customer-contractor relationships to British science policy circles and, together with developments that were already under way in some ministries, led to significant changes in the Whitehall machinery for formulating and executing research policy.

The language of the Rothschild Report should not, however, be allowed to obscure the fact that, although British government research establishments have, since 1972, had to learn to 'tender' for 'contracts' or 'commissions' from their ministries, the actual practice of the contract mechanism has been rather different from what an American observer might expect. First, as if to illustrate Hague's argument that the difference between a grant and a contract is largely a matter of institutional context, expectations and practices,[40] the post-Rothschild 'contracts' or 'commissions' placed by ministries with their own laboratories can perhaps best be understood as the formal output of a new, more stringent, but, with the exception of the Department of Industry, *intramural* programme evaluation and performance procedure.

A second difference from American practice is that, within the Department of Industry, the contract mechanism has been expanded to accommodate the introduction of non-governmental actors into positions of importance in the commissioning of research at government research establishments. This has occurred through the appointment of a majority of industrialists and academics to the research requirements boards, and through the provision that work done at those establishments should often be partly financed (and may even be wholly financed) by industry. Worthy though these developments may be, they seem remote from Blackett's position of 1967. They have done nothing directly to reduce the proportion of the national research effort which is conducted in government laboratories, although there are signs that some of the requirements boards are themselves anxious to move in that direction: in 1976 one board complained that it had received no research proposals from industrial companies, while a second spent 40 per cent of its funds in industry, and a third spent almost all its funds in industrial research associations or similar bodies.[41]

The post-Rothschild application of the customer-contractor principle derives, in most of the departments of British government, from a desire for enhanced public accountability in respect of research and development policy. That, however, is only partly true for the Department of Industry, where prior moves to introduce such a principle derived from both a belief in the need to gear the industrial research establishments more closely to industry's needs, and the problem of what to do with Harwell (and other laboratories) as they began to run out of work. This serves to illustrate that if, in an attempt to promote industrial technology through research and development, governments choose to set up their own research establishments, they do more than merely create laboratories. Specifically, they create for themselves two serious problems. The first is that of determining how best to employ those research establishments so as to assist industry. The second is what to do with those laboratories when the need for them appears to diminish. By that time they have probably become well-established features on the governmental scene, and their rundown is not easily achieved. That flexibility in the use of scientific resources which was explicitly sought in the United States through the introduction of the contract mechanism is not achieved any more easily in the Britain of the customer-contractor principle than it was before.

Notes

1. Bruce L.R. Smith (ed.), *The New Political Economy: The Public Use of the Private Sector* (London, Macmillan, 1975), p.8. See also D.C. Hague, W.J.M. Mackenzie and A. Barker (eds.), *Public Policy and Private Interests: The Institutions of Compromise* (London, Macmillan, 1975); and Bruce L.R. Smith and D.C. Hague (eds.), *The Dilemma of Accountability in Modern Government* (London, Macmillan, 1971).

2. See, for instance, Colin Turpin, *Government Contracting* (Harmondsworth, Penguin, 1972), p.260.

3. Don K. Price, *Government and Science* (New York, New York University Press, 1954), ch.3.

4. Ibid., pp.68-73.

5. Ibid., p.73.

6. Harold Orlans, *Contracting for Atoms* (Washington, Brookings Institution, 1967), pp.5-8.

7. Christopher Freeman, *The Economics of Industrial Innovation* (Harmondsworth, Penguin, 1974), pp.146-52.

8. Judith Reppy, 'Defense department payments for "company-financed" R & D', *Research Policy*, vol.6 (4, 1977), pp.396-410.

9. Cited in Orlans, *Contracting for Atoms*, p.9.

10. Don K. Price, *The Scientific Estate* (Harvard, Belknap Press, 1965), especially ch.2.

11. See S. Rosen (ed.), *Testing the Theory of the Military-Industrial Complex* (Lexington, Heath, 1973); Sam C. Sarkesian (ed.), *The Military-Industrial Complex: A Reassessment* (Beverly Hills, Sage, 1972); Carroll W. Pursell (ed.), *The Military Industrial Complex* (New York, Harper and Row, 1972); and Martin Edmonds, 'Accountability and the Military-Industrial Complex', in Smith, *The New Political Economy*, pp.149-80. See also, Martin Edmonds, 'Government Contracting and Renegotiation: A Comparative Analysis', *Public Administration*, vol.50 (spring 1972), pp.45-64.

12. Clarence H. Danhof, *Government Contracting and Technological Change* (Washington, Brookings Institution, 1968), p.5.

13. Ibid., p.451.

14. M.M. Gowing, *Independence and Deterrence: Britain and Atomic Energy 1945-1952*, vol.2 (London, Macmillan, 1974), pp.155-61.

15. These laboratories were: Building Research Station, Fire Research Station, Forest Products Research Laboratory, Hydraulics Research Station, Laboratory of the Government Chemist, National Engineering Laboratory, National Physical Laboratory, Road Research Laboratory, Torrey Research Station, Warren Spring Laboratory and Water Pollution Research Laboratory.

16. Norman J. Vig, *Science and Technology in British Politics* (London, Pergamon Press, 1968), ch.2 and *passim.*

17. *Committee of Enquiry into the Organisation of Civil Science* (London, HMSO, 1963, Cmnd.2171), paras.89-90.

18. Vig, *Science and Technology*, especially pp.34 and 83; and Sir Richard Clarke, 'Mintech in Retrospect', *Omega*, I (1973), pp.25-38 and 137-63, at p.26.

19. As listed in note 15, except for the Road Research Laboratory which went to the Ministry of Transport.

20. House of Commons, *Debates*, 702 (26 November 1963), col.216 (written answer).

21. Clarke, 'Mintech in Retrospect', p.139.

22. A.G. Mencher, *Lessons for American Policy-Making from the British Labour Government's 1964-70 Experience in Applying Technology to Economic Objectives* (Washington, National Science Foundation, 1975), Appendix 2.

23. Report of Address by Lord Blackett to the Parliamentary and Scientific Committee, *Nature*, vol.213 (no.5078, 1967), p.747.

24. The Rt.Hon. Anthony Wedgwood Benn, *The Government's Policy for Technology*, lecture given at Imperial College of Science and Technology, 17 October 1967 (London, Ministry of Technology, 1967); see also Ieuan Maddock, Selected Papers, available in the Library, London Graduate School of Business Studies.

25. See W. Marshall, 'The industrial research programme at Harwell', *Atom* (no.185, 1972); W. Marshall, 'Interaction between Government and industry: lessons from Harwell's experience', *Atom* (no.210, 1974); and Philip Gummett and Michael Gibbons, 'Redeployment and Diversification at Harwell', *Omega*, vol.6 (no.1, 1978), pp.1-5.

26. Albert H. Teich and W. Henry Lambright, 'The Redirection of a Large National Laboratory', *Minerva*, 14 (no.4, Winter 1976-7), pp.447-74, at p.448.

27. Marshall, 'Interaction between Government and Industry' (1974), pp.75-9.

28. Teich and Lambright, 'Large National Laboratory', p.472.

29. Ministry of Technology, *Industrial Research and Development in Government Laboratories: A New Organisation for the Seventies* (London, HMSO, 1970).

30. Sir Richard Clarke, *New Trends in Government* (London, HMSO, Civil Service College Studies, 1971), pp.95 and 95n.

31. Ministry of Technology, *Industrial Research and Development*, p.11.

32. By May 1971 these establishments were: National Physical Laboratory, National Engineering Laboratory, Warren Spring Laboratory, Safety in Mines Research Establishment, Laboratory of the Government Chemist, Torrey Research Station, and some of the laboratories (principally Harwell) of the Atomic Energy Authority. See Select Committee on Science and Technology, Session 1970-71, *Research and Development Activities of the Department of Trade and Industry* (London, HMSO, 1971, HC 525), p.3.

33. Ibid., question 14.

34. Select Committee on Science and Technology, Session 1971-72, *Research and Development: Minutes of Evidence and Appendices* (London, HMSO, 1972, HC 375), p.329 and pp.459-61, questions 11-18 and 23-27.

35. Lord Rothschild, 'The Organisation and Management of Government R & D', para.6, in *A Framework for Government Research and Development* (London, HMSO, 1971, Cmnd.4814).

36. Select Committee on Science and Technology, Session 1971-72, *Research and Development*, p.465, question 49.

37. Ibid., p.329.

38. Ibid.

39. See Michael Gibbons and Philip Gummett, 'Recent Changes in the Administration of Government Research and Development in Britain', *Public Administration*, vol.54 (Autumn 1976), pp.247-66; and Philip Gummett and Michael Gibbons, 'Government Research for Industry: Recent British Developments', *Research Policy* (1978), in press, on which the next three paragraphs are also based.

40. D.C. Hague, in Hague *et al.* (eds), *Public Policy and Private Interests*, pp.4-6.

41. Research and Development Requirements Boards, *Reports 1975-76* (London, Department of Industry, 1976), pp. 10, 29, 37.

5 BLIND LANDING SYSTEMS: GOVERNMENT-INDUSTRY INTERACTION IN INNOVATION

John Hartland and Michael Gibbons

Introduction

Much of the current discussion of the promotion and control of technology is based upon the notion of technology as an exogenous variable — that technology develops independently of its socioeconomic circumstances. Within this horizon, it should be possible — so it is argued — to prescribe certain social objectives, select the technologies appropriate to their attainment and then implement them accordingly. This, essentially positivist, view of the relationship of technology to larger social processes is faithfully reflected in contemporary economic orthodoxy in which the entrepreneur or manager, having determined business objectives, merely chooses — from a wide range of possibilities — the technologies needed to meet them. What is generally overlooked is that technology develops in a context and it is the objective of the narrative which follows to illustrate how, in the concrete, this happens.

In most industrial nations the context comprises a mixed economy operated by a partnership between industry, government and consumer; a context in which competition possesses an international dimension and in which technical virtuosity, supported often by government policy as well as price, determines who, in the long run, will be successful. In this context, as we shall see, no single agency explicitly *directs* technology. Rather, technology *emerges* from a sequence of closely interrelated decisions involving a number of participants, and it is only in hindsight, if at all, that technology is seen to have a direction — or to have been directed. Of course, it is precisely this dimension of 'technological emergence' that has provoked the search for more socially beneficial technology. It is argued that technology should emerge from a wider range of considerations than the purely commercial. One aspect of the innovation discussed in this chapter is to show that, to some extent, this occurs already and that the real problem is not to introduce noncommercial or supracommercial criteria into the decision-making sequence, but to evaluate critically those which do so enter.

The notion that technology emerges from a decision-making process has a long and respectable history in the study of technological innovation. It will suffice, here, to cite two key researchers whose ideas have had a formative influence on the study described herein. First, following Boulding,[1] technology is conceived as 'a complex set of ways of doing things with both human and material instruments'. What it offers is a capability. The outcome of a technological innovation is, therefore, not mere hardware, but the dual embodiment of a particular capability in a set of machinery and in the workers who operate this machinery. In the case of blind landing, the capability is embodied in a system comprising aircraft equipment, ground equipment, the radio signal between these two sets of equipment, and the pilot's role in monitoring the performance of the system and the circumstances of its operation.

Second, following Bela Gold,[2] innovation is conceived as an essentially incremental process of decision making. The continuing investment of resources in the development, procurement and operation of machinery, on which the introduction of new technology depends, may be regarded (he suggests) as the outcome of managerial decisions which, even in major developments, are not properly to be described as 'climactic actions' on the part of the innovating firm, but as 'elements in a stream of successive temporary commitments, each of which is heavily conditioned by the network of prior decisions and is subject to repeated later alterations on the basis of additional information, adjusted goals, and newly emerging pressures and alternatives'. A conceptualisation of this type must be distinguished carefully from the sense in which the term is commonly employed with mere reference to the technology, of whose emergence the decision-making process may be regarded as the vehicle. The process itself may consist of a single stream of decisions within a single firm or of several streams of interacting decisions within a number of commercial and governmental organisations.

In the case presented here, innovation is conceived as a complex flow of incremental decision making composed of six interacting currents (corresponding to the number of participant institutions: equipment manufacturer, aircraft constructor, airline, the Air Registration Board and the Board of Trade as joint safety authorities, and the successive Ministries of Supply, Aviation and Technology) from which separately crystallise five interrelated sequences of events: aircraft equipment development, airline procurement of this equipment, ground equipment development, airfield installation of this equipment, and safety clearance for the operation of the system in progressively lower visibilities.

The significance of Gold's description of the decision-making process is its tendency to discount, as a factor of assessment, any discrepancy between the outcome of an innovation — or, more precisely, its impact on the innovating firm — and the initial set of expectations on which a notionally discrete decision to innovate was based. What counts, rather, is 'the effectiveness of managerial responses to the changing determinants of successful performance'. As changes occur in the political, commercial or economic environment, so do these determinants. How rapidly does the firm perceive changes in its operating environment? How promptly does it respond to these perceptions? For microeconomic studies of innovation, one of the chief implications of Gold's description is that it is as much the timing as the substance of what appears, in retrospect, to have been key points of commitment in the decision flow which needs to be explained.

The definitions of technology and innovation outlined above provide the conceptual basis for the notion of technology as emergent from a decision-making process. The problem, then, with respect to any particular instance of innovation, is to account for the phenomenon — not so much in terms of the technology itself (its nature, origins and utility) — as of the gradualism and uncertainty characterising the process of its emergence and of the way in which a business organisation responds to its progressively sharpening perception of each of these characteristics.

What emerges from the historical reconstruction are six key decision points:

(i) Smiths Industries' decision to embark on the development of a new generation autopilot (1956-1957);
(ii) Smiths Industries' decision to accept the terms of BEA's specification for the Trident flight control system;
(iii) BEA's decision to *upgrade* their procurement commitment with regard to the operational capability of the Trident flight control system, first in 1963; and
(iv) second, in 1966;
(v) Smiths Industries' decision to reach an agreement with one of the four autopilot manufacturers in the USA — in 1963; and
(vi) to extend this agreement in 1967.

A full account of the innovational process would have to account not only for the emergence of these decision points but also for the timing and substance of these six decisions and, to some extent at least, their causal relations.[3] More important for our present concern is to probe the data organised in this way for what it can provide in the way of insight into the interactions between government and manufacturing industry in stimulating technological development. As a consequence of this interest, it will be most instructive to focus on certain aspects of the second, fifth and sixth decision points illustrated above. Before turning to the concrete details of the decision-making process, it will be necessary to clarify the requirements, governmental, industrial and technological, which constitute the context of the innovation.

The Context of the Innovation[4]

Government involvement in the innovation derives from three main factors governing the introduction of a new technology such as automatic landing into the civil aviation environment. First is the requirement for joint clearance of the design and operation of the airborne equipment by the British safety authorities: technical clearance in the form of a certificate of airworthiness issued only on the recommendation of the Air Registration Board, and operational clearance in the form of amendments to an aircraft's flight manual authorised by the Directorate-General of Safety and Operations at the Board of Trade. The second factor is government procurement and airfield installation of the necessary ground equipment, of a standard acceptable both to the safety authorities and to the airlines using the equipment. The third factor is the supply of pilots trained by the airlines and licensed by the Board of Trade for operating the system in progressively more difficult conditions.

These conditions have been categorised by the International Civil Aviation Organisation according to the height at which the pilot must decide whether or not he can see enough of the runway either to take over and land the aircraft himself after an automatic approach or to allow the aircraft to be landed by the automatic system. The limiting factor in both cases was the risk of something going wrong with the automatics. In 1959, a committee on landing aids — composed of representatives of all interested parties in the aviation industry and chaired by the Chief Technical Officer of the Air Registration Board — had decided that the use of an automatic landing system 'in the worst permitted circumstances' should not introduce a fatal accident risk greater than one in ten million in the last thirty seconds of flight. It was decided later that demonstrating compliance with this safety factor would require probably about 3,000 fully recorded automatic landings in scheduled service in conditions of visibility such that the pilot, in the event of the worst conceivable kind of system malfunction, would have adequate visual reference to recognise the occurrence of a malfunction and enough time either to initiate an overshoot or to take over and land the aircraft himself. Only when this proving period was completed satisfactorily could an aircraft be cleared for category 3 operations, which meant the ability to operate blind to the surface of the runway. This particular category was divided into three subcategories according to whether external visual reference was available to permit manual control of the ground run (category 3A, requiring a runway visual range of at least 200 metres), visual taxiing (category 3B, requiring a runway visual range of at least 50 metres), or nonexistent (category 3C). The runway visual range was the distance measured along the runway of the farthest visible light and, for categories 1 and 2, the relationship between this and decision height was based on the principle that the probability of having adequate slant visual reference at a given decision height should be as high as possible. Thus, a category 1 capability meant the ability to operate down to a decision height of 200 feet when the runway visual range was at least 800 metres, and a category 2 capability meant the ability to operate to decision heights between 200 and 100 feet with runway visual ranges between 800 and 400 metres. Pending the completion of this proving period, it was stipulated in 1965 that an automatic system should not be relied upon for landing an aircraft when decision height was lower than 150 feet. Attainment of this mid-category 2 capability was to depend, moreover, on evidence as to the satisfactory operation of the system in category 1 conditions.

How, though, did one set about designing any system to a one-in-ten-million safety factor? The conventional method of ensuring safety under automatic control was to limit the authority of the autopilot over the control surfaces of the aircraft by means of some kind of cutout device, so that – in the event of a fault in the automatics resulting in the most dangerous type of malfunction which drove a control surface hard in one direction – the system would cut out without imposing too difficult a corrective manoeuvre on the pilot. Clearly, this method was inapplicable for an automatic system required to land an aircraft in marginal visibility conditions, in which no height loss in the event of a fault could be tolerated. Moreover, control of sophisticated aircraft in the terminal phase of flight meant extending the authority of the automatics, not limiting it. The answer lay in the design technique known as redundancy – in other words, rendering the probability of a malfunction conditional on the occurrence of not one, but at least two faults in the automatic system during the critical period.

An autopilot could be provided with redundancy in the form of two or more absolutely separate subsystems, each of which was capable of controlling the aircraft on its own. The principle behind Smiths Industries' multiplex concept was that these independent subsystems should work in parallel. By multiplying the control channels in each axis, the system could be arranged so that no fault or sequence of faults in a single subsystem could affect overall performance. In a duplex system, the two subchannels in each axis would monitor each other. So long as their outputs were similar, the system would continue to operate. If a fault occurred in either of the subchannels, the discrepancy between their outputs would cause the whole system to cut out, but without causing the aircraft to deviate materially from its flight path as defined by the radio guidance inputs to the flight computers. It would, therefore, 'fail steady', and the aircraft would be in a safe condition for the pilot to take over. In a triplex system, three subchannels in each axis would monitor each other. A fault in one subchannel would be recognised by the two others, which would operate to cut it out, leaving the system at duplex level. A triplex system could, therefore, be described as 'fail-operative' in that it could survive a single fault and would fail steady on the occurrence of a second fault. The key issue was the probability of two faults occurring in more than one subsystem in the last thirty seconds of the landing manoeuvre. If, as Smiths Industries claimed, this probability could be shown to be less than one in ten million, a flight control system designed on triplex principles (in conjunction with ground equipment of a similar level of integrity) promised a genuinely blind category 3 landing capability to any airline ready to bear the cost of buying, proving, maintaining and carrying the weight penalty of the extra airborne equipment. An airline's readiness to do this would depend on balancing this total cost against the projected increase in the cost of disruptions to the passenger-carrying and maintenance schedules of its front-line fleet, as the projected units of this fleet became larger and more expensive. A Trident 2E, for example, was to cost BEA over five times as much as the price they had to pay for the Viscount.

Emergence of Specifications for the Automatic Landing Systems

In August 1959, after prolonged discussions with the aircraft manufacturers, BEA signed a £30 million contract with de Havillands (now Hawker Siddeley) for the delivery of twenty-four Trident I aircraft. From the point of view of Smiths Industries, who were to be subcontracted to manufacture the automatic landing system, the situation was less than ideal. It would have suited Smiths better if BEA had been more ambitious and decided from the outset to fit their new aircraft with triplex, fully automatic landing systems. In this way, they would be able both to capitalise on their undoubted technological lead in automatic landing systems as well as acquire some much needed government money to sustain rising research and development costs. In the event, however, the BEA specification, while recognising the potential requirement for an automatic landing system if adequate ground aids for lateral guidance to touchdown became available, was to provide automatic control to touchdown in the vertical plane only — using a radio altimeter. Smiths, no doubt, felt that this decision was shortsighted — involving as it must considerable technical problems when, later, modifications would have to be introduced to provide automatics for lateral guidance. Nonetheless, they accepted the specification because not to do so might jeopardise their considerable investment in avionics. Two developments specifically contributed to this judgement. First, to their surprise, a parallel contract for an automatic landing system for the VC-10 went to Elliott Automation, a relative newcomer to the avionics industry. And, second, their firm expectation of securing a contract for a triplex fail-operative system with an automatic landing capability in the Belfast strategic freighter aircraft to be built by Short Brothers and Harland for RAF Transport Command.

Before examining the details of Smiths' decision to supply automatic landing equipment for the Belfast, it will be instructive to investigate the background to the allocation of the flight control contract on the VC-10 to Elliott Automation. Not only does this case provide a fascinating glimpse into the nature of competition in this particular industrial context, but also it shows how governments may feel obliged to acquiesce in developments initiated elsewhere.

The VC-10 Contract

The prospect of offering their new autopilot to two domestic aircraft then on the drawing-board — the Vickers (now BAC) VC-10 and the de Havilland Trident — had given considerable impetus to Smiths Industries' early design work. For the past decade they had enjoyed a virtual monopoly in the British autopilot market for civil transport aircraft, and the multiplex development decision of September 1957 had been based on the tacit assumption that they were unlikely to be threatened by serious domestic competition for either of these contracts. In 1958 they submitted proposals for both aircraft. So also did Elliott Flight Automation who, only seven years earlier, had been struggling to get their newly formed aviation division off the ground. How, in the space of six years, had Elliott come to acquire the funds, technology and status to be able to challenge them?

In 1951, Elliott's sole experience of flight control (and their only contract) lay in manufacturing for the Royal Aircraft Establishment an RAE-designed single-axis stabiliser for the Jindivik pilotless target aircraft. Two unrewarding years spent struggling for contracts against Smiths Industries, Kent and Sperry resulted in a decision to seek association with one of the major autopilot manufacturers in the United States. In 1953, in exchange for the UK manufacturing rights on Bendix flowmeters and accelerometers, they sold 42 per cent of their equity to the American firm — an exceptionally opportune agreement, in that it was shortly followed by a Ministry of Supply procurement decision to fit the Bendix accelerometer to all fighter aircraft and by the award of a £1½ million contract to Elliott for the supply of Bendix flowmeters for the V-class bombers.

Meanwhile, through the experimental fitment of an improved Jindivik stabiliser to the Dassault Mystère, which enabled it to be the first European aircraft to exceed Mach 1, Elliott were securing a foothold in the European systems market for manned aircraft. This episode, though it aroused criticism in some quarters — notably the Ministry of Supply — over the exploitation of an RAE design to the benefit of a foreign manufacturer, established their name in the avionics systems field and put them in a position to discuss possible stabilisers for the Lightning with the English Electric design team at Warton. Elliott's initial proposal was for a single-axis stabiliser, which they then extended to three axes, and for this equipment, in 1954, just as the performance requirement for the aircraft was about to be extended, they were awarded a £400,000 development contract. The extension of the performance requirement, recommended by an operational research group in the Air Ministry, consisted of a programmed climb capability of 40,000 feet exceeding Mach 1 — which meant having full autopilot facilities. The revised contract, worth approximately £2 million, duly went to Elliott. By the end of 1955, with the build-up of their research and development facilities for the Lightning programme, they could claim technical parity in the military field with Smiths Industries and Sperry.

The award to Elliott of the Lightning autopilot contract marked

the beginning of a somewhat difficult readjustment of Ministry of
Supply procurement guidelines, which were based, in principle, on the
'proven capacity' of suppliers. Up to the last year or two, in the field
of automatic flight control, 'proven capacity' had been spelt out as
follows: *Smiths Industries* for the design and production of transport
aircraft and heavy bomber autopilots (providing a natural ground of
experience for the civil airline market), *Sperry* for the remainder of the
military field — mainly fighter and reconnaissance aircraft, *Newark* for
helicopter control systems and target aircraft autostabilisers, and
Elliott in the distinctly minor role of shadow manufacturer for target
aircraft autostabilisers. This readjustment was consolidated in 1956
with the allocation to Elliott of the Blue Steel guidance contract,
initially worth between £4 million and £5 million, against competition
from Smiths Industries, Sperry and Avro. A decisive factor in the
allocation of this contract was the high status in official circles of a
senior government scientist recruited by Elliott the previous year to be
deputy general manager of their aviation division with primary
responsibility for the direction of their research laboratories. But in
addition to this, over the preceding two years, also through recruitment
and notably in aerodynamics, Elliott had been considerably expanding
their range of technical expertise.

The next logical step was to challenge Smiths Industries in the civil
market. Again, exploitation of American technology — in the shape of
the Bendix PB-20 autopilot, for which Elliott's aviation sales manager
insisted he could get a licensing agreement from Bendix with full
technical support — was seen as the key to entry. But with BEA's
long-standing relationship with Smiths Industries and other wholly
British suppliers there seemed little hope of getting the Trident contract,
and there were serious doubts within the company as to whether the
VC-10 contract alone was worth going for. Smiths Industries' position,
it was argued, as the informally accredited supplier in this market in the
eyes of the government, who would be providing launching aid for both
aircraft, was virtually unassailable; also, de Havillands had declined to
bid for the aircraft on the ground that it would be unsaleable abroad if
built to the BOAC requirement.[5] If de Havillands proved to be right,
it would be impossible for Elliott to recoup the costs of development.
The opposing case, made out in ignorance of Smiths Industries'
multiplex development work, was founded on the operational
shortcomings of their SEP-2 autopilot. This (as Smiths Industries well
knew) was not technically comparable to the solid-state Bendix PB-20.
If the support of the aircraft constructor could be secured, official

procurement guidelines could (again) be overruled, and at least half of the £3 million to £4 million domestic civil market could be wrested from Smiths Industries. They should go through the motions of making a serious bid for the Trident contract, on the assumption it would strengthen their hand for the VC-10.

Experience in marketing the Viscount, combined with a certain anxiety to confound the sceptics with regard to the marketability of the VC-10, made Vickers highly receptive to the argument that a number of potential foreign customers would be likely to insist on the fitment of an American flight control system. Nor was there any resistance to the idea from BOAC – they were already buying Boeing 707s fitted with the PB-20, and adoption of the same equipment for the VC-10 would reduce overall operating costs by simplifying maintenance. Meanwhile, Elliott's aviation sales manager had left to join Bendix as managing director of their British subsidiary. From this position, he urged his parent company to license Elliott for manufacture of the PB-20; conceding their inexperience in what Bendix considered to be one of the most sophisticated areas of aviation technology, he questioned Bendix's ability to make direct sales in Europe in this market due to a general dislike in the industry for 'long-range engineering' (that is, dealing with a supplier of advanced technology systems, which were to be integrated operationally with a number of other systems, at a distance of several thousand miles). Finally, Bendix agreed to attach a three-man team to Elliott, with full technical support, if they could secure the contract.

After a number of meetings with Vickers' representatives in March and April 1958, Smiths Industries had submitted proposals for an integrated flight control system based on a fully triplex autopilot, and then, when Vickers decided this was too complex for initial installation, for a duplex system with facilities for re-engaging a single subchannel after cutout. The Ministry of Supply, who were providing development funds, were initially unyielding in their support of these proposals. But quite apart from commercial considerations (regarding the overseas sales prospects of the VC-10), there was a reasoned case to be made on technical and operational grounds against fitting a brand-new aircraft with an unproved control system. With the airline showing a mild but distinct preference for the American equipment, the Ministry of Supply were brought reluctantly to acknowledge the aircraft constructor's prerogative to make the decision. The contract, therefore, went to Elliott. Just before it was signed, Vickers endeavoured to secure from Bendix, through an exchange of letters, a formal guarantee of Elliott's performance.

The Belfast Requirement

Having failed to secure the VC-10 contract, and having failed to extract from BEA a more than tentative commitment to a triplex fail-operative capability in the Trident, Smiths Industries' incentive to comply fully with the terms of the Trident specification and to maintain the dynamic of their multiplex development effort, funded until then from their own resources, was critically strengthened in 1959 by the promulgation of a Ministry of Defence operational requirement for a blind automatic landing capability in the Belfast strategic freighter. In the course of that year, rising concern with the structure and efficiency of the aircraft industry — reflected institutionally in the merger of the aviation responsibilities of the Ministry of Transport and Civil Aviation and the Ministry of Supply, and their transfer to the newly-formed Ministry of Aviation — was beginning to result in a conscious effort to harmonise the characteristics of military and civil types of transport aircraft.[6] A government research establishment had already reported favourably on Smiths Industries' triplex fail-operative proposals for an automatic landing capability in the Trident, and for troop-carrying aircraft such as the Belfast it would clearly be difficult to justify acceptance of a less exacting safety requirement than that considered to be attainable and satisfactory for civil operations. The Belfast system should, therefore, also be triplex, and its development logically entrusted to Smiths Industries, to whom it was intimated that such a system would be the standard fitment for RAF Transport Command; in contrast to the situation in the civil environment, guidance could be provided by the leader cable system developed by the government's Blind Landing Experimental Unit (BLEU) and then being installed at a number of military airfields for the use of the V-bombers.

The fixed price development contract for the Belfast — the biggest development contract Smiths Industries had yet received from the government — was not finalised until July 1960. But, in the course of 1959, it promised to provide a framework for government technical support to the aviation division which would be of a long-term commitment to the development of a triplex system for the Trident. The Ministry of Aviation had already made available a Varsity aircraft to the aviation division's flying unit for flight control development work on a simplex automatic landing capability for the V-bombers; a second Varsity would now be made available to the flying unit for multiplex flight trials, and a Comet 2E to BLEU for performance evaluation of a full triplex system in high-altitude operating regimes.

Smiths Industries' confidence that the purpose of this support was to ensure 'a continuing British lead in (an) important field of endeavour' was to be reinforced by the substance of an address to the Royal Aeronautical Society by Mr Duncan Sandys, Minister of Aviation, in January 1960:

> By 1980, it is quite possible that ten times more people will be travelling by air. . .There will have to be major advances in air traffic control so that more aircraft can be handled simultaneously in the limited airspace available. At the same time, we must bring in fully automatic landing techniques which will make it possible to fly safely in all weathers.[7]

When the Trident contract was signed between BEA and de Havilland in August 1959, the latter had agreed to supply the aircraft fitted with flight control equipment in accordance with the airline specification, but not certificated to perform the automatic flare manoeuvre in scheduled service — they were 'understandably reluctant' to commit themselves contractually before clearly seeing how the requirement was to be met. Subsequently, there was to be a succession of alterations to the contract: initially to provide this certification, then to equip the aircraft and, still later, to certificate it for duplex and then triplex automatic landing, reducing the weather minima accordingly.

Smiths Industries were contracted only to de Havilland, and they, in turn, subcontracted to Sperry — as insisted by de Havilland, who had reservations about the ability of any one autopilot manufacturer to develop and produce the whole of the very complicated system required by BEA on the timescale involved — about 25 per cent in value of the total system; other instrumentation was subcontracted to Kelvin Hughes, a company Smiths Industries were to take over in 1961. Radio altimeters, developed from those produced originally in conjunction with BLEU, were to be supplied by Standard Telephones and Cables, and radio guidance receivers by Marconi. Certification of the equipment as airworthy, with respect both to design and performance, would be granted by the Air Registration Board in the form of amendments to the aircraft flight manual, on application from de Havilland and Smiths Industries. Licence to operate the certificated aircraft (under specific weather conditions in a specific airfield environment) would be granted by the directorate-general of safety and operations at the Board of Trade, on application from BEA's flight operations department who

would be required to prove their competence to operate safely in the
circumstances for which the licence was to be granted or extended.
Though there was no direct contractual link between BEA and either
Smiths Industries or the Air Registration Board, close informal contacts
would be maintained — as also with BLEU, who would be providing
experimental facilities for much of the development flying — through
the project and development branch of the airline's engineering
department.

Commercial Strategy: Smiths Industries' 1963 and 1967 Decisions

In 1963, Smiths Industries signed an agreement with Honeywell, one
of the four major United States autopilot manufacturers, whereby their
aviation division obtained UK manufacturing rights on certain advanced
instrument systems and control equipment of Honeywell design. The
decision to seek this agreement, as one means of safeguarding their
future in the world avionics systems market, coincided with the initial
impact on divisional operating performance of their massive
commitment from 1960 onwards to the Trident and Belfast triplex
automatic landing programmes.

In 1967, the agreement with Honeywell was extended to cover the
design, development, marketing and production of automatic flight
control systems and all-weather landing equipment, for commercial
aircraft in the 200-350 passenger class — namely the Douglas DC-10,
the Lockheed 10-11 and the European 'airbus', A-300B. The new
agreement aimed at promoting the far speedier development of a more
suitable system than could be achieved by either company operating
on its own, and it provided for the full exchange of technical
information. Honeywell were to lead the design and marketing teams in
North America, and Smiths Industries in Europe. For Honeywell,
Smiths Industries' multiplex expertise, painfully acquired on the
Trident and Belfast programmes, was a convenient platform from
which to extend their flight control interests into the civil field; they
agreed to partner the British firm without taking a shareholding. For
Smiths Industries, association with a major United States manufacturer
now seemed to be the only way of consolidating their position in the
rapidly expanding North American avionics market (as well as in other
markets which tended to buy American aircraft), of compensating for
any technological lag incurred through what some judged to have been
an excessive concentration of aviation division energies on a single giant
project, and of exploiting the prestige and skills they had derived from
a technically successful pioneering venture.

Smiths Industries' decision to seek this extended agreement must be seen in the light of their experience on the triplex development project which, in the absence of a BEA commitment, was tied to the Belfast programme, and of the national procurement context for civil and military aircraft. Not fitting triplex immediately to the Trident 1s had proved, for both airline and manufacturer, an expensive precaution: one serious design failure was discovered only after triplex flight trials had begun. Smiths felt that this design failure would have been discovered more quickly, saving about two years' development and a great deal of time if BEA had decided to fit the Trident 1s with a triplex system from the beginning. As it was, Smiths Industries' Aviation Division would remain heavily engaged for some time to come on an elaborate modification programme – to convert the duplex Trident 1s to triplex, and then to upgrade triplex-fitted aircraft to the performance level for which ARB Category 2 certification was subsequently to be obtained in September 1968. Costs, generally, had been much higher than anticipated, and a vigorous effort had had to be made to raise prices substantially above the level quoted initially. Part of the reason for this was that it had not been possible, as originally planned, to keep the Belfast programme ahead of the Trident programme so that the civil project could benefit from expertise gained on the military one. Problems had arisen in spring 1963 due to shortages of hardware for the military trials aircraft; the priority which was necessarily given from then on to difficulties in the Trident programme had the dual adverse effect of delaying further the Belfast programme and of requiring private venture funds for their resolution.[8] Coping with these problems, and attempting to make up for lost time, resulted in an even heavier commitment of divisional resources to the project than initially envisaged.

It should be noted that the competitive position of a European firm in this industry, in both foreign and domestic markets, was becoming critically sensitive to variations in the relationship between its volume of domestic sales and its absolute level of expenditure on research and development. The extent to which it could count, at the very least, on the relative medium-term stability of the defence procurement component in its domestic sales, and of the government-sponsored component in its overall research and development budget, might prove a decisive factor in the formulation of its commercial strategy. British manufacturers could count on neither. From 1954 to 1964, as Smiths Industries' aviation development expenditure was increasing, the proportion sponsored by the government was diminishing. In 1964, with the advent of the Labour government, came the simultaneous cancellation of the HS681, the P1154 and the TSR2. The last of these aircraft had been forecast to make the largest contribution of any aircraft, military or civil, to the domestic sales of the Aviation Division from 1965 to 1970. One of the severest blows, however, was the outcome of the Belfast programme.

In 1959, it had been the prospective allocation of this military triplex autopilot development contract, on the understanding that a triplex autopilot was to form the basis of a standard flight control system for RAF Transport Command, that had induced Smiths Industries to maintain the scale of their commitment to an ambitiously complex development programme, whose costs could only be recouped through the sale of sufficient aircraft to which the finished equipment was to be fitted. It was decided, subsequently, within the Ministries of Defence and Aviation, first that only 35 Belfast aircraft would be required, and then only 10;[9] finally, that Transport Command VC-10s should be fitted with an autopilot from another manufacturer.

Smiths Industries' decision to accept the Belfast contract had itself been in part the outcome of the confidence they had placed in de Havilland's 1959 estimate of the number of Trident aircraft to which the developed triplex equipment would be fitted, on the twin presumptions that BEA would eventually upgrade their procurement commitment to triplex level, and that other airlines buying the Trident would follow suit. In 1959, it was thought reasonable to plan on the basis of eventually fitting triplex equipment to about 200 aircraft; by 1969, 82 Tridents had been sold, and it was thought unlikely that more than 100 would be built.

Conclusions

The theme of government involvement in technological development — particularly advanced technology — is a perennial one in technology policy. In its simplest form, the discussion is about whether government, by means of some mode of intervention, can induce firms to allocate resources differently than they would if market pressures were allowed free reign. The innovation in automatic landing technology, as presented here, is less an example of government intervention in technology than one of government participation in a decision-making sequence. It is this aspect of participation that, in the introduction, prompted the suggestion that, at least in this case study, the technological capability emerged from the decision-making process rather than from any direct government action.

Yet there can be no doubt that government was involved, from the earliest, in the research of the BLEU and the RAE and, later, in the succession of contracts made to British industry by the Ministry of Defence. Finally, one ought not to forget the continuous government involvement in the setting of safety requirements and the provision of certificates of airworthiness — or, from another quarter, the development of civil airline requirements. Because the history has been constructed from the point of view of the firm, Smiths may appear to have been buffeted about unnecessarily or to have been the victim of circumstance. To a certain extent, this is true — but, as is so often said, innovation is a risky business and there is no gainsaying that, sometimes harsh, fact.

The central question is whether government presence alleviated or exacerbated the situation. This is, virtually, an imposssible question to answer since, in this case at any rate, government was a constituent of the situation from the beginning. The close, and fruitful, liaison of Smiths, BLEU, RAE and the Ministry of Defence in the development of the first automatic landing technology is indisputable, and probably the development would not have occurred at all without this initial government support. As always, problems appear when the industrial partner in prototype development decides to invest its own resources and move to full commercialisation. Still, government was involved because it was the government-owned airline (in this case, BEA) which specified what the technical specifications would be. It was airline requirements, first by BOAC for the VC-10, second by BEA for the Trident aircraft and third by the Ministry of Defence for the Belfast freighter that set the technical and commercial horizon for Smiths' aviation division. That horizon changed abruptly when Smiths lost the VC-10 contract; it changed again when the BEA Trident specification did not require a full triplex autopilot and finally it changed when the firm received the contract for the Belfast.

The most hotly debated issue in this series of events is, of course, whether the government was wise to allow the emergence of a second autopilot supplier, Elliott, when they knew well the extent to which the nascent Smiths Industries depended, at this stage in their research and development programme, on government funds. As the narrative makes clear, the Ministry of Supply had little choice but to acquiesce to the demands of the airlines as to what would increase the likelihood of selling the VC-10 abroad. In retrospect, though, the lack of a clear policy about encouraging civil avionics in Britain may be seen to have a positive aspect, for the lack of a clear and reliable home market for avionic equipment had the effect of making Smiths seek out new alliances — in this case, with Honeywell — with the consequent successful broadening of their market strategy from Britain to Western Europe and North America. The fact that the road to innovation was strewn with obstacles — some of them of government making — does not support the view that the situation would have been better, either if there had been more conscious planning on the part of the government, or if there had been no government involvement at all. In this, as in many other areas, a delicate dialogue of interests is required because no single agency can comprehend, let alone control, the totality of factors involved.

A final observation about methodology. To a certain extent, the conclusions reached about the close and continuous involvement of government and industry are a reflection of the way the process of innovation has been analysed. Too often, this process is depicted as the result of a few major decisions which can be seen, in retrospect, as either right or wrong. One consequence of thinking in terms of 'climactic' decisions is that it can create the impression of government acting unilaterally or arbitrarily at specific times. We have tried to show, on the contrary, that — by regarding technological innovation as a process of incremental decision making — the dialogue of government and industry in the process comes more clearly into view and, with it, more reasonable expectations about what can or cannot be accomplished through government intervention in the development of technology.

Notes

1. K. Boulding, 'The Emerging Super-culture', in K.E.M. Baier and N. Rescher (eds), *Values and the Future* (New York, Free Press, 1969), pp.336-50.

2. B. Gold, 'The Framework for Major Technological Innovation', in K.E.M. Baier and N. Rescher (eds), *Values and the Future* (New York, Free Press, 1969), pp.389-430.

3. For a fuller account, see J.E.H. Hartland, *Trident Blind Landing: A Study in Innovation* (unpublished M.Sc dissertation, Department of Liberal Studies in Science, University of Manchester), 1971.

4. This section is taken from J. Langrish, M. Gibbons, W.G. Evans and F.R. Jevons, *Wealth from Knowledge* (London, Macmillan, 1972), pp.429-32.

5. Vickers' forecast demand for the aircraft was 165. By the end of 1969, 53 had been built, of which 9 had been sold abroad.

6. See, for example, the policy statement to the House of Commons, 15 February 1960, by Mr Duncan Sandys, Minister of Aviation.

7. The exact date of the address was 12 January 1960.

8. The whole project was carried through the Trident programme, slightly

ahead of the Belfast programme, instead of the reverse. Delay in the Belfast programme reached the point where the Ministry of Aviation would have been entitled to claim penalties, though it did not, in fact, do so.

9. A costs analysis carried out in 1969 for the fourteen-year time scale 1959-72 showed a £400,000 profit for Smiths Industries on equipment sold for the ten aircraft built.

6 TECHNOLOGY POLICY AND THE MOTOR INDUSTRY

Peter Stubbs

The motor industry has been one of the prime movers of continued industrialisation in the world's advanced economies. As a growth industry it has been inextricably linked with the expansion of these economies, as their rising incomes manifested themselves in a rising demand for private travel, and the production of motor vehicles stimulated a vast supply train of smaller companies providing parts and materials for assembly into finished vehicles by the major manufacturers. The prosperity of cities like Birmingham, Detroit, Stuttgart and Turin has been due in no small part to their motor industries; and it has become common practice to employ the motor industry as an instrument of macroeconomic policy, in seeking to influence the general level of economic activity, the balance of payments and the balance of industrial activity between regions by inducing vehicle producers to establish plants in peripheral areas of high unemployment.

The factors which made vehicle production attractive to the advanced American and European economies in past decades now make it attractive to developing countries. Following the impressive example of Japan, motor industries are fast emerging in Brazil, Mexico, Iran, Korea and other countries. Thus the issues that we discuss in the British context are relevant to a wider audience, as industries in those countries face problems of growth and competition.

In this chapter we examine the importance of the motor vehicle, both functionally and as a source of economic activity; the technological and economic context of its production, and follow this with a case study of the motor industry in Britain. There we examine some of the problems faced by industry and government, and explore why the 'white heat of technological revolution' invoked as a *deus ex machina* by British politicians in the mid-1960s failed to energise the performance of the motor industry. Finally we offer some tentative observations about technology and the industry today, both in Britain and elsewhere for industrial success is a complex of interacting forces, in which technology, national governments and multinational corporations play vital roles.

The Significance of the Motor Vehicle

The motor industry is important for a host of reasons. Quite apart from the extreme visibility of the industry in the press and other media, it plays an economic role of great breadth and depth. In Britain this has been ably described in the report of the Central Policy Review Staff[1] and we shall return to it shortly, but first we must examine the role of the motor vehicle in the provision of transport.

Demand for transport is income-elastic: as personal incomes rise, the demand for travel commonly rises more than proportionately. It is also generally true that as income rises, so does the proportion of travel undertaken by road vehicle, particularly by private car. This is true of North America, Western Europe and Australasia, and the world in aggregate. Even in the developing countries, the car will play an expanding role in the foreseeable future. In land freight transportation, the road vehicle has also made absolute and relative gains.[2]

Many influences have contributed to the growing primacy of road transport over the period shown, including rising real income levels, falling real prices of vehicles and of fuel, scale economies in road freight vehicles and improvements in the infrastructure, notably the road system. Another key element in the advantage of road transport is its flexibility. Several of the other advantages mentioned have been eroded in recent years, but the attractions of flexibility remain. In the UK, where forecasts are published regularly, it is expected that car ownership will extend further, such that about 60 per cent of families will have cars by 1980, and 70 per cent by 1990.[3] There is no prospect in the short or medium-term future that the predominance of road transport will be seriously challenged by any other mode. Indeed, the latest forecasts of car ownership from the Transport and Road Research Laboratory[4] posit, on 'pessimistic' assumptions, a car population of 21.9 millions by 2010, compared with the actual figure of 13.7 millions in 1975. Under the least restrictive assumptions the figure for 2010 is envisaged as high as 30.5 millions.

At the moment road transport is dependent on petroleum fuels, which will become scarcer and more expensive. Nevertheless the private car will retain a powerful attraction, as a recent OECD research study[5] suggests:

> One is forced to the conclusion that for the majority of out-of-town trips the car has no effective substitute. Furthermore three-quarters of these car trips are for leisure purposes to which people evidently

Table 6.1: World Production and Ownership Statistics, 1975

Country	Cars in use, 1975 (millions)	Cars per thousand persons 1971	1975	Car output 1975 (000)	Commercial vehicle output 1975 (000)
USA	106.71	446	500	6,717	2,270
Canada	8.47*	323	377*	1,045	379
Australia	5.01	319	372	361	n.a.
Sweden	2.76	291	337	319	51
France	15.30	262	290	2,951	347
W. Germany	17.90	240	289	2,905	286
Switzerland	1.72*	231	267*	n.a.	n.a.
Belgium	2.61	212	267	798†	66†
Italy	14.30	209	258	1,349	110
UK	14.36	220	257	1,268	381
Holland	3.40	212	249	61	10
Japan	17.24	101	155	4,568	2,380
Spain	4.81	82	136	712	101
E. Germany	1.88	74	112	159	38
Czechoslovakia	1.50	65	102	175	36
Argentina	2.16*	71	86*	185	42
Yugoslavia	1.54	43	72	132	45
Mexico	2.40	26	40	262	100
Brazil	3.68*	29	35*	535	370
Poland	1.08	17	32	164	85
India	0.76	1	1	32	38
Bangladesh	0.03*	n.a.	0.4*	—	—
USSR	n.a.	n.a.	n.a.	1,201	765

Source: UN Statistical Yearbooks

Notes: n.a. not available; *1974 figure; † assembly only

attach great value, for they are not easily persuaded to give them up. The other quarter are for business trips, many of them quite short trips to or from rural areas or small towns, and sometimes carrying goods or equipment, for which any other mode would be much slower and less convenient.

This has implications not only for the car, but also for the limitations that radical improvements in telecommunications face: revolutionary and impressive though they are, they are only partial substitutes for personal mobility.

The question of fuel prices and sources remains an open one, though a recent research study[6] concluded that the two likeliest means of powering private cars in the first half of the next century are internal combustion engines using liquid fuel synthesised from coal (syncrude), and battery-powered vehicles. No one can be sure how far the efficiency of these two power sources may be improved, and whether the sodium-sulphur battery will become commercially practicable. Thus the future market shares of the two power systems must remain uncertain, but all available evidence we have, including studies investigating the possibility of free public transport,[7] leads to the conclusion that the car and road vehicles generally will still be much in evidence in the twenty-first century, and that the internal combustion engine will power many of them. Thus the business of manufacturing motor vehicles in a form generally similar to that at present will remain important for at least several decades to come. This has implications for Britain, Europe and many of the developing countries.

The State of the Industry

The industry is oligopolistic, in that it is dominated by a relatively small number of large corporations. Broadly speaking, the three American corporations are the biggest firms, General Motors, Ford and Chrysler, and they have the most advanced multinational ramifications. The major Japanese producers, such as Toyota and Nissan, are of the same order as Chrysler (the smallest of the American Big Three), but have concentrated their manufacture within Japan and their economies of scale have enabled them to become very successful exporters. In Europe the three leading car manufacturers are Renault, Fiat and Volkswagen, all capable of producing over 1½ million cars a year. In Britain, all the Big Three American producers have subsidiaries, and the only other sizable producer, British Leyland, was effectively nationalised when bankruptcy threatened and the National Enterprise Board (NEB) stepped in. As seen in Table 6.1, several countries outside the traditional automotive centres are fast increasing their output, such as Brazil, Mexico and the USSR, and others such as Iran and South Korea are likely to do so in the near future. Usually these countries have drawn on imported technology – in the USSR and Poland, Fiat provided it – and sometimes on imported capital.

In Britain, manufacture is stratified rather than vertically integrated, and makers of finished vehicles buy in about 60 per cent of the factory price of cars from outside suppliers; whereas in Europe, the United

States and Japan, the ratio varies from 25 to 40 per cent. International competition is severe, especially in Western Europe, where it has been intensified by the EEC, and in the United States; however it is restricted or nonexistent in Japan and many of the countries seeking to foster their domestic industries. In Western Europe, the British industry has proved particularly vulnerable to imports, which now hold almost half the market, compared with only a quarter in France and West Germany. The British component manufacturers, often considered the strongest in Europe, are also showing signs of competitive pressure. In all countries where manufacture occurs, the industry assumes major importance as a customer for other industries, notably iron and steel, non-ferrous metals, rubber, plastics, glass, paint and textiles. Thus recessions in the motor industry send depressive ripples throughout the economy: conversely, to correct a much-misquoted statement 'what's good for America is good for General Motors'.

It is perhaps misleading to consider the technology of the motor industry as a unity. Since the production of cars requires the amalgamation of literally tens of thousands of products, often themselves the result of technology applied in other industries, the sum of technology is more like a mosaic, some parts static, others in flux. However, in terms of dramatically revolutionary change the motor industry is not a source of great surprises. Whereas in the interwar period the industry could be portrayed as a leader in the technological race,[8] by 1971 an American economist could note[9]

> Perhaps the most striking thing about automotive technology in the postwar period has been the lack of fundamental change or advance. . .Even in the areas in which modern cars do differ from their early postwar predecessors, such as the widespread application of automatic transmissions and power-assisted equipment, the basic technology had been developed before the war, and postwar developments represented achievements in refining this technology rather than in any fundamental change.
> We are dealing with refinements of the technology, innovational advances to bring basic inventions to a marketable state, rather than with the basic inventions themselves. This process of refinement should not be taken too lightly. Significant progress often comes in a series of small steps.

This latter point would be well appreciated if one were to drive a 1946 model and switch immediately afterwards to a current type. White's subsequent points are well taken, too, that raw materials suppliers — steel, aluminium, copper, plastics, rubber, paints — have promoted their materials and fed technology into the assembly industry. In the United Kingdom this gradual sophistication of production technology, allied to powerful economies of scale, contributed to a steady reduction in the real cost of cars, while at the same time improving their physical characteristics.

The major vehicle manufacturers have emphasised product development more than applied research, and applied rather than basic research. Production technology corresponded also to these priorities. Indeed the technological status of the industry fits closely the pattern of events suggested by product cycle theorists such as Vernon[10] and Wells.[11] Since the product cycle is a useful analytical focus, it is worth summarising the concept.

The Product Cycle

Product innovations are first introduced in high-income economies with substantial industrial and scientific infrastructures. The dynamics of demand for new products suggest that, over time, total demand grows along a predictable course, corresponding fairly closely to a logistic growth pattern, or Gompertz curve. Moreover, the progression can be divided into identifiable phases, shown in Figure 6.1.

During the introductory phase, product design is still evolving. Product runs are relatively limited, techniques are changing and small-scale, and entry to the industry is easy, often helped by the optimism of innovators. Buyers of the product are relatively few and wealthy — effectively the upper end of the static demand curve, which corresponds to the lower end of the dynamic product cycle curve — and are more conscious of product-quality (novelty) than of price. Accordingly, cost-minimisation is much less important than the pursuit of scientific and engineering advance, in order to get ahead of other hopeful producers. This introductory phase is long past in the motor industry; it pre-dates the era of mass production of Henry Ford and Lord Nuffield in the United Kingdom. Yet the introductory phase could have a renewed interest as and when new forms of motive power are introduced to compete with the internal combustion engine.

The second or growth phase sees a sharp increase in demand. Growing public familiarity with the product through word of mouth, observation and advertising helps to boost demand; the early emphasis on science and engineering improves the quality and reliability of the product; the growth of output begins to yield productive economies

Figure 6.1: International Production under the Product Cycle

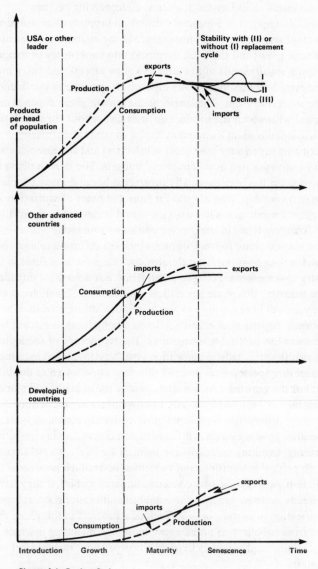

Phases of the Product Cycle

Source: Adapted from Vernon, 'International Investment'.

of scale which bring down prices (as with Ford's Model T or, more recently, electronic calculators). The weaker producers are weeded out, and managerial skills beyond science and engineering become increasingly important. Financial calculation supplants hunch and the accountant acquires as much importance as the engineer or scientist.

As scale grows and the weak disappear into bankruptcy or merger, the capital requirements of manufacture grow as well, and entry into the industry becomes much more difficult. It is a time of confidence for the successful firms. The length of the growth phase depends on the speed with which the product diffuses throughout the population, and this depends upon its inherent appeal to consumers (often reflecting its superiority over older substitutes) and the ease with which it can be incorporated into consumers' budgets. The growth phase for the private car has been especially protracted because many people aspire to ownership — we are still far from the point of saturation when all aspirants would actually own a car — and because it is one of the most expensive items in the average consumer's budget.

The mature phase follows, during which the diffusion rate of the product among consumers decelerates, and the growth of firms in the industry also weakens. For specialised firms, not diversified outside the motor industry, this phase has critical implications. Shareholders and employees will have come to expect continued strong growth. Given the normal dispersion of efficiency levels among firms, some will be weaker and less profitable than others. The technology of the industry shifts significantly: radical innovation gives way to modest increments of design interspersed with product differentiation, often of doubtful value; but the growing cost consciousness of the industry will stimulate process innovations, fed by steady improvements in production technology. Competition prompts other corporate responses typical of oligopolies: growing product differentiation is manifest in combative advertising, extolling brand virtues; mergers are likely, to yield strength through vertical integration, and to rationalise through horizontal integration, raising industrial concentration; companies, if they have not already done so, are likely to establish multinational operations; diversification is another option. Technical progress in this phase often comes from suppliers, as noted above by White, including machine tool manufacturers and suppliers in mutual competition, such as steel and aluminium.

The mature phase is difficult to delineate, and it may continue for many decades. Gold's research showed many cases where maturity led to an extended plateau of demand.[12] Beyond the point of saturation, there may follow a phase of stagnation in which the consumption per head is static, and any growth in output depends upon rising population and/or exports. In the case of durable goods, a replacement cycle may emerge: recent research in the United States, which is the country closest to saturation of demand, suggests that consumers' expenditure on car purchase is now influenced more by substitution between cars, other durable goods and housing than by the wealth and income effects.[13] The alternative, or successor, phase to stagnation is decline, which occurs when a superior substitute erodes the market for the original product. The pressing problems of maturity become the lethal ones of decline.

Technology, Trade and the Multinational Corporation

The product cycle has been used by Vernon[14] to explain the origins and international diffusion of innovations, and international trade theory in the past decade has become intertwined with industrial economics by authors such as Kindleberger, Hymer and Caves.[15] Vernon's emphasis has altered over the years, and his original formulation is synoptic rather than precise. Vernon suggested that the demand for new products will emerge in high-income economies, and a premium will attach to labour-saving products such as consumer durables. The most advanced market in this sense has been the United States, with the added advantage that it is also large and relatively homogeneous. Thus in such a market the product cycle will originate, and during the introduction phase manufacture will be concentrated close to the market, even though labour may be very expensive; for that phase displays an emphasis on innovative, technological competition and not so much on outright cost-consciousness, so that successful manufacturers will value rapid and accurate feedback of public reaction and the proximity of R & D competence. Once started as innovators, these successful domestic manufacturers have a growing advantage over late entrants. Figure 6.1 depicts the international life cycle of the product innovation.

Consumption follows in other advanced countries, which import from the pioneer country but may soon manufacture locally, especially if transport costs or tariffs counter the advantages of the pioneer. Developing countries with uneven income distribution may also import to satisfy the demand of wealthy inhabitants. However, as the product cycle advances, the pattern of manufacture changes. In the growth phase (corresponding to what Vernon calls the 'maturing product stage'), as the technology of the industry becomes more commonly agreed, and cost considerations impinge more strongly on corporate policy manufacture will extend among the non-pioneer countries, especially if they enjoy a modest cost advantage, as Europe did in labour costs when compared with the United States in the 1950s and 1960s. Exports from these non-pioneer countries will tend to grow, but once the product is standardised so that technology involved in its production is readily and cheaply available, production will rise rapidly in many of the developing countries, where rising income stimulates demand. They may generate a sizable export trade, especially if many of the assembly operations involved can be carried out on standardised machines operated by relatively unskilled labour.

The multinational corporation has been a prime vehicle for diffusing technology in this manner. Given the ethic of growth which pervades most of the large companies in market economies, the technological opportunities of the international product cycle coincide powerfully with the imperatives of oligopoly — especially research-based oligopoly — to expand into overseas manufacture. The most recent theories of multinational corporations have as their core the ready transferability of knowledge: Hirsch[16] constructs a simple model in which knowhow, both technological and commercial, takes the characteristic of a public good within the multinational; Buckley and Casson[17] also use the concept of internalisation of corporate knowledge in an attempt to formalise some of the earlier, amorphous contributions to the literature.

The British Case: an Established Motor Industry under International Pressure

We have dwelt upon the product cycle because many analyses of the British motor industry, consciously or unconsciously, seem to be drawn from it; moreover, it corresponds with the experience of many other industries, from textiles to electronics. The CPRS Report emphasised the growing challenge coming from the production of motor vehicles from countries which recently had no motor industries. To the policymaker it may matter little whether the technology passes along the multinational chain or has simply become so commonplace that internalisation is not important; but as we shall see the distinction is significant.

In recent years the performance of the British motor industry has been disappointing by international standards, and the competition that it faces from foreign manufacturers has sharpened to an embarrassing degree. However, the industry is such an important employer of labour and capital in the British economy, and a major source of exports, that it would hardly be an acceptable strategy to sanction its disappearance and satisfy the still-growing domestic demand for vehicles from efficient sources overseas. Motor manufacturing, selling, repair and maintenance account *directly* for 5 per cent of the total national workforce. In some regions the concentration of the industry makes it an even more significant employer: in the West Midlands in 1973, 16 per cent of the labour force was engaged in the motor industry. Moreover, direct employment figures are only a part of the industry's significance, since it buys in large amounts of materials from other industries: in 1974, it consumed £280m of metal goods, £240m of iron and steel, £140m of iron castings, £110m of non-ferrous metals, and significantly large amounts of other products including rubber, plastics, glass, paint and textiles. A serious running down of the industry would create additional problems of unemployment at a time when numbers out of work are higher than for four decades, and when a number of commentators such as Professor Christopher Freeman are seriously concerned that Western economies may be entering a prolonged period when technology will displace labour and preserve high unemployment rates for a decade and beyond.

If the rundown of the motor industry had a low opportunity cost, one might face it with equanimity: if the resources devoted to it could be readily redeployed, or if the economy were growing rapidly, the price might be payable; but not otherwise. Thus the public thirst for road transport and the key role its manufacture plays in the economy would seem to justify the view expressed in the 1976 White Paper[18] that vehicle production ought to remain an essential part of the economic base of the UK.

Government Policy and the Motor Industry

Wells has noted:[19] 'In every country, the automobile industry has been very dependent on government policies.' For example, tariff barriers were frequently erected against the United States mass-produced exports, and discriminatory taxation favoured small-engined domestically-produced European cars. Yet the British government was less interventionist than most, especially after 1950, when the industry, largely if temporarily relieved of Continental European competition, was buoyant and prosperous, and the demand for motor vehicles at home was manipulated as a macroeconomic policy instrument. No attempt was made to prevent US Ford buying out its 39 per cent British minority shareholding in 1960, though Ford gave certain undertakings on investment, exports, employment and dividends to the

British government.[20] The American company, Chrysler, took over the
ailing British Rootes group, acquiring a minority shareholding in 1964
and a majority one in 1966. In both the Ford and Chrysler cases (and
on subsequent occasions) the government was afraid that more
interventionist policies might deflect American investment to the
Continent instead.

Thus throughout the 1960s there was a clear increase in the
American penetration of the British industry, by a combination of
acquisition and increased market share of domestic output. The figures
shown in Table 6.2 are taken from two separate sources and the *exact*
degree of comparability is uncertain, but they show the growing share
of American-owned companies in both sales and employment, the
concentration on the motor industry relative to manufacturing as a
whole, and suggest that they enjoyed materially high output per man,
inasmuch as their share of sales was appreciably higher than their share
of employment.[21]

The attitude of government during the period was understandable.
Dunning had shown as far back as 1958 that American subsidiaries were
usually above the average level of efficiency of British companies,[22]
and subsequent research confirmed their advantages — concentrated in
industries more technological, more capital-intensive, more profitable
and above average in export performance.[23] Thus, with some
justification, it seemed that injections of United States capital would
contribute to the British balance of payments on capital account, and
could help the current account in future if United States managerial
competence could improve domestic productivity and exports.

Despite the fact that it was the Ministry of Technology that took
over responsibility for government relations with the motor industry
from the Board of Trade in 1966, as far as technology was concerned,
government policy was one of *laisser-innover*, to use Freeman's phrase.
He shows that by 1968-9 the motor industry was tenth in a league table
of 31 industrial groups ranked by their R & D expenditure as a
percentage of net output;[24] the industry spent £45.7m on R & D, which
was 7 per cent of the national industrial total; however, only 3.2 per
cent of that £45.7m was financed by government — a trivial proportion
when compared with the research monies used to promote technology
in aerospace, electronics, scientific instruments and other 'strategic'
spheres. The picture was substantially similar by 1972-3, the latest year
for which detailed figures are available; indeed, the proportion financed
by government and public corporations appears even lower, at just
below 1 per cent,[25] though it is not clear on what basis the earlier figure

Table 6.2: United States Participation in the British Motor Industry

	1963 (%)	1973 (%)	1973-4, actual
(a) SALES			
US share in vehicles	21.5	29.4	£1,722m
of which motor vehicle manufacture		41.2	£1,675m
other vehicle production		2.6	£47m
US share of total manufacturing		12.8	£7,940m
(b) EMPLOYMENT			
US share in vehicles	15.4	21.2	164,754
of which motor vehicle manufacture		33.1	157,633
other vehicle production		2.4	7,121
US share of total manufacturing		9.7	740,261

Sources: 1963 figures, unpublished Board of Trade figures, quoted by Hodge, *Multinational Corporations and National Government*, p.182. 1973 figures, Economists Advisory Group, *US Industry in Britain* (London, 1974).

was calculated.

Why was the policy of *laisser-innover* applied? There are several plausible reasons. First, there was no strong historical precedent for technological support to the industry. The real point of take-off for the industry had been in the interwar period, and its continued growth through the postwar period had been demand-induced. The characteristics of the product cycle help to explain this. In the case of private cars, the cycle is a very extended one; purchase is so expensive that it is likely to be at least a century from the introduction of cars in Britain before saturation of demand occurs. The major product innovations, having occurred early, give way to incremental and process innovations. By contrast, aerospace and electronics have crucially important military applications; they are much less constrained by the budgetary limits of the ordinary citizen, and wars, hot and cold, have persuaded governments to invest prodigally in R & D.

Secondly, the technology of the motor car is humdrum compared to the glamour of high technology. Any industry which is dominated by the necessity of having to assemble thousands of contributory parts to construct a whole, will display an emphasis on development rather than the more 'intellectually respectable' areas of basic and applied research (see Table 6.3). Even where government has acknowledged that the

Table 6.3: R & D in Britain and the USA, Government Support in Selected Industries

| Industry | Percentage by area | | | Percent financed |
	Basic	Applied	Development	by government[1]
(a) Britain (1972-3)				
Motor vehicles	0.6	11.4	88.0	1.0
Aerospace	1.1	3.3	95.6	84.6
Electronics and communications	3.7	13.9	82.4	53.1
Pharmaceuticals	7.4	52.4	40.2	0.2
All industry	3.4	21.4	75.2	42.6
(b) USA (1970)				
Transport equipment, inc. MV[2]	n.a.	81.8		17
Aerospace	1.2	9.6	89.2	79
Electronics and communications	4.9	15.4	79.7	53
Drugs and medicine	15.4	38.9	45.7	3
All industry	3.3	18.4	78.3	45

Notes: 1. UK figures refer to government finance for R & D conducted within the industry.   2. Includes ships and railroads.

Sources: (a) Central Statistical Office, *Research and Development Expenditure* (London, HMSO, 1976); (b) National Science Foundation, *Research and Development in Industry 1970* (Washington, NSF 72-309, 1972).

emphasis on high technology has been excessive, it has been difficult to redeploy its support.[26]

Table 6.3 shows similar predispositions of both British and United States governments to back high technology, with the notable exception of pharmaceuticals, a complex case with an unusual emphasis on science. The British government clearly regarded the motor industry very differently from aerospace or electronics, and the contrast with the United States government's degree of support for R & D in transportation equipment is striking.

The attitudes outlined above bear upon the third cause of *laisser-innover*, namely the difficulty of stimulating R & D in a strictly commercial and competitive environment, where the government is not the primary customer. Not only does this raise the thorny questions of control and accountability but also the potentially more difficult issue of the distribution of benefits. The problems which loomed in many minds are plainer than the solutions. What methods should the government employ to stimulate private industry to innovate? Since it is immanent among multinational corporations to transfer knowledge more or less freely to their sisters overseas, how could one guarantee that the rewards to government-sponsored R & D would not be drained away? Might it not be a distortion of a reasonably efficient market system: perhaps the multinationals, by sourcing some R & D here and some there, were cost-minimisers, and the government support of increased local effort would be nugatory: knowledge might be bought cheaper abroad. Given the powerful trend towards 'world-wide sourcing' and the integration of production among subsidiaries in many countries, did it make sense to contemplate national policies? And how might one reconcile the unprofitable nationalised passenger transport industries to the encouragement of their fiercest competitor? One traditional role of sponsorship, the encouragement of basic research the results of which could be disbursed neutrally to all the oligopolistic members of the industry, was not an easy one because of the limited scope for such research in the industry. In 1972-3, for example, research association basic research in the industry was £163,000 compared with the corporate figure of only £133,000.

Against this complexity, it is not surprising that the most prudent policy would seem to be to leave the industry to keep its own technological affairs in order. However, by the mid 1970s the industry had become massively unprofitable, and the government had to intervene to rescue two of its four biggest companies.

The Recent Performance of the Industry

The CPRS Report analysed the recent performance of the industry, and its causes, with chilling clarity. In the two subsequent years the situation has worsened in many respects. Imports accounted for about 5 per cent of the domestic car market in 1965 and rose to 35 per cent by the time of the CPRS Report in 1975, but by the closing months of 1977 penetration was almost 50 per cent. Part of this rise can be ascribed to free trade in cars, but also to the uncompetitiveness of British cars, since other European manufacturing countries did not witness such deep penetration. Moreover, a similar trend has begun to emerge among commercial vehicles, with rising imports and declining exports. Three of the four biggest British manufacturers — Leyland, Vauxhall and Chrysler — have suffered heavy losses for several years, and could not generate enough cash internally to finance their capital investment programmes.

The causes of the industry's plight, briefly, are poor product availability, weaknesses in the distribution chain especially overseas, poor product quality and a cost structure which has become uncompetitive with European levels, despite markedly lower wages in the British industry. The CPRS Report calculated in 1975 that a car made in Britain at £1,150 factory cost excluding finance charges would only cost £1,020 in Europe.[27] Part of the cost disability was attributable to managerial weakness, especially in failure to rationalise so that fragmentation of model ranges and plants increased overhead costs per vehicle very severely. Most of the industry's problems have little to do with technology, and much to do with mutual problems of management and labour, leading to overmanning, slow workpace, production-line breakdown, and undercapitalisation. But even where Ford, the most efficient of the British makers, had machines identical with continental companies, output per man was only half as much: this state of affairs apparently still applied in early 1978 when a separate investigation was conducted.[28]

The general problem of the industry's downward competitive spiral has created technological problems. The British industry over the past two decades grew more slowly than its competitors, partly because of managerial shortcomings and partly because its domestic market was growing more slowly and was affected by 'stop-go' policies of government macroeconomic management. Poor sales put the industry at a disadvantage against more dynamic firms abroad, which can afford to introduce new models more often. Moreover, the problem was compounded in the late 1960s and early 1970s when much of the development work in the industry had to be devoted to satisfying the United States and EEC regulations concerning safety and exhaust emission levels: at a time when resources were needed to develop new models this essentially defensive R & D pre-empted them, but wealthier foreign firms could more easily meet these costs without disruption. Across the period 1966-7 to 1972-3, R & D spending in the industry, corrected for inflation, declined by about one tenth, R & D employment fell, and there was a very sharp drop in capital expenditure on R & D, amounting in real terms to some two thirds and implying that firms were cutting back on the use of modern equipment in their R & D. Pratten[29] has shown that the heavy fixed costs of introducing new models have to be covered in one of two ways: either the models must be produced in great quantity over a relatively short period, or the models must be kept in production for very long periods. The British industry has had little choice but to accept the second alternative and has thus suffered a severe handicap.

New models are essential elements of competition in the industry. Other factors, such as extensive and efficient dealerships, product reliability and durability, and competitive prices, are important, but the Ford Model T and Volkswagen Beetle eventually had to bow to product innovation. The fact that the motor industry uses face lifts to differentiate its products should not be allowed to cloud the fact that the industry is fiercely competitive and that the succession of model changes is likely to bring about tangible improvements in car design and performance — better cruising speed, acceleration, fuel economy, handling, accommodation and so on. The British industry has been disadvantaged by its inability to keep pace with the new products of Europe and Japan.

The Emergence of New Priorities

Hard facts forced the government in the mid 1970s into a far more active role in the industry than ever it could have contemplated in the 1960s. Then it was content to vet foreign takeovers and, through the Industrial Reorganisation Corporation, act as broker in the Leyland-BMC marriage. In 1975 it was obliged to save the bankrupt Leyland by transferring the majority shareholding to the National Enterprise Board, and following the recommendations of the Ryder Committee[30] to underwrite a £1,000 million capital expenditure programme for Leyland's car division. At the end of 1975, Chrysler's British subsidiary was also on the brink of collapse, and was also rescued by loan money from the government, and guarantees to meet part of the subsidiary's future losses; only to be sold to Peugeot in 1978.

The Leyland rescue was controversial, and drew critical comment from the House of Commons Expenditure Committee,[31] but the Chrysler rescue was even more so. It involved backing a foreign multinational, much the weakest of America's big three producers; it was arguably the most marginal of Britain's big four producers, so that rescuing it was very much at odds with the finding of the CPRS Report that there were too many manufacturers in Britain for all of them to achieve the minimum economic scale of output; it could not be readily nationalised (though Chrysler reputedly offered it to the government) because Leyland was already effectively nationalised, and to have two such corporations in outright competition would have been politically unacceptable; yet the integration of Chrysler into Leyland was not an operational possibility. But counter-pressures were strong, and real enough to sway a divided Cabinet. Jobs would be lost, many in politically sensitive areas; exports would be lost, and imports would fill, in part, the vacuum created by a departed Chrysler, not only among customers but also among dealerships. Thus where technological economy might have written Chrysler off, political economy sustained it until the Peugeot takeover in August 1978.

The government has gradually taken an increasing interest in the affairs of the industry, culminating in its present commitment, stated in 1976, to improve the efficiency of the industry. The means to increase efficiency are very problematic, but if the stated policy of the government is to seek a viable industry, every means merits consideration. It is not enough to expect a general revival of the British economy to pull the motor industry along in its train, because the industry's failure has been a very specific one. Thirlwall has calculated income elasticities of demand for motor vehicle imports which exemplify the past shortcomings of the British industry: between 1963 and 1974, a 1 per cent increase in incomes in Britain was associated with a 3.9 per cent increase in imports of motor vehicles, whereas a 1 per cent increase in world income only witnessed an increase of 0.9 per cent in British motor vehicle exports.[32] No other British industry examined had such a wide disparity, which might be interpreted as a rough measure of the scope for improvement.

The CPRS Report, no less relevant today, shows that the key improvements must include superior management, better labour relations and practices, and a slimmer but better range of products, more efficiently produced. In this, technology is important for, notwithstanding the spread of vehicle production to countries like Iran and South Korea, technological competence confers competitive advantage. For example, Volkswagen in Germany has its own wind tunnel, which has helped to improve its cars' aerodynamics, thus improving high-speed economy and stability, whereas the British industry has been restricted to the tunnel at the Motor Industry Research Association. In Japan, Soichiro Honda has emphasised research in his company ever since he visited Britain in 1953 and was chastened to see motor-cycle engines with much better specific power outputs than his own; this has paid off in various directions, not least with the stratified charge combustion chamber which satisfied United States emission requirements without complex catalytic exhaust systems, and with high-pressure aluminium diecasting, significantly reducing the need for machining. Indeed, Japanese industry as a whole has been particularly adept at acquiring technology from overseas and using it as a base to develop its own increasingly significant R & D.[33]

The *concept* of employing technology as an instrument in the revivification of the British motor industry seems to meet general acceptance; but it prompts the questions, how much, and how? R & D already enjoys tax allowances, and some work is being done under the aegis of the Department of Transport, but it is appropriate here to consider some of the basic principles of allocating money for technological improvement.

The first point to be made is that technology – knowledge applied to the production of artefacts – is much wider than the narrow notion of formalised R & D. Some technological benefits will flow from the general support given to the motor industry by the British government. Another important point is that the optimal application of science and technology requires equilibrium of supply and demand: the supply of technology must not be overemphasised if the marketable demand for that technology is so remote as to be insignificant or unlikely; and the simple fact that a market is large cannot guarantee that new technology will be applicable to it. Thus a promising focus for technology would be one where knowledge can be seen to be applicable, and where there is a likely market for its product. Past overemphasis on high technology of low commercial potential was highlighted by Sir Ieuan Maddock,[34] when he showed that Japanese civil R & D, in 1972 appreciably greater in total than British, was much more closely related to the pattern of the economy's industrial output than was Britain's R & D. For example, R & D expenditure on motor vehicles was more than twice the British figure. Similarly in West Germany there has been a greater congruence between R & D and industrial application, and perhaps a greater appreciation of the richness of technological inputs arising out of a proven system of technical education.

A third point is that the market mechanism is unlikely to prove adequate, since the leading members are extremely hard pressed for investment funds. In these circumstances, R & D is the most vulnerable area of investment. Debtor companies like Leyland and Chrysler are even more constrained than usual to seek early profits. British companies generally in their private allocation to R & D exhibit a strong bias towards projects with an early return,[35] and in recent years national expenditure on R & D in Britain and the United States has displayed a downward trend. One may conclude that R & D is a potential source of weakness in the British motor industry, and that if government wishes seriously to encourage the industry, more explicit

policies towards R & D are advisable. Although the government avoided
a direct role in the technology of the industry in the 1960s, there is
today some involvement, albeit modest.

Apart from selective assistance used to induce companies to invest
in development areas, as in the recent case of Ford's engine plant for
Bridgend, South Wales, it is possible under the Science and Technology
Act for government funds to be used in joint R & D ventures. In
August 1977, a Product and Process Development Scheme was
announced covering projects between £25,000 and £1m, and proposals
from firms are beginning to appear at the Department of Industry.
More long-term research, of the sort of which companies might
normally be suspicious, is also desirable. In this area the Department
of the Environment is contributing £400,000 towards extramural
R & D on sodium-sulphur batteries during 1977-8: work has been going
on in this area for several years, also involving the Department of
Industry, the Electricity Council and the Chloride Group of Companies.

A technology policy for the industry should have two aims: first to
assist the short and medium-term effectiveness of the industry, through
incremental product and process innovation, and second to assist in the
promotion of more radical long-run technology. However, many people
express scepticism at the very concept of a technology policy, and it is
only likely to succeed if it can be linked to a more explicit industrial
strategy than the current one. The recommendations of the National
Economic Development Office sector working parties have been
detailed and useful, and more realistic than the ambitious optimism of
the National Plan of 1965. But the present strategy seems more tactical
than strategic, in that it includes a very wide range of industries and
lacks the element of careful selection implicit in strategic choice. Such
choices *were* made by MITI – the Ministry for International Trade and
Industry – in Japan.

This paper is not intended to produce instant prescriptions for
policy, merely to suggest that technological options for the industry be
explored to the full. Broadly one can agree with many of the suggestions
made by Pavitt about the redeployment of British technological effort,[36]
but some additional points need to be made:

(i) Government should not be too punctilious about the distribution of
benefits of the R & D involved. If they went substantially into
corporate profit, this would not be a bad thing for British industry,
and in any event corporation tax would claw back much of it.
(ii) Careful attention would have to be given to the modes of incentive

to be employed. These have been explored by a number of commentators[37] and may include joint ventures, contracts, fiscal incentives, credits and grants and co-operative research. It is difficult to imagine that the scope for all of these has been exhausted or even fully explored, and the motor industry may suffer because it is remote from the Research Requirement Boards.

Schott has observed recently[38] that her econometric model suggests that in Britain corporate tax reductions are the likeliest means to stimulate industrial R & D — more effective than juggling patent life-span, or adjusting interest rates, investment allowances or R & D allowances; however, in their present unprofitable state, some of the major British manufacturers are unlikely to find that general conclusion useful to them.

(iii) We have not considered the problems in encouraging R & D in multinational corporations, which might transfer the resultant knowhow. There are some grounds for optimism about this. Government relations with the multinational motor companies in Britain appear to be good, and British design capabilities are well regarded. It is true that all three multinationals are now sourcing their cars and components throughout Western Europe, but added technological expertise in Britain can only augment her attraction as a productive base. Moreover, if Britain were to decline as a centre of design, it would ultimately affect her component makers, which have in the past sometimes benefited at least as much as the manufacturers out of their associated innovation: thus Leyland got much glory but little profit out of the Mini but GKN, who patented elements of the transmission, have since become profitable suppliers to many European front-wheel-drive cars. Multinationals are concerned about their image and their relations with local governments, and it should be possible to devise a system of arm's length pricing to gain realistic returns to contributions from British subsidiaries.

(iv) One must concede that an increased R & D effort as a means to higher efficiency is at best hollow piety and at worst rank misallocation if it is not backed by technological commonsense. In 'the application of knowledge to the production of artefacts', it would seem that throughout many segments of British industry there is enormous scope for improvements in quality control, the application of value analysis, and other techniques which could go far towards raising British standards of reliability and quality up to those currently achieved by Germany and Japan. The best designed product will still fail commercially if it is badly assembled, and there is much evidence of this shortcoming in British industry.

(v) Long-run technology policy may have to face the possibility that new organisational forms may be necessary if radical innovations are to succeed, as one hopes they will if Britain is to withstand competition from developing countries producing standardised products. It has been suggested earlier in this chapter that the internal combustion engine and the battery-powered vehicle will coexist in the early part of the next century. Present vehicle manufacturers may succeed in making the transition, but if they are sluggish to adopt battery-powered vehicles (and the marketing and maintenance of some designs might be markedly different from existing patterns) it may be desirable to encourage non-vehicle companies into an industry where the barriers to entry are formidable.

Some General Conclusions

The lessons for the industrialised countries are that technology is widely important, in more than high technology areas. Technological strength is a necessary, though not a sufficient condition for industrial competition, especially if less developed nations begin to enter the 'simpler' areas of the industry, often helped by multinational corporations. The example of the motor industry has a wider relevance, in that industries which today appear healthy are liable to similar erosion of their position.

For other countries, too, there may be relevance. Those countries currently fostering or aspiring to motor industries must become aware that, in the future, technology as well as sheer scale of output is important. Expected shortages of fuel will affect the emphasis of technology, and technological capability will be vital in the search for more economic variants of both the liquid-fuelled and the electric vehicle. The multinationals will continue to dominate technological dissemination, but it would be a doubtful act of faith for any government to delegate this function to the companies alone.

Notes

1. Central Policy Review Staff, *The Future of the British Car Industry* (London, HMSO, 1975), ch.1.

2. A.H. Tulpule, *An Analysis of some world transport statistics*, TRRL Laboratory Report 622 (Crowthorne, Berks., Transport and Road Research Laboratory, 1974).

3. *Transport Policy: a consultation document*, vol.1 (London, HMSO, 1976), ch.2.

4. J.C. Tanner, *Car Ownership trends and forecasts*, TRRL Laboratory Report 799 (Crowthorne, Berks., Transport and Road Research Laboratory, 1977).

5. *The Future of European Passenger Transport* (Paris, OECD, 1977), p.590.

6. P. Chapman, G. Charlesworth and M. Baker, *Future transport fuels*, TRRL Supplementary Report 251 (Crowthorne, Berks., Transport and Road Research Laboratory, 1976).

7. Several studies have assessed the significance of zero fares, by a variety of means, but none has suggested that zero fares would enable public transport to supplant the private car. See, for example P.H. Bly, *The effect of fares on bus patronage*, LR 733 (Crowthorne, Berks, Transport and Road Research Laboratory, 1976), and A.J. Daly and S. Zachary, *The effect of free public transport on the journey to work*, SR 388 (Crowthorne, Berks, Transport and Road Research Laboratory, 1977).

8. L.T. Wells, 'Automobiles', ch.11, in R. Vernon (ed.), *Big Business and the State* (London, Macmillan, 1974), especially p.236.

9. L.J. White, *The Automobile Industry since 1945* (Cambridge, Mass., Harvard University Press, 1971), ch.13.

10. R. Vernon, 'International investment and international trade in the product cycle', *Quarterly Journal of Economics*, vol.80 (1966), pp.190-207. The model is extended in his *Sovereignty at Bay* (Harmondsworth, Penguin, 1973).

11. L.T. Wells (ed.), *The Product Life Cycle and International Trade* (Boston, Harvard University Graduate School of Business Administration, 1972), chs.1 and 3.

12. Bela Gold, *Explorations in Managerial Economics: Productivity, Costs, Technology and Growth* (London, Macmillan, 1971), ch.11.

13. A.C. Hess, 'A Comparison of Automobile Demand Equations', *Econometrica*, vol.45 (1977), pp.683-702.

14. R. Vernon, 'International investment', n.10, *supra*.

15. See C.P. Kindleberger, *American Business Abroad* (New Haven, Yale University Press, 1969); R.E. Caves, 'International Corporations: the Industrial Economics of Foreign Investment', *Economica*, vol.38 (1971), pp.1-27. Hymer's major contribution was an unpublished Ph.D dissertation, 'International Operations of National Firms' (MIT, 1960).

16. S. Hirsch, 'An International Trade and Investment Theory of the Firm', *Oxford Economic Papers*, vol.28 (1976), pp.258-70.

17. P.J. Buckley and M. Casson, *The Future of Multinational Enterprise* (London, Macmillan, 1976).

18. *The British Motor Vehicle Industry* (London, HMSO, Cmnd.6377, January 1976).

19. L.T. Wells, ch.11, in R. Vernon (ed.), *Big Business and the State* (London, Macmillan, 1974), p.232.

20. These are quoted and the circumstances discussed more fully in M. Hodges, *Multinational Corporations and National Government* (Farnborough, Saxon House, 1974), pp.186-91.

21. Though the figures may be influenced by different degrees of vertical integration in companies, the higher level of productivity in American subsidiaries is not in dispute.

22. J.M. Dunning, *American Investment in British Manufacturing Industry* (London, Allen and Unwin, 1958).

23. See, for example, M.D. Steuer and J.M. Dunning, 'The Effects of United States Direct Investment on British Technology', in J.M. Dunning (ed.), *Studies in International Investment* (London, Allen and Unwin, 1970).

24. C. Freeman, *The Economics of Industrial Innovation* (Harmondsworth, Penguin, 1974), pp.34-5.

25. *Central Statistical Office, Research and Development Expenditure* (London, HMSO, 1975), pp.114-15.

26. K. Pavitt, 'The choice of targets and instruments for Government support of scientific research', in A. Whiting (ed.), *The Economics of Industrial Subsidies* (London, HMSO, 1975), pp.114-15.

27. Central Policy Review Staff, *Future of British Car Industry*, p.93.

28. *Sunday Times*, London, 5 March 1978, pp.17-19.

29. C.F. Pratten, *Economies of Scale in Manufacturing Industry*, University of Cambridge, Department of Applied Economics, Occasional Paper No.21 (London, Cambridge University Press, 1972).

30. House of Commons, HC 342, *British Leyland: the next decade*, 23 April 1975, ch.14.

31. House of Commons, HC 617, Fourteenth Report of the Expenditure Committee 1974-5, *The Motor Vehicle Industry*. The CPRS Report also included a section devoted to the control of British Leyland's investment programme, *Future of British Car Industry*, pp.136-40.

32. A.P. Thirlwall, 'The UK's Economic Problem: A Balance of Payments Constraint?', *National Westminster Bank Quarterly Review*, February 1978, p.31.

33. See R. Caves and M. Uekusa, *Industrial Organisation in Japan* (Washington, Brookings Institution, 1976), ch.7.

34. Sir Ieuan Maddock, Seventh Royal Society Technology Lecture, 12 February 1975, reproduced in *Proceedings of the Royal Society*, vol.345 (30 September 1975).

35. K. Schott, 'Investment in Private Industrial Research and Development in Britain', *Journal of Industrial Economics*, vol.25 (1976), pp.81-99.

36. K. Pavitt, 'Choice of targets'.

37. *The Aims and Instruments of Industrial Policy* (Paris, OECD, 1975).

38. K. Schott, 'The Relations between Industrial Research and Development and Factor Demands', *Economic Journal*, vol.88 (1978), p.100.

Part Two

THE CONTROL OF TECHNOLOGY

7 THE CONTROL OF TECHNOLOGY THROUGH REGULATION

Judith Reppy

Perhaps the most distinctive feature of modern industrial societies has been their rapid rate of technological change. New technologies and new uses of old technologies have conferred economic growth and substantial increases in the standard of living on the populations of the industrially advanced countries; they have also created a host of related problems, such as pollution of the air and water, increased hazards from toxic chemicals, and strains on the social and political fabric, as a consequence of changes in communications and transportation. Meanwhile, institutional arrangements for assigning property rights and responsibilities have lagged behind the pace of technological change. Faced with an increasing public activism across a range of environmental and safety issues, it is not surprising that the response of governments to many of the undesired side effects of technological change has been an increase in the scope and variety of government regulation.

The tendency for governments to intervene to moderate the hazardous side effects of new technologies or products can be traced back in history to such early examples as the banning of the use of sea coal in English cities in the thirteenth century[1] and the establishment of the Alkali Inspectorate in 1863. The dominant regulatory activity during the late nineteenth and early twentieth century, however, was concerned with controlling monopoly positions in the markets for transportation and public utilities, industries which were considered to be 'clothed in the public interest'. In the United States, for example, this resulted in the establishment of the Interstate Commerce Commission (1887) and the Federal Communications Commission (1934). There was also concern at the national level about certain public health problems, resulting, for example, in the passage of the Pure Food and Drug Act of 1906. In the last ten years there has been again a substantial upsurge in the use of regulation by the United States and other Western governments to offset the adverse effects of technology directly in such fields as nuclear power, motor vehicle safety and environmental pollution — indeed, in most of the areas where the benefits of new technology have been accompanied by

135

substantial costs in terms of health and safety. This chapter discusses
this trend towards increased regulatory activity, focusing on the
experience of the United States, with particular reference to the impact
of regulation in the American automobile industry.

Some Theoretical Considerations

Regulation can be defined broadly to mean almost any action by the
government to control corporations or individuals; examples are the
structure of charges for public utilities set by public commissions, laws
passed by legislatures requiring motorcyclists to wear safety helmets,
and even the more general fiscal and monetary policies of the
government which 'regulate' the environment in which corporations
and individuals make decisions. For our purposes, however, it is useful
to confine the term to those actions of the government aimed at
controlling directly market price or conditions of entry into an industry,
or to regulating specific features of products or industrial processes.

In a country like the United States, which relies for the most part
on a free market to allocate resources, the theoretical argument for
government intervention must be made in terms of market
imperfections or market failure.[2] Market imperfections, notably the
presence of monopoly power, were the focus of an earlier wave of
regulatory activities in the United States, when, for example, the
railroads were brought under the control of the ICC and telephone
service under the FCC. In these cases the remedy of regulation was
directed towards controlling prices, the quality of service, and entry
(for example, by allocation of routes). Of course, the original source
of monopoly power in an industry may be a dominant technology
which is efficient only in large-scale operations, so that, in effect, a
public utility is created. Moreover, the effects of government regulation
on such an industry will include an impact on the choice of future
technology in the industry, both because the structure of charges
provides the financial base for future investment and because it may
introduce a bias in the type of technology chosen.[3] Nevertheless, in
general, the control of technology in these cases is only incidental to
the regulatory process, which is aimed principally at substituting
public decisions for private ones in order to mitigate the economic
effects of monopoly power.

In the case of market imperfections based on imperfect information
and in the broad category of market failure, the impact of regulation
on technology is typically more direct. The more recent expansion of
government regulatory activity has been in these areas. For example,

a whole range of consumer issues involves problems of information: the public at large is not able to judge the dangers of various chemicals or the design hazards which may be present in a complicated piece of machinery like an automobile. Individual choice may then entail unrecognised social costs in terms of health and safety. It is far easier to control the characteristics of a consumer product during manufacture than to educate the whole population to its potential dangers and to rely on market forces to eliminate the hazards.[4] Regulation of the marketing of drugs, safety standards for automobiles, and the banning of unsafe toys are all actions designed to protect consumers by limiting the hazards of products at the manufacturing stage.

The failure of the free market to place a price on the costs and benefits of 'unowned' resources and byproducts provides another large field for government regulation. If disposal of wastes into the atmosphere or public streams is not taxed or prohibited, private industry will have every incentive to use the natural environment as a dumping ground. The classic example of this type of problem has always been the smoky chimney, but modern technology has created many more lethal situations in which industrial chemicals and pesticides of unsuspected toxicity have been dumped into the air or water supplies. Similarly, the benefits of a healthy work environment do not accrue directly to the firm, so there is little incentive for it to invest in improved working conditions. In such cases, there is a *prima facie* case for government intervention to moderate private action to serve the social good.

Given an argument for intervention, the range of possible government actions is, in theory, broad. If the total costs, including social and ethical considerations, for a specific problem are not large, the best course is probably to do nothing, since regulation itself carries costs. At the other end of the spectrum lies nationalisation of the industry, a course of action which shifts decisions from private to public hands. The judgements on optimal rate structure, acceptable levels of effluents and necessary safety characteristics still have to be made, but the conflict between private gain and public good is eliminated. Of course, in many Western countries, although not in the United States, major industries as well as public utilities are nationalised.

Regulation as a policy lies in the middle ground between doing nothing and more drastic measures like nationalisation. As such, it has had great appeal in the American political context, supplying a response in those issues where public opinion demands that the government do something. The regulatory process also offers a solution to the problems posed by the technical complexity of many of the issues at stake. Congress can pass a law declaring that public policy requires a solution to the serious problems of pollution and safety, and then turn the job of implementing the policy over to a regulatory agency, which is staffed with experts. Special expertise seems necessary (if not sufficient) to deal with many of the problems, either because of their origin in new technologies, like nuclear power, or because their solution seems to require a 'technological fix'. Indeed, a hallmark of the regulatory approach in the case of externalities is the implicit faith that a technological solution is possible: that automobiles can be designed to reduce injuries; that scrubbers can substantially reduce air pollution from stationary sources; that effective pesticides which do not persist in the environment can be developed. Finally, regulation may be instituted because the target industry, as well as the government bureaucracy, has a preference for this form of government control. Interest groups on all sides of an issue may believe that they will have more opportunity to influence favourably the policy outcomes in a regulatory framework than in any other.[5]

One consequence of the faith in the technological fix is that it seems reasonable for the government to mandate standards for products and processes. An alternative approach, favoured by economists, but not by politicians, is indirect regulation of undesired side effects of market activities through monetary incentives. For example, effluents may be regulated directly via an absolute standard, or an effluent charge may be levied. In the latter case the polluting enterprises have a motive for reducing their effluents up to the point where the marginal cost of further control is greater than the tax on the effluent. By varying the tax, in theory any level of control can be achieved; indeed, it may be possible to reach a lower level of pollution via the tax method than by an absolute standard, since some producers may find it easy to reduce their effluents drastically, while a uniform standard must be set high enough not to impose too great a burden on the industry as a whole, including the weaker firms. Similarly, it has been proposed that, in place of the multitude of regulations issued by the Occupational Safety and Health Administration (OSHA), worker safety on the job might be better served by imposing an injury tax on employers.[6] Other variations on the theme of designing an interventionist policy to rely on the market include proposals to auction pollution rights (up to a predetermined acceptable level) and systems of subsidies or bribes to producers not to pollute.[7]

These arguments for promoting allocative efficiency through

monetary incentives are not, however, politically popular. There are practical difficulties:

> Thus, a number of control policies can be used for pollution. And they are equally efficient, except where information about costs and benefits is incomplete and where there are administrative costs involved — which is to say, except in the real world.[8]

There are also political difficulties. Effluent taxes and similar devices carry an appearance of inequity, with large corporations given a 'licence to sin', which is not compatible with the crusading zeal which has characterised the extension of government policy into the areas of environmental quality and safety. In some cases the goal is not to reduce levels of industrial pollution to tolerable levels, but to eliminate completely very toxic substances, and in these cases an absolute standard set at or near zero is appropriate. Charles Schultze has argued further that the tendency to employ direct regulation is in part a result of the government's desire to be able to retain some case-by-case control over policy, for example by amending standards, rather than relying on impersonal market forces.[9] Finally, to the extent that regulation is in support of social policy, considerations of economic efficiency are only one factor in the choice of a policy tool.

The Effect of Regulation on Future Technology

If the perspective shifts from questions of allocative efficiency in the short run to the effects of regulation on technological change in the long run, new problems appear. Government regulation has been accused of biasing research and development efforts by corporations. We have already mentioned the effect which rate structures set by regulatory commissions may have on capital investment and, hence, on technological innovation. The control of entry in the field of telecommunications through allotment of the microwave spectrum is another example of regulatory decisions which can mould the shape of future technology.

Regulation through standard-setting has even more obvious effects. The search for a technological fix often requires innovation; for example, the requirement that industries install anti-pollution devices has shifted resources towards investment in specific kinds of technologies and away from other kinds. US industries complain that much of their R & D is now 'defensive', aimed at protecting the companies against possible trouble with regulatory agencies; this complaint is especially prevalent in the drug and chemical industries where research generally results in new compounds which must be extensively tested for safety before being cleared for sale.[10] The form of the regulation matters: a standard which sets an early deadline for compliance virtually requires that current technology rather than a new approach will be used; conversely a distant deadline may induce inaction.

There tends to be an implicit assumption in these discussions that defensive research is inherently less innovative than R & D in unregulated markets and therefore less desirable. This assumption is, perhaps, just a measure of the extent to which goals like safety and reduced pollution are not fully integrated into the value systems of persons concerned with industrial R & D. Because the benefits of regulation are difficult to quantify, there is probably a tendency to undervalue them in business decisions, even after government action has 'internalised the externalities' by assigning legal, and therefore economic, responsibility to the firms. And because quantification is at best incomplete, the argument over the returns to R & D devoted to meeting the regulatory standards cannot be settled by reference to a balance sheet.

Regulation may also reduce the resources devoted to R & D. The costs of meeting standards and of showing compliance increase current expenses and thus may reduce the funds available for new developments. To the extent that regulations increase consumer prices, growth in demand will be affected; if the regulations have been wisely designed there will be a net increase in social benefits, but the individual firm's incentives, as well as its ability, to invest in future growth may be reduced. This is particularly a problem for small firms, which lack elaborate test facilities and for whom the paperwork associated with government regulations is a heavy burden, but large firms complain too. General Motors Corporation has claimed, for example, that it spent $1.3 billion in 1974 to meet government regulations.[11]

Regulation, however, may also increase incentives to innovate. Some technologies or materials may be prohibited, but new ones are required: the ban on fluorocarbons in aerosol containers, for example, required a shift in materials for a whole industry; the US motor vehicle safety standards for restraint systems created a new market for seat belts and air bags. Where such developments represent an actual increase in resources devoted to innovation, and not just a reallocation of existing programmes, the rate of technological growth will have been enhanced.

In the long run, it seems likely that economic growth without unacceptable social costs in pollution and health hazards will be possible, if at all, only through the mechanism of technological change.[12] Population increases alone ensure that pressures on the environment will increase unless much more effective methods for reducing and controlling waste products are developed and implemented. Thus any effect of regulation in diminishing or biasing of investment away from these areas must be a matter for concern; but, given the mixed impact of regulation on incentives to innovate, it is not possible to generalise about the net effect of regulation on the rate of technological development.

Procedural Aspects of Government Regulation in the United States

A different kind of critique of the regulatory approach has focused on the shortcomings of the process in practice. In the United States, federal regulations are issued by independent regulatory commissions, such as the FCC and the Civil Aeronautics Board, or by agencies, such as the National Highway Traffic Safety Administration and the Food and Drug Administration (FDA). The independent commissions are theoretically independent of Congress and the President and have a number of members, appointed for fixed terms, who are jointly responsible for reaching decisions; the regulatory agencies are lodged in the executive branch and have a single administrative head who serves at the pleasure of the President.[13] Regulations issued by these bodies are announced in the Federal Register, following procedures laid down in the Administrative Procedure Act. Depending on the agency, the process may call for a formal hearing before a hearing examiner with cross-examination of witnesses and other courtlike procedures, or it may follow informal procedures, requiring only publication of the proposed regulation, with an opportunity for comment by interested parties. In both cases after publication in final form the regulation becomes law, unless it is successfully challenged administratively before the issuing agency or, if that fails, in the courts.

The old-line regulatory commissions such as the ICC and FCC have been accused of being slow to reach decisions, of favouring large companies and interest groups over smaller ones (because of the cost of carrying a case through the lengthy appeal procedures), of attracting only mediocre personnel, and of labouring under an excessively vague Congressional mandate while lacking the capacity, themselves, to formulate a coherent overall policy. Most seriously, they have been charged with promoting the interests of the industries which they regulate over the public interest — the 'captured agency' syndrome.

The capture takes place through the exchange of personnel between agency and industry and through the gradual identification in the minds of the regulators of the industry's (and agency's) interests with the public good (chapter 11).[14]

These problems with regulatory agencies and the regulatory process have been widely discussed in the academic literature and in the press. Criticism reached a cyclical high in the early 1970s with the report of President Nixon's Advisory Council on Executive Organization (the 'Ash Report'), which was issued in February 1971, accompanied by a crescendo of attacks on the regulatory agencies and on the Ash Report itself for not being critical enough.[15] It is significant, however, that the criticism of the Ash Report was directed at the old-line regulatory commissions, those concerned with control of market monopoly situations, and its main recommendations called for reforming their quasi-judicial procedures and replacing the collegial form of the commission boards with a single administrative head. Most of the new regulatory agencies, were, of course, hardly yet in place at the time the Ash Report was released and were not affected by its strictures on the effectiveness of the commission structure. At any rate, acknowledged shortcomings of regulation as a policy tool did not preclude the extension of regulation to new areas, once they become national issues.

The 'New' Regulation, 1965-75

In the 1960s a series of new concerns moved onto the political agenda in the United States. The civil rights movement and the Vietnam war were the issues which dominated political life in this decade, but there was also a widespread reaction against the pollution and other environmental and social costs of a highly technological society. Evidence of the long-term effects of industrial pollution and the hazards associated with modern technology was accumulating in accident statistics and wildlife populations, and by the 1960s had reached a level which impinged on the national consciousness. A cynical observer might also suspect that the environmental and safety issues were taken up with relief by the middle class and elected politicians as a substitute for the more explosive problems of racial equality and the war;[16] at the very least the idealism of the civil rights movement created an atmosphere in which the consumer and environmental movements could flourish. In each case the catalyst bringing an issue to the fore seems to have been a specific precipitating event, such as the thalidomide tragedy; the 1962 publication of *Silent*

Spring by Rachel Carson; Ralph Nader's book *Unsafe At Any Speed* (1966) and General Motors' subsequent harassment of him personally; the oil blowout offshore at Santa Barbara, California.

The response of the government, once these issues were raised at the federal level, was to create new regulatory bodies with authority to set national standards. Table 7.1 lists chronologically the new agencies created from 1965 to 1975, with their principal responsibilities. Legislation also increased the responsibilities of existing agencies like the FDA. With the exception of the Consumer Product Safety Commission, all the new regulatory bodies were placed in the executive branch rather than being constituted as independent commissions, the form favoured in the past.

The new areas of concern reflected a public perception that the spread of technology had brought in its wake new dangers and social costs. Industrial practices which had gone unhindered, almost unrecognised, were now excoriated in the press and public meetings and were subject to direct regulation. Thus, standards for safety features of motor vehicles, solid waste disposal, air quality, water quality, exhaust emissions from automobiles, the design of toys, and conditions in the workplace came, one after the other, from the federal government. In some cases these standards were patently unrealistic and had to be postponed or weakened; nevertheless their broad effect was to establish new rules of the game for US industry. Their impact went further, particularly in the motor vehicle industry, because imported goods had to meet the relevant standards to gain entry to the US market. Furthermore, in a kind of demonstration effect, public activism on the environmental and nuclear issues spread to Western Europe and Japan; in some cases US activists were a direct link, as they travelled abroad to help organise citizen protests in other countries.[17]

By 1974, however, the economic and political climate had changed. Economic problems became paramount, as recession and inflation simultaneously took hold in the aftermath of the OPEC oil embargo and price increases. The result was a general drawing back from earlier goals, such as cleaning the environment, because it was perceived that pursuing these goals might have an adverse effect on employment or prices. Regulatory activities, new and old, came increasingly under attack, not for favouritism to the industry or for procedural delays, but for their economic costs, both in higher prices to consumers and higher costs to producers.

In November 1974 President Ford issued an executive order

Table 7.1: Major New Federal Regulation in the United States,
1965-76

Year	Legislation	Agency	Principal regulatory responsibilities
1965	Water Quality Act	Federal Water Pollution Control Administration (after 1970, EPA)	Federal approval of standards for ambient water quality
1966	National Traffic and Motor Vehicle Safety Act	NHSB (after 1970, NHTSA)	Motor vehicle safety standards
1966	Highway Safety Act	Federal Highway Administration jointly with NHSB (later NHTSA)	Standards for highway design, vehicle registration, and vehicle inspection
1967	Air Quality Act	National Air Pollution Control Administration	Oversee state standards for air quality. National standards for automobile emissions
1970	Clean Air Amendments	EPA	Threshold values for pollutants. Stricter standards for automobile emissions
1970	Occupational Safety and Health Act	OSHA	Health and safety standards in the workplace
1972	Federal Water Pollution Control Act Amendments	EPA	Direct regulation via permit of effluents at the source
1972	Noise Control Act	EPA and Federal Aviation Agency	Noise emission standards for aircraft, railroads and motor carriers.
1972	Consumer Product Safety Act	Consumer Product Safety Commission	Safety standards for consumer products
1975	Energy Policy and Conservation Act	NHTSA	Fuel economy standards for automobiles
1976	Toxic Substances Control Act	EPA	Regulate the manufacture and distribution of industrial chemicals

EPA = Environmental Protection Agency
NHSB = National Highway Safety Bureau
NHTSA = National Highway Traffic Safety Administration
OSHA = Occupational Safety and Health Administration

requiring that all new regulations be accompanied by an inflation impact statement. The Council on Wage and Price Stability, itself created to try to halt inflationary price increases, was given the job of reviewing these impact statements, and in several significant instances it opposed new regulations on cost grounds. For example, the Council came out against the National Highway Traffic Safety Agency's (NHTSA) proposal for mandatory passive restraints (a position the Council later dropped), and it also opposed the Environmental Protection Agency's proposed standard for heavy truck noise. Unwilling to reimpose mandatory wage and price controls during this inflationary period, the Republican administration put heavy emphasis on the benefits of deregulation, which promised to be a policy which would both lower business costs and reduce the role of government.[18] Both themes struck a responsive note in corporate offices, especially in those industries which had newly come to be regulated. For example, in November 1974 in the midst of the recession, Lee Iacocca, president of Ford Motor Company, claimed that federal regulations had added $500 to the price of a Ford Pinto and called for a moratorium on all further regulations.[19] Ironically, business leaders of the transportation industries, which were the chief target of the push for deregulation, were ambivalent or openly opposed to a reduction in the degree to which the government controlled their markets. The reaction of the trucking industry is typical: 'We're not against competition, we're against unbridled competition.'[20]

President Ford's initiative against regulation stimulated the Congressional and bureaucratic supporters of the regulatory agencies to fight back. The Democratic Party caucus adopted a position favouring deregulation of prices in the old line agencies, but strongly defending the need for safety and environmental standards:

We note, however, that while 'regulatory reform' is a cliché whose time has come, one person's regulatory reform is another's environmental, consumer rip-off, unconscionable cancer risk, or return to the robber baronies of yesteryear. We note also, that the shrill defense of small business freedom can sometimes mask the effort to preserve the unrestrained freedom of giant corporate conglomerates to dominate and manipulate markets.[21]

The Environmental Protection Agency (EPA) collected data to defend itself against the charge that regulation meant fewer jobs: it claims a net increase in employment as a result of its standards, with 75,000 jobs in the new pollution control equipment industry and 92,000 jobs in construction of waste water treatment plants, which are heavily subsidised by the federal government.[22]

The prospect that deregulation would be extended to include the new regulatory agencies was considerably reduced by the election of Jimmy Carter. He had received strong support from the consumer movement during the election campaign, and many of his appointments to the regulatory agencies were persons who had been actively involved earlier in the efforts to win Congressional action on environmental and safety matters. Actions which had been ignored or delayed during the Nixon-Ford administrations were now pursued more vigorously — e.g. passive restraints for automobiles, investigation of carcinogens in the workplace — but any further expansion of government regulatory powers seems unlikely in the near future. Despite vigorous lobbying, Congress did not pass a Nader-supported bill establishing a Consumer Protection Agency in 1977 or in 1978. The situation thus seems one of temporary stability, with no new large initiatives likely, but no retrenchment likely either, except in the widely supported moves to reduce price regulation in transportation markets, for example, in airline rates. The newer agencies, obeying the bureaucratic imperative as well as responding to the challenge of unfinished business, will doubtless continue to issue new regulations and to amend existing standards.

Regulation of the American Motor Vehicle Industry

The experience of the automobile industry in the United States since 1966 provides a case study of the extent to which government regulatory activities have expanded into new policy areas. Before the National Traffic and Motor Vehicle Safety Act of 1966 the American motor vehicle industry was virtually unregulated. By 1977 the industry was responsible for meeting federal motor vehicle safety standards, automobile exhaust standards and fuel economy standards for its products, as well as new standards for pollution control and work safety in its factories.

Given the central position of the automobile in American culture, it was inevitable that the industry should be affected by the new concerns for health and safety in the 1960s and 1970s. In 1965 public opinion polls briefly listed highway safety as number eight in a list of ten pressing issues facing American society;[23] in subsequent years environmental concerns would occupy a similarly high position in the polls. The National Traffic and Motor Vehicle Safety Act was one of the early successes of the new activism, and its unanimous passage by Congress was a symbol of the new political potency of the consumer movement and of Ralph Nader's rising star. The motor vehicle industry, with its few large and powerful firms, was an easy target for the populist strain in the consumer movement, and, somewhat atypically for the new regulation, the 1966 legislation singled out the industry, rather than cutting across industry lines as the environmental legislation did.

The theoretical, as distinct from political, argument for government regulation of automobile safety is based on the social costs of injuries and deaths in crashes, costs which typically exceed the private costs, even when there is complete insurance coverage, by the public contribution to hospital care and rehabilitation services and by the intangible costs to family and friends. The argument for government intervention is strengthened by the failure of the general population to carry full insurance protection, by the lack of competition in the automobile industry, and by the failure of the manufacturers to offer a range of safety options on their products. The industry's argument has always been that 'safety doesn't sell' (a self-fulfilling prophecy, given the industry's negative attitude towards marketing safety features), and the economics of mass production preclude offering safety options to only a few consumers. Thus, in the unregulated situation, the individual consumer may not be able to maximise his private preference with respect to safety, any more than under regulation. Government regulation, by imposing a single standard on the whole industry, in effect removes safety from the market.

The 1966 Safety Act embodied a new principle: that motor vehicles could and should be designed to reduce injuries in crashes. Heretofore, government policies towards traffic safety had concentrated on highway building, licensing procedures and enforcement of traffic laws, all activities for state and local governments in the United States. The 1966 legislation established a federal authority to regulate the motor vehicle itself, shifting responsibility to the industry to meet the new safety standards which were issued under the Act, and focusing attention on automobile design.[24]

The initial impact of the safety standards on technology was not great: by law the first set of standards, which took effect on 1 January 1968, were modelled on existing standards, such as the voluntary standards of the Society of Automotive Engineers, and the result was only to enforce on all manufacturers the current 'best practice' with respect to safety design. In an industry notoriously indifferent, even hostile, to safety features, however, this was in itself a significant achievement, and since 1966 the death rate per 100 million miles driven has dropped steadily from 5.7 to 3.3 in 1976 as the population of automobiles has come to be dominated by models built under the motor vehicle safety standards.[25]

The one motor vehicle safety standard which did present a major technological challenge to the automobile industry was the requirement for passive restraints, and the standard has been vigorously opposed. First proposed by the NHTSA in 1969 it is now due to take effect in 1981 for full-sized automobiles of model year 1982.[26] Passive restraints, for example airbags, are systems which do not require any action by the vehicle occupant to be effective; in this sense they represent the ultimate in a technological fix. The strongest argument in their favour has been the continuing low rates of seat-belt use in the United States, that is the low rate of response to efforts to modify behaviour.

The opposition of the industry to the passive restraint rule (which is commonly supposed to require airbags, although it can also be met through passive seat belts) has been so fierce and prolonged that some explanation beyond the technical difficulty of meeting the standard seems necessary. Indeed, the argument that meeting the standard was not 'reasonable or practical' was explicitly rejected in an early court case on the matter;[27] it became patently inapplicable after General Motors began to market airbag-equipped automobiles in 1974.

The source of industry opposition appears to be a confluence of factors, including a uniform resistance to all the new government regulations which the industry has faced, a special concern about company liability for the performance of the airbag in a time when consumer legal actions against the industry have been rapidly increasing, and a fear that the costs of the airbag system would meet consumer resistance. As technical difficulties were solved, the industry's arguments shifted to economic problems, emphasising the cost of airbags relative to seat belts, and the effect of regulation-induced price increases on the industry's sales and employment.

For much of the Nixon/Ford administrations the opponents of passive restraints were successful in delaying a final rule on the issue. In December 1976, just before leaving office, Secretary of Transportation William Coleman issued a 'final' decision which declared passive restraints to be capable of saving 12,000 lives annually; nevertheless, he refused to mandate them on the grounds that the public was not ready to accept them. Instead, a large-scale fleet demonstration of airbag effectiveness was proposed, an action which would further delay rule-making by at least two years.

The situation changed dramatically with the election of Jimmy Carter. The new head of the NHTSA was Joan Claybrook, long a supporter of passive restraints, and, after yet another round of public hearings (there had already been two major public hearings, in addition to Congressional hearings), Secretary of Transportation Brock Adams issued a ruling, requiring passive restraints in large-sized automobiles by 1981, with medium and small-sized cars to follow in successive model years.

Ironies abound in this sequence of events. Opponents of airbags have included those who, apparently sincerely, oppose any government intervention into individual risk-taking, but also those who argue against airbags, only to recommend mandatory seat belt use laws instead. The same companies which argued that the standard could not possibly be met with existing technology, are now introducing passive seat belts far ahead of the deadlines — General Motors displayed sixteen candidate models in February 1978. Mandatory seat-belt laws have been rejected as impractical in the American political context, although they have been adopted in most West European countries as well as Canada and Australia.

One of the leading developers of airbag systems, Eaton Corporation, announced it was leaving the field, after Secretary Adams' ruling in favour of passive restraints; it is not clear whether this decision was prompted more by an unwillingness to risk further exposure in a market subject to the vagaries of government regulation or by a perception that the outside suppliers' share of the market would not be large enough to justify further investment.[28]

The federal safety standards as a group tend to add weight to the automobile, working against the goals of fuel economy mandated under the Energy Policy and Conservation Act of 1975. Similarly, measures to meet the exhaust emission standard have reduced engine efficiency and fuel economy. In each case regulation has been directed towards a desirable policy goal, but with little regard for the trade-offs between them. It is, however, difficult to evaluate the seriousness of the potential conflicts between these goals, since the automobile manufacturers have repeatedly declared that federal standards were technically impossible, only to meet them a short time later.[29]

A final irony can be found in the role played by Congress. In 1974, only eight years after the unanimous passage of the National Traffic and Motor Vehicle Safety Act, Congress voted to overturn a regulation of the NHTSA requiring ignition interlocks, a device designed to prevent operation of a vehicle unless its front seat belts were fastened. Setting aside the arguments on expertise which favour leaving technical decision to the specialised agencies, Congress also reserved to itself veto power on any further rule requiring passive restraints; a determined attempt by airbag opponents to overturn Secretary Adams' 1977 ruling was, however, unsuccessful. For many, in and out of Congress, the airbag had become a symbolic issue, pitting big government against the rights of the citizen, a conflict all the more powerful because the automobile itself is a symbol of freedom and privacy to many Americans.

The passive restraint standard was not the only standard attacked by the automobile industry, although it was the most bitterly opposed. In many respects the provisions of the Clean Air Amendments of 1970 placed a greater demand on the available technology than the safety standards did, but the issue of air pollution was seen largely as a conflict between industry and the public interest and thus it was politically difficult to attack the goals of the legislation. Demands for cleaner air did not raise the issue of the individual's right to determine his own level of exposure to risk, as the safety regulations did, since clean air was universally perceived as a classic public good. The automobile industry, therefore, although claiming it could not meet the proposed standards concentrated its efforts on getting the best arrangement it could with respect to the details of the standards and compliance procedures; to the extent that the standards were difficult to meet, the industry has been successful in winning a reprieve.[30] The public demand for lowered air pollution meanwhile has been dampened by the realisation that the promised technological solution — catalytic converters — was both less effective and more costly than expected. Enthusiasm for cleaner air does not seem to extend to a willingness to change patterns for use of private automobiles.[31]

Regulation setting limits on damageability (the bumper standards) is another area in which the manufacturers have protested strongly, only eventually to comply. The history of the bumper standard illustrates some of the pitfalls of regulation by standard; clearly intended to reduce repair costs for low impact crashes, the original standard, effective in 1972, was issued under the guise of the National Traffic and Motor Vehicle Safety Act and couched in terms of damage-ability to safety-related components.[32]

The American manufacturers' response to the bumper standard, unfortunately, was to install heavier bumpers, adding to both the weight and costs of the automobile, and increasing repair costs in high impact crashes in which the bumper itself was damaged. Only the designs utilised by foreign manufacturers such as Volvo and Opel demonstrated that a less costly alternative was feasible; nevertheless in 1974 and 1975, during a period in which automobile sales were down in the United States, and concern over fuel economy was at a pitch, there was considerable, although ultimately unsuccessful, pressure for a roll-back of the bumper standard's requirements.

Ten years of product regulation have produced many changes in motor vehicles. Automobiles produced for sale in the United States are now safer, have lower exhaust emissions, and, on the average, have better fuel economy than they had in the 1960s. The industry's spending on research and development has increased, more than doubling between 1967 and 1973.[33] Manufacturers have invested heavily in new tooling for smaller automobiles, spurred on by the fuel economy standards, and by the need to meet OSHA and EPA noise standards.[34] Concern over fuel economy has spurred development of new lightweight materials.

But automobiles also cost more, and industry spokesmen continue to attribute the price increases to federal regulation; although in an inflationary period with other design changes also occurring, it is difficult to assign an accurate cost to any single change or set of changes. Certainly the company estimates for the cost of airbags have been sharply challenged, and their other cost claims may be similarly inflated.[35] Many have urged that explicit cost/benefit analyses be made of proposed regulations before they are adapted, and the inflation impact statements now required for new regulations have generally supplied such estimates. The difficulty of attaching any reasonable value to human life or health, however, has made the application of the cost/benefit calculus to safety standards a dubious proposition. Such calculations have been made by the NTHSA to support its preference for the passive restraint standard, but they were used only to demonstrate the superiority of the airbag technology over seat belts, given low rates of seat belt use. There was no effort to say how much should be spent to save a single life, and indeed, the legislative history of the National Traffic and Motor Vehicle Safety Act shows that Congress rejected such a formulation. The determination of how far to carry motor vehicle regulation in pursuit of various public benefits remains, as it should, a political question.

Conclusion

The motor vehicle industry represents, perhaps, an extreme example in its exposure to the full range of regulations emanating from the United States government in the last ten years. Its prominent position in the social and economic organisation of the country ensured that it would be a target for the new concerns for safety and the environment; externalities associated with a technology as ubiquitous as the automobile are likely to be significantly large. The oligopolistic structure of the motor vehicle industry, its traditional indifference to safety and the problem of incomplete consumer information about a technically complex product added to the arguments for government intervention in the design of motor vehicles.

The government regulations have had a direct effect on the product, as described above. Their impact on the development of technology in the long run is less certain. Prior to the onset of government regulation of the automobile, R & D in the US industry was at a low level; since the Second World War most innovation had come from adaptation of developments in other industries or from foreign manufacturers.[36] Regulation necessitated an increased effort by the American manufacturers; the standard for passive restraints, for example, gave a real impetus to the development of airbag technology. It must be added, however, that the ensuing political struggle over the implementation of the standard largely negated this advantage, while inhibiting company interest in alternative technological approaches. Similarly, meeting the near term exhaust emission standards by 'add-ons' to the gasoline-powered internal combustion engine has perhaps introduced a bias against a more radical technological approach.[37] It is almost certain, however, that without regulation the motor vehicle industry would not have undertaken even this 'defensive' research and development. From the point of view of the progress of the economy as a whole, it may not even matter very much, since rapid technological change is more likely to be associated with new industries, growing from new technological opportunities, than to occur in a mature industry like that of automobile manufacturing. The companies' most sensible strategy is probably to continue to rely on innovations from other industrial growth points (chapter 6).

It may still be argued that a different governmental approach might have been more effective than regulation in achieving social goals, while avoiding the problems of industry hostility and the implicit conflicts between standards set by different agencies which characterise the

current situation. It is not clear, however, that this is the case.
Co-operation between the industry and the government along the lines
of the British model would surely be politically unacceptable; given
the industry's image of caring only about selling new styling, its
sincerity in pursuing broader social goals would be questioned. Use of
effluent taxes might be preferable to rigid standards on exhaust
emissions, but such taxes seem hardly less coercive than standards
when one considers the reliance of all income groups on automotive
transport. Any attempt to address the problems caused by American
reliance on the private automobile by radically reducing that
dependence faces formidable political and social opposition; the cure
might well be worse than the disease. In sum, all potential governmental
policies carry some liabilities so that a pragmatic strategy is indicated.
In particular, while regulatory standards clearly are imperfect tools for
social policy they should not be discarded except in specific cases
where an alternative policy measure can be shown to be superior.

Notes

1. Jean Gimpel, *The Medieval Machine: The Industrial Revolution of the Middle Ages* (New York, Penguin, 1977), p.82.
2. Market imperfections are defined with reference to the ideal of perfect competition and include the presence of monopoly power, incomplete information about products and prices, and restrictions on entry. When the activities of a unit (firm or individual) affect the welfare of another without the market assigning a price to the activity, then we have market failure. Externalities or spillover effects − for example the effect of industrial waste disposal in streams on downstream water supplies − fall into the category of market failure. Both market imperfections and market failure lead to a divergence between social and private costs.
3. The theoretical tendency is towards overly capital-intensive technology because regulated rates have traditionally been set to allow a 'fair rate of return' on invested capital. See F.M. Scherer, *Industrial Market Structure and Economic Performance* (Chicago, Rand McNally, 1970), pp.529-37.
4. A further argument can be made. Even if complete information were available in these cases, it may be that the consumer is unable to weigh adequately his individual risk in a situation where there is only a very small probability that any single individual will be adversely affected. Nevertheless, summed over the whole population, the social costs may be great. See T.C. Schelling, 'The Life You Save May Be Your Own', in Samuel B. Chase Jr. (ed.), *Problems in Public Expenditure Analysis* (Washington, DC, Brookings Institution, 1968), p.144.
5. See Howard Margolis, 'The Politics of Auto Emissions', *The Public Interest*, vol.49, p.17.
6. Albert L. Nichols and Richard Feckhauser, 'Government Comes to the Workplace: An Assessment of OSHA', *The Public Interest*, vol.49, pp.64-7.
7. See Anthony C. Fisher and Frederic M. Peterson, 'The Environment in Economics: A Survey', *The Journal of Economic Literature*, vol.XIV(1), pp.12-15,

for a summary of the literature.

8. Ibid., p.13.

9. Charles L. Schultze, *The Public Use of Private Interest* (Washington, DC, Brookings Institution), pp.71-2. Schultze's discussion is thoroughly embedded in the US context. In the UK, case-by-case flexibility is a more prominent characteristic of government regulation, and it is achieved through industry-government co-operation rather than mandatory standards. See chapter 11.

10. Glenn Schweitzer, 'Regulation and Innovation: The Case of Environmental Chemicals' (Ithaca, NY, Program on Science, Technology and Society, Cornell University, February 1978), pp.5-8. See also Roger G. Noll, *Reforming Regulation: An Evaluation of the Ash Council Proposals* (Washington, DC, Brookings Institution, 1971), pp.33-9.

11. 'News Release', Motor Vehicle Manufacturing Association of the United States Inc., 14 July 1976, p.1.

12. Schultze, *Public Use of Private Interest*, pp.26-7.

13. An example illustrating the difference between the two forms is the scope of President Carter's order of 23 March 1978, requiring that government regulations be written in 'plain English'. The rule applies to all agencies in the executive branch, but is only advisory for independent agencies, which legally are supposed to be free from executive branch influence.

14. See Marver Bernstein, 'Independent Regulatory Agencies: A Perspective on Their Reform', *The Annals of the American Academy of Political and Social Science*, 400, pp.14-26, for a summary of these arguments. See also US Senate, Committee on Governmental Affairs, *Study on Federal Regulation*, V (Washington, USGPO, 1977).

15. For example, Noll, *Reforming Regulation*, pp.12-14.

16. Elizabeth Drew suggests that this was the case with the automobile safety issue. See 'The Politics of Auto Safety', *Atlantic Monthly* vol.218, no.4, pp.95-102.

17. With varying degrees of success, however. See Cynthia H. Enloe, *The Politics of Pollution in a Comparative Perspective* (New York, David McKay, 1975), pp.280-3.

18. For example, in April 1975 President Ford claimed in a speech that federal regulation was costing the American family $2,000 per year – a figure which was, however, never substantiated. *Washington Post*, 18 May 1975, p.1-N.

19. James W. Singer, 'Regulatory Report 9/Product Efforts Challenged as Being Too Costly', *National Journal Reports*, vol.7, p.658.

20. Robert Shertz of RCL Corporation, quoted in *New York Times*, 2 January 1978.

21. *Congressional Record*, 26 June 1975, p.S-11686.

22. Eckardt C. Beck, 'Ending Pollution Blackmail', *New York Times*, 8 May 1978, p.A-19.

23. *Gallup Political Index*, 1 June 1965.

24. The 1966 National Traffic and Motor Vehicle Safety Act also included provisions for compliance testing, used motor vehicle safety programmes, labelling requirements for automobile tyres, research in traffic safety, and defect notification (safety recall programmes). Companion legislation, the Highway Safety Act, provided for federal standards for state programmes in such areas as vehicle registration and road design.

25. Manufacturers had already introduced some of the new safety features before the standards took effect. The clear safety advantage of post-1967 automobiles has been documented in a study by Leon Robertson, 'State and Federal New Car Safety Regulation: Effects of Fatality Rates', *Accident Analysis*

and Prevention, vol.9, 1977, pp.151-6. See also the report of the General Accounting Office, 'Effectiveness, Benefits and Costs of Federal Safety Standards for Protection of Passenger Car Occupants' (Washington, DC, 7 July 1976, CED-76-121).

26. Assuming that the rule issued by Secretary Brock Adams in October 1977 withstands the court challenges which have been lodged by those who think the rule is too much, too soon, and by others who argue it is too little, too late.

27. *New York Times*, 6 December 1972, p.1.

28. *Automotive News*, 16 January 1978, p.4.

29. The most striking example is General Motors' about-face on the catalytic converter. See Ralph Nader, 'Washington Under the Influence', 23 February 1976 (mimeo.), p.40.

30. Margolis, 'Auto-Emissions', pp.15-16. Legislation in 1977 extended the deadline for meeting the stricter standard of the 1970 Clean Air Amendments from 1977 to 1979.

31. Bruce Kovner, 'Cleaning the Air', *The Public Interest*, 50, p.139.

32. Separate legislation, the Motor Vehicle Information and Cost Savings Act of 1972, allowed for direct regulation of damageability, but the standard issued under this Act took effect only in 1978.

33. National Science Foundation, 'Research and Development in Industry, 1973' (Washington, DC, 1974, NSF-75-315), p.3.

34. In 1976 the 'Big Four' manufacturers claimed they would have to spend $2 billion between 1975 and 1980 to meet the OSHA and EPA standards. *Automotive News*, 7 June 1976, p.14.

35. John Z. DeLorean, a former General Motors vice-president, estimated in 1976 that a full front-seat airbag system could retail at only $127 compared to the automobile manufacturers' public figures of up to $371 during the same time period. Insurance Institute for Highway Safety, *Status Report*, 12 October 1976, p.9.

36. Laurence J. White, *The Automobile Industry Since 1945* (Cambridge, Harvard University Press, 1971), pp.211-16.

37. Allen V. Kneese and Charles Schultze, *Pollution, Prices and Public Policy* (Washington, DC, Brookings Institution, 1975), p.65.

8 CONTROL OF THE ENVIRONMENTAL IMPACT OF TECHNOLOGY

Dave Eva and Harry Rothman

Over the past two decades most industrialised countries have witnessed a great increase in governmental activity on the control of environmental pollution. In this chapter we shall trace the background to this increased activity and describe the main forms of governmental control.

'Environmental' concerns have on the whole been limited to the effects of pollution on the atmosphere (air), hydrosphere (water), lithosphere (earth) and biosphere (life)[1] of our globe. Furthermore, it is the effects of the wastes of human activity on the biosphere, of which humans are a part and on whose functioning they depend, that has been the focal concern in discussions of environmental pollution. A World Health Organisation (WHO) Report[2] states that pollution occurs

> when environmental changes create or are likely to create nuisances or hazards to public health, safety or welfare, or when they are harmful to domestic, industrial, agricultural, recreational or other legitimate uses of environmental components, or to livestock, wild animals, fish, aquatic life and other biological species.

This statement also illustrates the socioeconomic nature of the perception of pollution. What is perceived as pollution and the way in which the dangers of pollution are assessed will depend on the social and economic values ascribed to particular elements of the biosphere or to specific activities. Not only will different societies have differing perceptions but different social interests within specific societies will perceive pollution problems differently, and no doubt suffer them to different degrees. For example, the importance of the detrimental side effects of a pesticide on bees will be perceived differently by beekeepers and naturalists compared with the pesticide manufacturers, the farmer who uses the pesticide for economic reasons and the employees of manufacturing firms who may lose their jobs if the chemical is banned.[3]

It is important that the existence of such differing perceptions be recognised since they have often created problems for governments

156

attempting to control pollution and deciding on priorities for pollution control. This difficulty has often been compounded by the problems of defining many of the long-term effects of pollution.

The Growth of Pollution

Human settlements have always caused some pollution of the environment. In many countries, however, the scale of pollution has increased dramatically since the nineteenth century with the growth of industrialisation and urbanisation and the expansion in volume and variety of technological production.

During the nineteenth century, and indeed until the mid twentieth century, awareness of the dangers of pollutants came chiefly through acute ill-effects on people, or occasionally, on animals. Limited medical and scientific understanding of poisoning, and poor analytical techniques, meant that only the more obvious pollutant-effect relationships were detected. The response of governments was, in general, to frame *ad hoc* legislation dealing with those specific problems which had created the greatest public outcry; accordingly anti-pollution laws tended to be piecemeal reactions to disaster. The post Second World War period witnessed another great expansion in industrial production, especially in the chemical industry.[4] The use of new synthetic chemicals, especially in agriculture, began to create new environmental problems. The inadequacies of governmental control systems began to become widely apparent and were an issue of great public interest and hence political importance during the late 1950s and early 1960s. Two main factors contributed to this.

First, governmental control systems were still in many cases only reacting to disasters rather than trying to prevent them, yet developments in mass communications led to a greater awareness of disasters, both national and international. Such well-publicised disasters as Minimata or the London Smog emphasised the failure of governments all over the world to do more than react to problems which affected thousands of people.[5]

Second, developments in the scientific field also began to raise questions about the performance of governments with regard to pollution control. The control of pollution requires first the ability to detect disturbances in, or harm to, the environment or people. The rapid improvement in analytical techniques during the 1950s made it possible to detect pollutants in human tissues and potentially dangerous substances in food, urban air and the water supply.[6] Further, epidemiological statistics demonstrated that chronic diseases such as cancer had become a prime cause of death in industrial society. While decreased death from infectious disease could account for much of the increase in chronic disease, some people related increased chronic illness to the chemical insult of environmental pollution.

In support of this belief, toxicology began to supply experimental evidence of possible causal relationships between particular hazards and chronic diseases. Moreover, the demonstration that chemicals could cause cancer, mutation and teratogenesis raised many fears about the possible effects of chemical pollution.[7] Finally, the parallel advancing development of ecology began to produce evidence of environmental disruption due to pollution, and also provided explanations of the mechanisms of disruption, thus enabling predictions to be made of the possible long-term effects of pollution. The demonstration of, for instance, the way in which food chains concentrate toxic chemicals and pass them on to humans, and the widely read 'popular' writings of Barry Commoner[8] and Rachel Carson[9] have done much to raise public consciousness of the delicate and systemic nature of the environment. Indeed, as Egler[10] observes, it was predominantly through the efforts of pressure groups and a very few scientists (unaided by the major scientific organisations) that such information was brought to public attention.

Evidence that public concern about pollution increased in the late 1960s can be found in opinion polls taken in various countries. In the USA[11] the percentage of people polled who thought that water pollution was a serious problem increased from 35 per cent to 74 per cent between 1965 and 1969. The percentage that would like to see more political effort put into pollution problems increased from 17 per cent in 1965 to 41 per cent in 1971. In 1971, 83 per cent of those polled felt that the US Federal Government should spend more money on pollution control. A Canadian[12] poll in 1970 showed that 69 per cent of Canadians considered that the dangers of environmental pollution were 'very serious'. In the same year another poll found that the reduction of air and water pollution was named the top domestic problem by 65 per cent of respondents. Similar trends were evident in Swedish and Japanese polls.[13]

The New Politics of the Environment

The failure of governments to protect the environment adequately fostered the growth of environmental pressure groups from the late nineteenth century. The first environmental pressure groups were essentially conservationist, concerned either about the disruption of their recreational use of the environment (e.g. bird watching) or about the effects of pollution on their livelihoods (e.g. beekeepers and fishermen). These groups were often able, due to their social position, to gain the ear of government and achieved some limited success.[14] However, in the face of the industrial expansion of the post Second World War period they were on the whole powerless to provoke much governmental action, and their energies were usually applied to the protection of their specific interest rather than to pollution as a whole.

The 1960s, however, witnessed the rise of a new form of pressure group, particularly in the USA, whose aim was to expose governmental inactivity over pollution. Thus, in the USA, the policy of such groups as Friends of the Earth, the Environmental Defense Fund and Nader's Raiders has been to confront the government in the courts and to research into and expose the inefficiencies of government control.[15] The purpose of this activity has been to press for the opening of decision-making and enforcement procedures to public scrutiny and public involvement. These pressure groups have engaged wide public support and it is worth briefly outlining the reasons for this. First, the failures in government control and the involvement of industrial interests with government have made the public wary of government assurances that it is protecting their interests.[16] Second, the obvious lack of scientific understanding of many hazards, and the widely differing interpretations of scientific evidence that occur, create a situation in which the basis for decision making is not clear-cut.

Accordingly, there exists a sufficiently ambiguous situation with regard to the 'facts' of pollution for groups with differing perceptions of the risks in question to challenge the government's selection, interpretation and evaluation of the evidence (chapter 11).[17] Finally, some have felt that their interests are not being looked after and their point of view not considered and, therefore, have sought access to the decision-making process.[18] Those that fail in this have often attacked the governmental process for being undemocratic and dominated by industrial interests.

Pressure groups have played an important part in both the discovery and collection of information on the effects of pollution and in bringing this information to the attention of government and the public. Egler[19] has pointed out that much of the scientific information on pollution was available for many years before it came to public notice. Even when it became public it was mainly through the efforts of pressure groups or science journalists rather than practising scientists. Thus, it could be argued that pressure groups have played an essential part in bringing a wider range of views and information to governmental attention than would otherwise have been available. The limitations of pressure-group activity are, however, great due to lack of resources and access to the decision-making process.[20] The control of knowledge through control of its production and dissemination rests with government and industrial bodies and this raises important questions. Limited public access to information and the inability of environmental pressure groups to sponsor research produces a situation in which public control over government regulatory bodies and the ability to monitor their performance becomes limited. One may question whether, without the involvement of pressure groups representing diverse social values and perceptions of pollution, decision-making bodies can adequately and fairly discuss and assess the hazards of environmental pollution.[21]

Measures for Pollution Control[22]

The control of pollution and its effects can take place at a number of stages in the process by which pollutants affect the environment. The main stages of control are:

(i) Control at source.
(ii) Control at the discharge stage (e.g. treatment of waste before discharge).
(iii) Control in the environment (e.g. addition of dispersants to polluted waters).
(iv) Prevention or reduction of human exposure (e.g. protective clothing).
(v) Prevention or reduction of adverse effects (e.g. immunisation).
(vi) Treatment of affected groups.

Generally, control at the source of pollution is most effective in that it prevents the entry of pollutants into the environment.

Most government attention is now focused on the first two of these stages in order to prevent the introduction of pollutants into the environment, although action at the other stages is still often necessary. Three general approaches can be identified as important to control at stages (i) and (ii).

The Development of Less Polluting Processes

This is one of the most obvious methods of control at source. However, work in this area is, on the whole, in its infancy. There are some examples, such as the use of desulphurised fuels, where pollution has been reduced, but most alternatives are still in the early stages of research. There are often great barriers to the development and use of alternatives. For example, in the field of pest control much work has been done on 'biorational' methods of pest management. Yet the problems of implementing such methods have meant that they have little commercial attraction.[23] The investment needed to develop and market alternative technologies means that, unless state intervention occurs, private industry must see a commercial opportunity in these technologies. Thus, if alternative technologies appear less commercially viable or attractive than polluting technologies it is unlikely that industry will invest in them unless under some duress or provided with incentives.

Waste Management[24]

Waste management covers a wide range of techniques concerned with the collection, storage, treatment, disposal and recycling of wastes. The simplest forms of waste disposal are dumping (e.g. landfill or down mineshafts), dispersal (e.g. dilution in water or air) and destruction (e.g. incineration). All these can, however, be sources of rather than answers to pollution.

With the realisation of the effects of pollutants and the fact that the natural degradation mechanisms of the environment are incapable of dealing with particular pollutants or the scale of their production, there has been pressure to develop artificial systems to degrade and control them. Such systems may either entirely control the pollution at source by collecting it and rendering it harmless or may treat the wastes so that they are more easily dealt with in the environment. These systems may either utilise natural systems under artificial conditions (e.g. the use of bacteria to degrade toxins in sewage works) or use artificial chemical and physical treatments. Another approach has been the treatment and collection of wastes for the purpose of recycling raw materials or utilising the constituents of waste for further production.[25] Such recycling has begun to be used industrially on a small scale. The main obstacle to such technologies again appears to be economic as they are often expensive to implement. Their development has so far outstripped their use though there is evidence that the separation and recycling of some wastes can be an economic proposition.[26]

Monitoring[27]

The monitoring of pollutant levels is an essential part of the control process. It is necessary for a number of reasons:

(1) To determine the effectiveness of the control process.
(2) To detect sources of pollution and pollution trends.
(3) To enable retrospective assessment of the effects of particular levels of pollution.

Monitoring may be either direct, measuring pollutant levels in samples, or indirect, using biological indices such as the health of heavily exposed or extremely sensitive species. The resources necessary for comprehensive monitoring programmes are great in terms of money, technical staff and equipment. Monitoring schemes, therefore, need substantial governmental commitment if they are to be effective.

Mechanisms of Governmental Control of Pollution

Legislation

Most countries have a constitutional structure that defines, through laws and regulations, the rights and duties of citizens and of the authorities with regard to pollution control. In many countries attempts to introduce new environmental legislation or to improve environmental standards have resulted in intense political conflict. In most countries there has been substantial pressure from industrial interests to minimise the impact of pollution laws because of the costs that industry would have to face.[28] The power and political influences of the industrial lobby, and the importance of industrial performance to national economies, has placed great pressure on both legislative and enforcement agencies and it should be remembered that environmental control measures are designed and implemented in this context.

The particular nature of a legal system, the content of its laws, the powers of the enforcing authorities and the basic philosophy of control vary between nations. Many countries have begun to replace the previously piecemeal legislation dealing with environmental matters with comprehensive environmental legislation. For example, the USA has the National Environmental Protection Act (NEPA) 1969, Sweden[29] has passed an Environmental Protection Act (EPA) 1969, and the UK the Control of Pollution Act 1974.[30] There has also been a greater centralisation and co-ordination of control of environmental matters in countries that have not yet passed comprehensive legislation, such as Japan and Canada.

(i) Direct control. Direct control of pollution means that governments lay down requirements as to the action that polluters must take to control pollution. The exact stage at which control may be required can vary. The law may define the technologies that may or may not be used (control at source, stage i), the emissions that are allowed (stage ii), the level that a particular pollutant may reach in the environment (stage iii), the level it may be in products sold for public consumption (stage iv), or the level it may reach in the human body itself (stage v).

The many technical and economic problems of pollution control have meant that most governments have assumed that absolute environmental purity is impossible to achieve. Government activity has, therefore, concentrated on determining 'acceptable' levels of pollution and attempting to gradually improve environmental quality. This has usually involved a two-fold strategy of establishing standards for pollutant emissions and/or environmental levels and defining the technologies that must be employed in control.

Emission or environmental standards may be set in a number of ways. First, standards may be set at 'desirable' levels, i.e. as low as technically possible. Second, they may be set on the basis of what the environment can absorb without ill-effect. Such levels, usually called hygienic standards,[31] are however very difficult to calculate because of lack of knowledge of the effects of most pollutants, especially in the long term. Third, and more usually, levels may be set on the basis of a compromise between biological, technical, economic and political requirements. That is, a balance is struck between the costs and effects of avoiding pollution and those of allowing it to occur. Thus, a certain degree of damage or risk is judged 'acceptable' in the light of the benefits that accrue from the polluting activity. The question this immediately raises is, 'acceptable' to whom? Who makes such decisions, and on what basis? The means by which 'acceptable' levels are determined have been the source of some controversy.[32]

Requirements as to the technologies of control follow the same basic pattern. First, governments can require pollution to be controlled by the use of the *best available* technology. Polluters must then employ the most up-to-date techniques of control. This will be the requirement of the US NEPA from 1983. Second, they may require the use of *best practicable* technologies, the present US requirement. In other words polluters must take all practical steps to control pollution regardless of cost. Third, all *reasonable* or *reasonably practicable* steps to prevent pollution may be required. This is the approach used by many governments and it is especially widely used in the UK and Canada. As with 'acceptable' levels, it means that the costs of controlling pollution must be balanced against the hazards of pollution and some compromise reached. Again, questions arise over who makes such decisions, and how.

(ii) Indirect control. Indirect control usually constitutes the provision of incentives, primarily economic, not to pollute. Some governments have attempted to reduce resistance to control measures by providing grants, loans or tax relief for investments in pollution control activities. For example, the Swedish Environmental Protection Board made grants available for 25 per cent of the costs of investments in anti-pollution technologies during the five years after the introduction of the Swedish EPA.[33] Another indirect approach, based on the concept of 'social costs', is pollution charges.[34] Polluters pay either in the form of a tax or some other levy related to the type or level of pollution, for their polluting activity. The idea is that provided the charges are calculated correctly they will not only act as an incentive not to pollute but will also provide the state with financial resources for pollution control. Indirect incentives are usually used in concert with direct methods of control although the balance varies between countries with charges dominating in some (e.g. France and Netherlands) and only being used occasionally in others (e.g. Norway has a tax related to the sulphur content of fuels).[35] The problem with indirect measures is that they may not act as incentives and indeed may be seen as 'buying' the right to pollute.

(iii) Anticipation. A third legislative route through which governments have tried to increase their control over pollution is by requiring that new products and processes be assessed for their environmental impact. Schemes designed to assess the effects of specific products such as pesticides have operated in several countries since the 1950s. More recently, countries have begun to extend such assessment from specific products to the majority of chemicals.[36] The exact requirements of national schemes vary widely but all reflect the concern to anticipate the health and environmental effects of industrial products by requiring that biological and environmental information be collected on compounds prior to their commercial use. Unfortunately, the cost of acquiring this information has meant that industrial interests have resisted such schemes. Some governments have extended the principle of anticipating environmental impact to other areas. In the USA, the NEPA requires full environmental impact statements to be provided for

all Federal proposals, thus increasing the scope for the assessment of the environmental effects of governmental action. However, it remains to be seen whether the provision of impact statements will achieve this aim in the USA unless they are carried out by groups independent of the sponsoring body.[37] On the other hand project sponsors often claim EPA procedures unduly delay their projects. In Sweden the EPA requires that plans for new industrial plants or alterations to existing plants in a number of industries be submitted for approval to the National Franchise Board for the Protection of the Environment (NFBPE). The NFBPE functions like a court of law and applications to it must be published so that all interested parties may submit evidence to it. It can set levels of emissions and specify the control procedures to be used. Not all plans, however, have to be submitted to it and companies can apply for exemptions.[38]

Enforcement

Standards and laws are, of course, meaningless without enforcement. Enforcement authorities often play an important role in determining 'acceptable' levels or 'reasonably practicable' technologies. This is more often the case in countries such as Canada and the UK where few mandatory standards for emissions or environmental levels are laid down and inspectorates develop their own guideline standards for enforcement. This may involve inspectorates in making decisions on the acceptability of pollution on the public's behalf. The argument usually advanced for general requirements in law rather than mandatory standards is that they allow 'flexibility' in enforcement. However, it has been argued that unless the inspectorates' actions are open to public scrutiny such flexibility could act against the public interest given the pressure that industry can bring to bear on an inspector.[39] It is, of course, true that making standards mandatory does not guarantee their enforcement either but at least it allows the public some possibility of ensuring that inspectorates act when pollution reaches a particular level.[40]

The 'styles' of enforcement agencies also differ greatly and we shall discuss this more fully later. Some inspectorates, for example in Britain, act in a spirit of consultation and gradual improvement; others, for example the US Environmental Protection Agency, act more in a policing fashion.[41] The openness and accountability of agencies also varies as do their institutional location and areas of responsibility.

International Aspects of Governmental Control

The problems of cross-border pollution and the pollution of the global environment have only recently begun to receive attention. Although international disputes over pollution have occurred since the turn of the century only a few channels exist for settling them. Bilateral and multilateral treaties have been the usual approach to such problems.[42] More recently concern that differing national laws might act as non-tariff trade barriers has increased governmental interest in the harmonisation of laws at both the regional and the global levels.

Regional collaboration and harmonisation of environmental policy is probably most developed in Europe, although differing national approaches to regulation have caused problems even within the European Economic Community.[43] Attempts to harmonise legislation and approaches to pollution have also been initiated within the Organisation for Economic Co-operation and Development (OECD).[44] There are also some cases in which nations have formed collaborative bodies to deal with specific problems of common interest as, for example, with the International Committee for the Protection of the Rhine.[45]

The first world conference on environmental pollution was held, on the initiative of Sweden, by the United Nations (UN) in Stockholm in June 1972. The conference recommended a wide range of international measures for the monitoring, evaluation and control of pollution.[46] Some of those have been taken up by the UN agencies, especially WHO and the Food and Agriculture Organisation (FAO). However, the commitment of governments to these programmes is questionable, and international agreements are in any case notoriously difficult to enforce. Another problem has been the conflict between the control of environmental pollution and the industrialisation of the underdeveloped nations.[47] Many such nations have been concerned that harmonised international standards may in fact be to their detriment because of the costs of meeting them. The agreement of a global environmental policy is, therefore, problematic; it remains to be seen what can be achieved at this level.

Decision Making, Enforcement and Non-governmental Activity

As we described earlier, the control of pollution, and indeed many other areas of the control of technology, have over the last two decades become highly politicised subjects. Failures in governmental regulatory systems and the obvious lack of understanding of and disagreement over the exact nature and potential hazards of pollution have created problems for governments. The power of the industrial lobby, in terms of resources, expertise and political influence, the visibly close relationship between government agencies and industry often accompanied by a lack of public scrutiny of agencies' activity, and a lack of public involvement in decision making have contributed to a decline in public faith in the regulatory agencies. Another result, as we have argued, has been the growth of politically more 'activist' pressure groups seeking greater public participation in the decision-making process. The politicisation of environmental issues has presented government agencies and decision makers with the problem of maintaining their political credibility.

Governmental Responses to the Problems of Environmental Decision Making

The extent of public participation in and scrutiny of the decision-making process varies widely between nations. At one end of the spectrum lie countries with 'closed' systems, such as the UK and Canada, where administrative discretion and secrecy are great. At the other end lies the USA with its Freedom of Information (FOI) Act and its more open style of government.[48]

Pollution laws in the UK and Canada leave much to the discretion of the enforcement agencies. Policymakers tend to regard the public as passive and as accepting what is good for it — an approach Tinker has described as 'Nanny knows best'.[49] Responsibility for determining the 'public interest', what information the public may be given, whether enquiries will be held and who may present evidence lies with ministers who delegate much of this authority to non-elected civil servants. The normal process of decision making under such circumstances is selective consultation with particular interests, and with no requirement to keep the general public informed. Indeed, the participants in decision making are often bound by the Official Secrets Act and hence prevented from divulging information should they wish to. The system is essentially closed, therefore, to all but a very few selected outside groups. This method of decision making has become the subject of public attack in many countries and, therefore, governments have sought more publicly acceptable methods.

Some governments have increased their utilisation of eminent but 'independent' (usually academic) experts as inputs to, and observers of, the decision-making process in order to assure the public of the scrupulousness and legitimacy of the process. However, it may be difficult to convince the public of the independence of experts and in any case their existence only provides legitimation of the process if the process itself is *seen* to be fair. The success of independent experts depends greatly on the public's ability to scrutinise their performance and evaluate the arguments leading to consensus.

Another approach has been to attempt to define more 'rational' approaches to decision making. For example, techniques such as cost-benefit analysis, technology assessment, risk assessment and systems analysis (chapter 9) have all been advocated as the basis for risk/safety decision making.[50] However, such techniques can only provide evidence as to the nature and costs of risk rather than its acceptability or not. Therefore, in recognition of the political nature of decisions on the acceptability of risk some countries exhibit some sort of separation in their decision-making process between 'scientific' and 'political' aspects.[51] For example, in several UK regulatory schemes a scientific sub-committee presents the 'facts' about risk to a 'political' committee which makes decisions about acceptability. Increasing pressure from interest groups has begun to see a wider range of interests represented on 'political' committees even in the UK. However, this has not entirely resolved controversies. The problem with this approach, as with the use of 'rational' decision-making techniques, remains that the scientific data are themselves usually contentious. Some interests may still, therefore, not feel adequately represented in the decision-making process especially if it is they who face the risks under discussion.[52]

Such problems have led some people to advocate adversary decision making in which all interested parties argue their case before some independent arbiter. This process is employed in the USA and Sweden although some other countries use it occasionally and on a limited basis in the form of a public enquiry. The Swedish and US systems of involvement are not, however, exactly the same. In Sweden participation by the general public is limited to those cases which come before the NFBPE. In the hearings, which are publicised in local newspapers, pressure groups may submit evidence. However, there are ways around this procedure which companies can use to reduce the effectiveness of the system.[53] The US constitution and legal system give much greater scope for public involvement, allowing the public to take direct legal action against polluters, and also allowing for the improvement of governmental standards through legal action. Environmental decision making in the US is thus based on bargaining between political lobbies in an adversarial system, and the openness of the system is increased by the FOI Act. This situation goes a long way towards explaining the greater power and activity of pressure groups in the US.[54]

There are, nevertheless, some problems with this approach. While it increases the potential for public participation, its success depends on the access of the public to sufficient technical, legal and financial resources to compete with governmental or industrial interests. The choice of independent arbiters may also be difficult. Public scepticism of the judiciary may mean that judges' decisions may not lead to increased public consensus. This scepticism may be increased if such enquiries are held behind closed doors with little or limited public access to the evidence submitted.

Enforcement Agencies and the Public

Similar problems arise in the enforcement of pollution laws. The nature of regulatory work means that enforcement bodies often have to develop a close relationship with those being regulated (usually industry). The nature of this involvement is not always open to public scrutiny and often leads to complaints of collusion with industry or undue industrial influence on enforcement agencies. If the public is ignorant of the standards used in enforcement, as was the case in most countries until recently, and is not involved in or able to view the reasoning behind decisions, it is inevitable that suspicions of bias and collusion between regulators and regulated will arise. Such suspicions will generally increase when a single government agency both sponsors and regulates industry in a particular area. The regulatory activity of an agency may become compromised by its close relationship to the polluters in its sponsoring capacity. In the Soviet Union, for example, the pressure on government departments for good production figures has meant that environmental considerations, often given less priority anyway, tend to get ignored.[55] Such problems also occur regularly in Japan and the UK where they tend to be compounded by secrecy laws that prevent or excuse inspectorates from divulging information to the public.[56]

This has led in some instances to governments attempting institutionally to separate the roles of sponsorship and control, and thereby to remove enforcement agencies from special interest pressures. For example, in the USA the Environmental Protection Agency was formed and given an independent institutional location partially to remove the control of pollution from the US Department of Agriculture where it was felt that agricultural interests might influence the Agency. Similarly the Nuclear Installations Inspectorate in the UK was established independently of the Atomic Energy Authority. Other methods have included giving inspectorates greater powers and explicit commitments *only* to regulation. The public accountability of agencies can also greatly be increased by ensuring their openness and laying down strict standards and procedures to be enforced. The FOI Act partially performs this function in the USA by requiring that government documents and reports be made publicly available.[57]

Conclusion

The nature of decision making in the area of environmental pollution control creates severe problems for governments. Decisions as to the 'acceptability' of risk and whether to allow pollution at all are often made the basis of perceptions of the benefits of the polluting activity and the nature of the risks involved. Such decisions involve inherently political and social values, and decision making on the basis of the 'facts' alone becomes impossible. Faced with such problems, and with increasing public dissatisfaction with closed decision-making processes, governments have begun to allow increased public participation in and scrutiny of the decision-making process.

Public participation is not, however, merely a reaction to public hostility; it can improve decision making and lead to better informed and more consensual decisions. The participation of pressure groups is a source of additional evidence to decision makers and can raise wider issues in terms of their own perceptions of the particular problem. Without public participation those who are affected by pollution may only receive indirect representation by people whose perceptions are not theirs (chapter 9). If pressure groups and the public at large know that their interests are actually or potentially represented in the decision-making process then their trust and faith in that process is enhanced. Such faith is reinforced if the process is open to public view and the enforcement of decisions is carried out in the open by publicly accountable bodies particularly if, as too rarely happens today, active measures are taken to seek out and adequately inform all the parties that may be affected by a decision (see chapter 9). The development of decision-making systems that encourage participation is, therefore, a trend which is likely to extend to countries that at present do not have such systems.

Complicating the picture, however, is the argument[58] that the successes of the environmental pressure groups in thwarting particular projects are causing the assessors employed by industrial organisations and government executive agencies to present far more sophisticated and elaborately analytical defences of their sponsors' goals. It is therefore likely that all the easy environmentalist victories have already been won. Environmentalists are now faced with the necessity

of improving their analyses of environmental impacts. However, given
the gross disparity of resources between most public pressure groups
and vested industrial or government interests, how likely is this?
Consequently we would argue strongly that those governments which
genuinely desire to serve the public interest ought to seek means to
ensure 'parity in technology assessment techniques so that disputations
between public and sectoral interests are not unbalanced'.[59]

The complexity of modern society and the potential social
impact of technologies such as microelectronics[60] and nuclear power
emphasise the necessity of fully appreciating the consequences of
technological developments and devising appropriate control systems.
The control of environmental pollution is one of the first areas of
public concern to raise the question of control of technology and as
such can provide an important lesson. The failure of governments to
do more than react to the detrimental consequences of technical
developments points to the necessity for the development of systems
for the anticipation and assessment of the biological, social, political
and economic effects of technological change. Decisions as to the
necessity for or benefits of particular technologies can no longer be
left in the hands of industrial interests whose actions have, as we have
seen in the environmental context, endangered human life and
necessitated government intervention.

Notes

1. The biosphere is the zone of life that films the planet; it extends into and
interacts with each of the other systems. It is largely based on the photosynthetic
activity of plants and algae trapping part of the energy that the sun radiates.
2. WHO Expert Committee Report, *Health Aspects of Environmental
Pollution Control* (Geneva, 1974), pp.8-9.
3. Disparate approaches have been used to examine the problem of the
socioeconomic roots of pollution and its perception; ranging from those theorists
who judge the nature of the socioeconomic formation to be of minor importance
(for example, D.R. Kelley *et al.*, see note 13) to those who believe it to be
fundamental (for example, H. Rothman, see note 5). The importance of the social
nature of risk perception for an understanding of current debates over
technological hazards is illustrated in H. Nowotny, *Social Aspects of the Nuclear
Power Controversy* (International Institute for Applied Systems Analysis,
Research Memo – 76-33. Laxenberg, Austria, 1976).
4. For estimates of the increase in chemical production and use in the
postwar period, see H.W. Gerarde, 'Occupational Medicine Research and
Industrial Toxicology', *Journal of Occupational Medicine*, vol.8 (1966), p.167.
5. For details of such disasters, see H. Rothman, *Murderous Providence:
a Study of Pollution in Industrial Societies* (London, Hart Davis, 1972), and
A. Tucker, *The Toxic Metals* (New York, Ballantine Books, 1972).
6. G. Zweig, 'The Vanishing Zero: the Evolution of Pesticide Analysis', in
F.R. Blood (ed.), *Essays in Toxicology*, vol.2 (London, Academic Press, 1970).
Zweig shows how important improved analytical techniques were in stimulating

awareness of pesticide pollution. See S.S. Epstein, *Cancer Research*, vol.34 (1974), pp.2425-35 for the cancer data.

7. Indeed government reports in the USA and UK demonstrate how little was known about toxic effects of most pollutants. See *House of Representatives Select Committee to Investigate the Use of Chemicals in Food and Cosmetics* (Washington DC, 1951), and *Working Party on Precautionary Measures Against Toxic Chemicals used in Agriculture: First Report* (London, HMSO, 1951).

8. B. Commoner, *Science and Survival* (New York, Viking Press, 1963); also *The Closing Circle* (New York, Knopf, 1971).

9. R. Carson, *Silent Spring* (Harmondsworth, Penguin, 1972; original issue 1963).

10. F. Egler, 'Pesticides in Our Ecosystem', *American Scientist*, vol.52 (1964).

11. All the following figures from H. Erskine, 'The Polls: Pollution and Its Costs', *Public Opinion Quarterly*, vol.35 (1971), p.120.

12. Quoted in L.J. Lundqvist, 'Environmental Policies in Canada, Sweden and the United States', *Sage Professional Papers in Administrative and Policy Studies*, vol.2 (1974), p.9.

13. For Swedish polls see Lundqvist, 'Environmental Policies'. For Japanese see D.R. Kelley, K.R. Stunkel and R.R. Wescott, *The Economic Superpowers and the Environment* (New York, W.H. Freeman, 1976), p.140.

14. For a discussion of UK pressure groups see P.D. Lowe, 'Environmental Pressure Groups: a study of their organisation and effectiveness' (unpublished M.Sc thesis, Department of Liberal Studies in Science, Manchester University, 1972).

15. For example, Ralph Nader's group have produced several reports on environmental issues. J. Eposito, *Vanishing Air* (New York, Grossman, 1970); D. Zwick and Y. Benstock, *Water Wasteland* (New York, Grossman, 1971); H. Welford, *Sowing the World: Pesticides and the Public Interest* (Washington, Centre for the Study of Responsive Law, 1971).

16. For an example of such problems in the UK see M. Frankel, 'The Alkali Inspectorate: the Control of Industrial Air Pollution', *Social Audit Special Report* (London, Headley Brothers, 1974).

17. See Nowotny, *Social Aspects*. The interpretation of evidence, given what some would see as the inherently political and value-laden activity of assessing risk and safety, presents governments with severe problems. See also P.B. Hutt, 'Public Participation in Toxicology Decisions', *Food, Drug and Cosmetic Law Journal*, vol.32 (no.6, 1977), p.275.

18. P.D. Lowe, *Environmental Pressure Groups*, ch.1.

19. F. Egler, 'Pesticides'.

20. G. Wootton, *Interest Groups* (London, Prentice-Hall, 1970).

21. This point is discussed in more depth in Council for Science and Society, *The Acceptability of Risk: The Logic and Dynamics of Fair Decisions and Effective Controls* (London, 1976).

22. 'Environmental Engineering: A Guide to Industrial Pollution Control', *Chemical Engineering*, 27 April 1970.

23. C. Djerassi, 'Insect Control of the Future', *Science*, vol.186 (1974), p.596.

24. A.N. Neal, *Industrial Waste: Its Handling, Disposal and Re-use* (London, Business Books, 1973).

25. H. Rothman and D. Bartlett, 'Sewage – Pollutant or Food? An assessment of alternative ways of disposing of sewage', in P.D. Wilmot and A. Slingerland (eds.), *Technology Assessment and the Oceans* (Guildford, IPC, 1977), pp.161-7.

26. United States Congress Committee on Interstate and Foreign Commerce: Subcommittee on Transportation and Commerce. Symposium on Resource Conservation and Recovery (Washington, US Government Printing Office, 1976).

27. WHO Expert Report (1974), *Health Aspects*, p.29.

28. For example, in the USA the Control of Toxic Substances Act was resisted very strongly by industry. N. Wade, 'Control of Toxic Substances: an Idea Whose Time has Nearly Come', *Science*, vol.191 (1976), p.541.

29. Lundqvist, 'Environmental Policies', ch.1.

30. *The Law and Practice Relating to Pollution Control in the United Kingdom* (published for the European Economic Community by Graham and Trutman Ltd, 1976). Other countries in this series are Belgium, Denmark, France, Ireland, Italy, Luxembourg, Netherlands and West Germany.

31. For a discussion of these see Rothman, *Murderous Providence*, p.276.

32. See Council for Science and Society, *Acceptability of Risk*.

33. Lundqvist, 'Environmental Policies', p.27, and Organisation for Economic Co-operation and Development, *Environmental Policy in Sweden* (Paris, OECD, 1977).

34. OECD, *Pollution Charges: an Assessment* (Paris, OECD, 1976).

35. OECD, 'Paying to Pollute', *Environment*, vol.18 (no.5, 1976), p.16; for a strong critique of market calculus approaches to pollution problems see K.W. Kapp, 'The Implementation of Environmental Policies', *Development and Environment* (1972), pp.67-94.

36. Such schemes have been introduced in Japan, Canada, USA, Sweden, Switzerland and Norway. M. Idman, 'Anticipating the Effects of Chemicals: an Evolving Concept', *Ambio*, vol.5, (no.9, 1976). In the UK a scheme has been proposed, see *Proposed Scheme for the Notification of the Toxic Properties of Substances*, Health and Safety Commission Discussion Document (London, HMSO, 1977); see also 'Health Hazards from New Environment Pollutants', *WHO Technical Report*, Series No.586 (Geneva, WHO).

37. R. Gillette, 'NEPA – How well is it working?', *Science*, vol.176 (1972), p.176; N. Lee and C. Wood, 'Environmental Impact Assessments of Projects in EEC Countries', *Environmental Management*, vol.6 (1978), pp.57-71.

38. Lundqvist, 'Environmental Policies', pp.27-33.

39. Frankel, 'The Alkali Inspectorate', p.14.

40. Ibid., p.45.

41. T. O'Riordan, *Environmentalism* (London, Pion, 1976), ch.7.

42. See for example the articles on air and water pollution by D. Harris, in A.D. McKnight, P.K. Marstrand and T.C. Sinclair (eds), *Environmental Pollution Control* (London, Allen and Unwin, 1974).

43. A. Tucker, 'Secrecy Widens Gap', *Guardian* (18 March 1978).

44. OECD, *Environmental Standards: Definitions and the Need for Harmonisation* (Paris, OECD Environmental Directorate, 1974).

45. WHO (1974), pp.54 and 128.

46. United Nations, 'Report on the UN Conference on the Human Environment' (June 1972).

47. United Nations, 'Impact of Environmental Policies on Trade and Development in Particular of the Developing Countries', *UNCTAD TD/130* (13 March 1972).

48. See for example O'Riordan, *Environmentalism*, ch.7.

49. J. Tinker, 'Britain's Environment – Nanny Knows Best', *New Scientist* (9 March 1972), p.551; see also R. Gregory, *The Price of Amenity* (London, Macmillan, 1971).

50. Such methods are recommended in WHO (1974) and *Health Hazards from New Environmental Pollutants* (WHO Technical Report 586, 1976); technology assessment is recommended by D. Medford, *Environmental Harrassment or Technology Assessment?* (Amsterdam, Elsevier, 1973); systems analysis and risk assessment by K.R. Hammond and L. Adelman, 'Science, Values and Human Judgement', *Science*, vol.194 (1976), p.389.

174   *Control of the Environmental Impact of Technology*

51. W.W. Lowrance, *Of Acceptable Risk: Science and the Determination of Safety* (Los Altos, Calif., William Kaufman, 1976). See also Council for Science and Society, *Acceptability of Risk.*

52. For an overview of such problems see J. Primack and F. Von Hippel, *Advice and Dissent: Scientists in the Political Arena* (New York, Basic Books, 1974).

53. Lundqvist, 'Environmental Policies', p.33. Applications for exemptions outnumber those going to public hearings by 6 to 1.

54. O'Riordan, *Environmentalism*, ch.7, and Kelley *et al., Economic Superpowers*, p.154.

55. Kelley *et al., Economic Superpowers*, p.166.

56. For the UK see O'Riordan, *Environmentalism*, p.237, and J. Bugler, *Polluting Britain: A Report* (Harmondsworth, Penguin, 1972). For Japan see Kelley *et al., Economic Superpowers*, pp.180-92.

57. There have, however, been problems with the FOI Act. See N. Wade, 'FOI Act: Officials Thwart the Right to Know', *Science*, vol.175 (1972), p.498.

58. Medford, *Environmental Harassment*, p.321.

59. Ibid., p.325.

60. C. Freeman, J.D. Bernal Memorial Lecture, reported in *Financial Times*, 24 May 1978, p.17.

9 TECHNOLOGY ASSESSMENT: INFORMATION AND PARTICIPATION

Michael Gibbons

Introduction

There is an essential ambiguity in the notion of controlling technology, After all, technology is the science of controlling forces, both natural and social, to produce desired effects. What, then, can be the meaning of controlling the science of control? The ambiguity is lessened, if not removed altogether, when it is recognised that much of the rhetoric about the control of technology expresses concern for undesirable social, economic or political situations which are presumed to be the result of previous technological decisions. Control of technology, in this sense, is concerned with controlling the effects of technology — where effects are presumed to derive from decisions made somewhere in society and at a certain time.

But, surely, it is argued, no one invests money or time in creating a technological capability without a very precise idea of the effects to be attained. In a certain sense — i.e. when considered solely from a particular vantage point — this is true. Because any society is a complex of interdependencies, it can happen that looking at effects from a single perspective may obscure their impact in other sectors, or simply take time before the consequences of a decision begin to manifest themselves. It is this concern with remote or second-order effects of technological decisions which has motivated interest in technology assessment.

The notion of technology assessment emerged in the late 1960s, a time when most industrially advanced nations, the United States in particular, were experiencing a modest romantic revival.[1] This revival found expression, at least in part, in a revulsion against the environmental and human consequences deriving from what was perceived to be unconstrained technological progress and the promotion of a contemporary view of Rousseau's 'noble savage' with its concern for a simpler life based on less complicated technology. Technology assessment enthusiasts were only incidentally involved in this revival; rather, they expressed their fundamental belief in that version of technological optimism so characteristic of those who see more (not less) technology as the key to most of our social problems.

175

The immediate audience for technology assessment was the political and administrative systems, rather than the commune; government, as custodian of the public interest, would have to bear the brunt of rising social awareness concerning the consequences (some of them adverse) of technological development. This is not to say that environmentalists or other groups had no role to play in this development; they certainly did, but not perhaps in the way they originally intended. For one thing, it soon became clear that there was no 'proper machinery' for handling groups who frequently predicated their cases on technical assumptions different from those of the establishment. If technology assessment is not simply to be a further extension of the bureaucracy, these views will have to be considered. There is more involved here than the provision of more information; there is also the need to increase public participation in the decision-making systems that evaluate or in some way make use of this information.

From its earliest days, as we shall see, technology assessment has possessed this dual requirement: additional information about the social consequences of technology *and* the utilisation of this information in the decision-making apparatus. To a considerable extent the future of technology assessment rests on the successful marriage of these two features. Information without participation is just as undesirable as participation without information. In what follows, an attempt will be made to clarify both of these aspects and suggest a possible method for their integration.

The Development of the Notion of Technology Assessment

At first glance, technology assessment might seem to be a straightforward concept. After all, everyone possesses at least common-sense notions about both technology and assessment, so that their conjunction should present no major barrier to what is meant. Unfortunately, this is not the case. Throughout the last decade, there has been much discussion about the meaning of the concept and its implications for action.[2] Broadly speaking, there are those − based mainly in the United States − who believe that technology assessment represents a new methodological stance supported by new technologies while, on the other hand, there are others, mostly Europeans, who assert that technology assessment is, and long has been, carried out, although perhaps under a different name.[3]

While the major part of this section will be concerned with clarifying the meaning of the concept of technology assessment with a view to describing its scope and purpose, it will be useful beforehand to discuss some of the terms which will be needed in this clarification. First, 'technology' will be used in the sense of technological capability, the complex of organisational and individual skills which operate on hardware to produce a capability. Second, the notion of 'impact' is inseparable from the rhetoric of technology assessment. In fact, this term conveys an inaccurate image because the effects that technology assessment seeks to articulate are precisely those which appear only when a technology has become embedded in the social, physical, economic and political matrices of society and this may take a considerable time. As a result, reference is made here to the consequences, for physical, social, economic and political processes and trends, of the application and absorption of a technological capability. Third, assessment is taken to mean the evaluation of these consequences; some of these may be good, others bad. It is virtually certain that none will be neutral and so, in the end, judgements must be made. These judgements (or lack of them) will, in turn, reflect and be reflected in the kind of society we want to have.

With these few preliminary clarifications in hand, we turn now to examine more fully the notion of technology assessment – its historical origins, its relationship to decision-making processes and, finally, to set out the further notion of the technology assessment system. The technology assessment system, as we hope to show, goes some way towards resolving the dichotomy arising out of the informational and participatory viewpoints on technology assessment.

Historically, the notion of technology assessment is linked to political and social developments that occurred in the United States during the middle and late 1960s. It was during this period that the cumulative effects of technological developments, set in train many years previously, emerged into social consciousness. While it is not part of this paper to describe these events, it remains a fact that, from the early 1960s onward, Americans became collectively more conscious of the decay of their cities, the pollution of their environment and the incipient violence of the ghettoes. In brief, they became conscious of the deterioration in their 'quality of life'. Rightly or wrongly, the cause of much of this blight was placed on the doorsteps of the large public and private institutions whose technologies, it was claimed, were being implemented without due consideration of possible adverse effects which might occur in the future.

Technology Assessment in the US Congress

This was the general context in which Congressman Emilio Q. Daddario prepared the Bill which resulted, eventually, in the establishment of 'an Office of Technology Assessment for the Congress as an aid in the identification of existing and possible impacts of technological application'.[4] The Office of Technology Assessment was intended, essentially, as another information input to the legislation process and, perhaps because of this, has seen its role primarily in terms of data gathering and the preparation of objective and comprehensive reports. Since its inception, the office has carried out a wide variety of assessments, including a comparative analysis of energy technologies and an analysis of marine pollution caused by spills from large oil tankers.[5]

Technology Assessment in the Executive Branch

A slightly different view of technology assessment, but one which, in the last analysis, may be more relevant to the European context, can be gleaned by examining the views of those concerned with establishing the activity of technology assessment in the executive branch of the United States Government. The American political system, it should be remembered, is composed of three branches: the legislative branch (Congress), the executive branch (containing the Office of the President) and the judicial branch (containing the Supreme Court). For the purpose of this discussion, one needs to keep in mind that all programmes involving the expenditure of public funds (and these, of course, include some with a large technological component) are presented by the executive branch to Congress which acts as the final arbiter on whether resources will be voted to them. It can happen, as in the case of the supersonic transport programme, that expenditures requested by the President are rejected subsequently by Congress.

In the European context, decisions concerning expenditures on large technological projects are more usually taken by ministers (with the advice of top civil servants) in Cabinet and not in Parliament. Because of this, it is perhaps more germane to ask about the effectiveness of the executive in assessing technology before one concedes the necessity of legislation to create a separate body like the Office of Technology Assessment parallel to, or at least, independent of the executive. The views discussed in the following few paragraphs, then, tend to be based on the premise that technology assessment is an adequate description of much that is already going on within the departments and agencies of the executive branch.

An important and fundamental notion of this aspect of the discussion concerns the nature of governmental decision making. From the point of view of the executive branch, a technology assessment system should provide the administrative and procedural framework for continuing assessment within the everyday process of programme formulation, review, decision and implementation. The policy-making process, it is contended, involves a continuous interaction of each of these activities and could not function as effectively if an outside, or parallel, body or agency attempted to evaluate the programme. The argument is based upon the premise that no outside group or agency would have the resources to assess either the quantity or the complexity of the information with which the executive branch is organised to deal. Any such external agency would be required to make a technology assessment on only partial information and would inevitably introduce unnecessary delays in the due execution of government policy.

None the less, it is freely admitted that the executive branch suffers from serious drawbacks if it attempts to perform technology assessment.[6] First, most assessments of the consequences of introducing a technology are incomplete if not superficial. Commonly, they include few external consequences (those lying outside an agency's programme interests or statutory responsibilities). By comparison the technical and economic analysis of internal consequences (those lying within those interests and responsibilities) is much more thorough. Second, the resultant information is not consistently used in policy decisions because technology assessment is not recognised as a continuing responsibility of most agencies. Third, prevailing assessments are often inadequate because they are conducted by agencies committed to a particular technology or industry; they are vehicles of advocacy rather than impartial analyses. Negative or undesirable effects tend to be discounted, overlooked, or dismissed without the same intense examination devoted to favoured courses of action. Fourth, because no agency has any responsibility, nor is appropriated any money, to deal with problems outside its legislative charter, 'full impact' assessments of the broadest public interest and importance are neglected. The range of consequences is not broadened significantly by the establishment of interdepartmental or interagency committees. These committees seem able only to press for a review of a department's technical and economic analysis, rather than insist that analysis be extended to a wider range of considerations.

It is because of difficulties like these that some have suggested that the principal function of technology assessment should be an adversary one, putting forth all the reasons why a certain programme should be stopped.[7] Since, it is argued, there is no shortage of institutional pressures to launch new technological programmes, technology assessment should become a kind of counteracting force against indiscriminate technological expansion.

This is not the place to evaluate this proposition, except to point out that it has been this sort of stance that has given to the activity of technology assessment a certain anti-technological connotation.

In the light of these remarks, we can put forward a second definition of technology assessment. Technology assessment describes

> the activity or the means by which information now available can be used, within a given decision-making structure, to increase the perception and wisdom of decision makers with respect to the consequences of technology.[8]

We can bring together now the two definitions of technology assessment, adumbrated above, and present the definition which will be used in this paper. Technology assessment is defined as an activity to provide information about, and systematic analyses of, the internal and external consequences (short, medium and long-term) for a society of the application and diffusion of a technological capability into its physical, social, economic and political systems. The information and systematic analyses are to be so structured and presented as to aid the decision makers charged with the responsibility of operating those systems.

This definition encompasses two distinct processes: the collection and analysis of information and the improvement of decision making with respect to technological programmes. With regard to the collection and analysis of information, a technology assessment may draw on a wide range of techniques developed initially for other purposes. A useful outline of the techniques available has been presented by Coates in her study of technology and public policy.[9] Perhaps the most novel technique, developed in connection with technology assessment itself, is cross impact matrix analysis. This technique is a derivative form of consensual forecasting which makes it possible to explore the effects of interactions between different kinds of *potential* events.

More important for the purposes of this paper are the ways in which information and analysis might be used to influence decision making and to a brief discussion of this we now turn.

Technology Assessment and its Relationship to Decision Making

The simple availability of information of whatever kind is no guarantee that it will be used in the way the analyst intended, when a group of decision makers is engaged in the process of choice. None the less, there is a widespread belief that the more complete the information about a given prospect the better will be any decision about it. This belief in its most articulate form gives rise to what is sometimes called the rational approach to decision making, the main elements of which exhort the decision maker to:

(1) identify, scrutinise and put into consistent order those objectives and other values which he believes should govern the choice of a solution to the problem;
(2) comprehensively survey all possible means of achieving those values;
(3) exhaustively examine the probable consequences of employing each of the possible means;
(4) choose a means — that is, a particular policy or combination of policies — that will probably achieve a maximum of the values or reach some acceptable level of achievement.

This normative description usually presumes that it is desirable to gather as much information as possible that might be relevant to a given decision but assumes also that the decision makers possess both the intellectual capacity and the time to process it in some meaningful way. Further, it overlooks the fact that information about consequences is, at best, partial. Finally, rather than helping the decision maker to limit the range of relevant consequences, it forces him to face an open system of variables, a world in which all consequences should, but cannot, be surveyed. The inherent limitations of the rational model prompt one to review critically any activity such as technology assessment which stresses the need to investigate all the consequences of a given technological application.

A less demanding description of decision making has been outlined in the strategy of 'disjointed incrementalism' advanced by C.E. Lindblom. Disjointed incrementalism seeks to adapt decision-making strategies to the limited cognitive capacities of decision makers and to reduce the scope and cost of information collection and computation. Lindblom has summarised six primary requirements of the model in this way:[10]

(1) Rather than attempting a comprehensive survey and evaluation of all alternatives, the decision maker focuses only on those policies which differ incrementally from existing policies.

(2) Only a small number of policy alternatives are considered.

(3) For each policy alternative, only a restricted number of 'important' consequences are evaluated.

(4) The problem confronting the decision maker is continually re-defined. Incrementalism allows for countless ends-means and means-ends adjustments which, in effect, make the problem more manageable.

(5) Thus, there is no one decision or 'right' solution but a 'never-ending series of attacks' on the issues at hand through serial analysis and evaluation.

(6) As such, incremental decision making is described as remedially geared, as it is oriented more to the alleviation of present concrete social imperfections than to the promotion of future goals.

This model is believed by Lindblom and others to be a more realistic description of what actually goes on when a decision maker is faced with a problem which he must solve more or less quickly; he moves incrementally, making adjustments to existing policies at the margin. According to Lindblom a measure of co-ordination among a multiplicity of decision makers is accomplished through the mechanism of 'partisan mutual adjustment'.[11] This mechanism, in effect, compensates on the societal level for the limited capacities of the individual incremental decision maker and for the society's inability to make decisions effectively from the centre. In summary, Lindblom, among others, believes both that incremental decision making is a realistic account of how most pluralistic societies decide policy issues and that it represents the most effective approach to social decision making.

Now, if the rationalistic and incremental models are regarded as the two ends of a spectrum, the most interesting discussion is that now being carried on over the contours of the middle ground by policy analysts such as Y. Dror and A. Etzioni, among others.[12] Perhaps the most succinct expression of a viewpoint which tries to weave what seems both credible and possible in the extreme positions into a coherent model of the policy-making process belongs to Etzioni who has developed the notion of mixed scanning. This notion must now be introduced because it will form an integral part of our model of the technology assessment system which will be discussed in the next section.

Basically, the notion of mixed scanning is derived from the empirical observations that societies, represented in the policy-making process by governments, do, from time to time, initiate major changes. While it would be true to argue that these initiatives do not derive from the sort of comprehensive analysis suggested by the rationalistic model, neither are they derived simply from the incremental process of give and take which Lindblom describes as partisan mutual adjustment. According to Etzioni, it is necessary to distinguish fundamental decisions from incremental ones:

> Thus while actors make both kinds of decisions, the number and role of fundamental decisions are significantly greater than incrementalists state, and when the fundamental ones are missing, incremental decision making amounts to drifting — action without direction. A more active approach to societal decision making requires two sets of mechanisms: (a) higher order, fundamental policy-making processes which set basic directions and (b) incremental processes which prepare for fundamental decisions and work them out after they have been reached.[13]

The process whereby this is accomplished is described by Etzioni as mixed scanning. As a strategy for decision making, it involves two distinct but related activities. First, fundamental decisions are made by 'exploring the main alternatives the actor sees in view of his conception of goals but. . .details and specifications are omitted so that an overview is feasible'. Second, 'incremental decisions are made but within the *contexts* set by fundamental decisions (and fundamental reviews)'.[14]

Examples of mixed scanning seem easy to identify. One has to think only of decisions such as the one to establish the health service in Britain, the Anglo-French co-operation in the development of supersonic air transport, or the decision, also made in Britain, to build the advanced gas cooled reactor. In each of these cases, the 'fundamental' decision constituted the context within which subsequent 'incremental' decisions were taken. From the point of view of technology assessment, it is the 'fundamental' decision, the one that sets the context, that needs a thorough analysis across a broad front, so that its unexpected, or second-order, effects may be identified and examined.

Before going on to elaborate the notion of the technology assessment system, it will be useful to relate what has been said about information and decision making to some empirical research. It should be clear, however, that, while it is useful, for theoretical purposes, to separate the informational from the decision-making aspects of technology assessment, no empirical research could be adduced in which the separation was complete. None the less, it is valid to maintain that, in most studies, one or other aspects predominate. For example, the study by Hittman Associates Inc., which describes itself as a technology assessment, says very little about the decision-making systems which would evaluate the range of technological scenarios proposed.[15] The same might be said of the otherwise excellent work of R. Bowers and his colleagues at Cornell University. Their earlier work on solid state microwave devices, as well as their more recent work on communications for a mobile society, discusses technological evolution largely independently of the matrix of decision making which will, ultimately, articulate the various possibilities.[16] A similar trend is observable in the application of cross impact matrix analysis to technology assessment.[17]

Turning to the decision-making perspective outlined above, the three types of model discussed — rational, incremental and mixed scanning — are also difficult to identify in their pure form. For example, the rational model is well exemplified for such topics as automotive emission controls, computer-communications networks, enzymes, sea farming and water pollution by Strasser in his attempt to identify the impact of these technologies on society.[18] By contrast, much of the work undertaken by the Science Council of Canada is structured within the perspective of mixed scanning in which major initiatives, such as the laying of major new pipelines, are seen as an occasion to involve the decision-making apparatus at both federal and local levels. This aspect of technology assessment is discussed more fully in the next section.

The Notion of the Technology Assessment System[19]

From the outset, a distinction has been drawn between the informational and decision-making aspects of technology assessment. The distinction is, admittedly, somewhat artificial in that, in practice, the two exist in a kind of symbiotic relationship: information influences decision making, but the perspectives of the decision maker dictate what information shall be considered relevant. The problem is to find ways to improve practice and this is the function of the technology assessment system. This system, we think, provides a concrete way forward for technology assessment, uniting as it does, in a single operation, both the information-gathering and the participatory dimensions of assessment.

In our usage of technology assessment, a specific technological capability stands at the centre as the focus for the interests of a number of groups, more or less loosely coupled together. Thus, a technology assessment system comprises those social groups which are (or should be) concerned with developing a given technological programme. The elements which make up this system may, or may not, be bound together by any formal arrangements: coupling is affected by their mutual interest in the development and diffusion of a given technological capability. In addition, the composition of the technology assessment system varies with the technology under consideration.

Within the technology assessment system it is possible to identify three different classes of actor, distinguished by their degree of involvement with the development of a technological capability. The *core* actors are those intimately and continuously involved in the process of development; they are the main actors and there are only a few of these. Less intimately involved are the rather more numerous collection of *supporting actors*. They may have an interest in one or more aspects of the development of a given technology but, by and large, they affect it only tangentially. This is not to say that at some time during the evolution of a technology one of the supporting actors cannot so intrude into the process as to alter the outcome desired or narrow the range of possibilities available to the core actors. The emphasis, here, is on the continuity of concern rather than on the likelihood of concern. A further group of actors — ones important to the ideal of technology assessment — are those that *should be* but are not involved in the technology assessment process. It is one of the expressed aims of technology assessment to canvass as wide a range of interests as possible and at least some of these may be expected to be sufficiently large to affect the path of technological development but not to be politically organised. The problem is how to involve these groups more closely.

These three main types — the core actors, the supporting actors and those that should be but are not yet involved — comprise the technology assessment system. The system itself is supposed to have no specific goals other than those derivable from the decisions of the actors themselves. (This conforms to Lindblom's definition of good decisions as those with which the decision makers agree.) As a first approximation it is assumed that the goals of the technology assessment system are describable as a combination of the individual goals of the core actors. The goals of the system need not be static but may alter as new information and new actors enter it.

Individually, the actors are presumed to behave according to the mixed-scanning model of decision making. Accordingly, each actor is concerned with the degree to which he is being successful in attaining his primary goal, such as producing petroleum at a profit large enough to satisfy his board of directors, and he evaluates his success in attaining his secondary goals in terms of, or with respect to, his primary goal. In the event that things are proceeding satisfactorily one might expect that no new initiatives would be likely to result. On the contrary, according to Etzioni, the decision maker scans his horizon looking for both problems and opportunities which, if identified, are monitored continuously. It is possible that one or more of these will come to be of sufficient importance to constitute a major change in policy relative to the primary goals. Such a policy initiative has been referred to previously as a 'fundamental decision' and it may provide the context for a whole range of subsequent incremental decisions. It is, at least partly, through this scanning function that individual actors become aware of the need for information and new studies may be commissioned as a result of the identification of a new problem or opportunity. The information thus collected, if it is circulated, may have the effect of attracting the attention or changing the perspectives of other actors involved and so lead to fundamental decisions at points quite far removed from the original enquiry.

Before going on to discuss the technology assessment system outlined above, it is perhaps important to point out that the idea has been taken up in at least one country as a basis for carrying out technology assessments.[20] Several case studies now exist which show clearly that it is possible to identify the various types of actors, define their individual perspectives and goals and determine the degree to which attention is being given to the longer-term consequences of technological development. In particular, the work of Auerbach and Voyer[21] in studying the technology assessment systems operating (or not operating) in the economic development of the Canadian north show clearly the benefits of this approach. Although there is a considerable way to go before we could say with confidence that in respect of northern development, Canada is carrying out adequate assessments of technological projects there, Auerbach and Voyer are at least able to identify where the problems are (or are likely to be) and to suggest areas where more detailed research will be necessary. They also recognise that it is not necessary, nor is it within their institution's resources, to carry out all the empirical work themselves. This is important because, as we have already seen, one of the positive deterrents to technology assessment is the fear on the part of decision makers that 'independent' research will not be able to command the resources available to a ministry or firm and, as a consequence, any analysis will be weaker for that. It is also important to note that the kind of 'assessment of the assessment' with which Auerbach and Voyer are involved is being carried out within the Science Council of Canada. Because the Council is a Crown Corporation it enjoys the unusual position of being close to, but not part of, the civil service; this places it in a very favourable position from which to orchestrate, but not necessarily execute, technology assessment in Canada.

Concluding Remarks

This chapter has sought not merely to review developments in technological assessment over the last decade but also, and more importantly, to provide a modest justification for the notion of the technology assessment system. This justification has both theoretical and practical aspects. Theoretically, the technology assessment system is based on a model of societal decision making which seems to be founded on empirical fact; that is, both fundamental decisions and the subsequent chain of incremental decisions can be identified. Practically, the notion acknowledges the role of perspectives (and hence values) in problem formulation, data collection and analysis, and implementation. Thus, it accepts that independent, value-free enquiry is largely a myth.

Still, there are many caveats one should make about existing technology assessment systems and the style of organisation they encourage. For example, the introduction in the United States of the requirement that all major technological programmes requesting federal resources should include an environmental impact statement[22] is intended to encourage executives to look more widely at this implication of their proposals, and thus may be regarded as one type of technology assessment system. But as it turns out, these analyses are relatively short-term ones looking at the immediate, most likely or most dangerous *environmental* consequences involved.[23]

Although environmental impact statements are not required to do more than they do, to qualify as outputs of an authentic technology assessment system in the sense we are using the term here, they would have to be broadened both to include non-environmental aspects of major new technological programmes and to interact more closely with the various agencies involved. Environmental impact statements should be regarded as a type of specialised technology assessment, the frequency of which may be expected to increase in the future as the implications of government regulations in respect of pollution, resource utilisation, energy conservation and health and safety at work begin to emerge.

Second, one of the principal fears outlined above concerned the danger of separating too starkly the informational and decision-making aspects of technology assessment. Still, it does not follow that the technology assessment system solves the problem completely. The way in which organisations make decisions of any kind is ill understood and, by implication, so is our understanding of the role of information in this process. Merely to identify groups by their interest in a particular development does not guarantee participation in any real sense. This is particularly true of that group of actors whom we have called the 'should be' actors − those groups who are not yet a part of the technology assessment system but should be. These groups are the ones most likely to be ill-organised and financially weak and so unable, realistically, to participate in the decision-making process. One way of meeting this situation which has been explored, again, in Canada, involves voting federal funds to pay for legal and other forms of information in preparing a submission to a royal commission. In this way one is able to prepare the views of minorities − in this case those of various groups of Eskimos and Indians − into the sort of 'professional' case being put by other more organised groups.

Third, even if one is completely satisfied that all the actors have been duly identified and represented, there is still the problem of language. There is a problem of language in two senses: technical and perspectival.[24] The technical aspect of the problem arises from an inherent tendency within technology assessment to cast all problems − even obviously social ones − in a form amenable to measurement. The close alliance, in this respect, of the social indicators movement with technology assessment has been pointed out by Wynne and deserves further comment.[25] What is at issue here is the wisdom of formulating social issues in this way and, Wynne argues, the mere attempt at casting issues in a form amenable to numerical analysis conditions the type of answer one gets. The implication is that the range of possible answers is considerably reduced thereby and that this is probably not a good thing.

Equally fundamental problems are raised when we realise that knowledge often reflects group interests. This not only calls into question the possibility of an independent, neutral, value-free type of report but, more importantly, the difficulty of communicating the significance of one group's findings to another. The first issue is concerned with the notion of objectivity in the social sciences, a deeply philosophical problem which we might be excused from dealing with here, but the second issue, the fact of differing perspectives, is crucial to the notion of the technology assessment system. If communication is hindered because groups occupy different perspectives, what, then, are the chances of consensus? The answer is, we suspect, that groups do not necessarily see the world from mutually exclusive perspectives and that communication would be possible if all reports were written in 'appreciative' rather than technical form, as has been suggested by Vickers.[26] With the growth of appreciation of another viewpoint, the way lies open to persuasion and, perhaps, consensus. It is for this reason that the technology assessment system needs a centre or steering mechanism of some kind — someone to take an overview, someone to bridge the gap created by differing perspectives. This problem is not a simple one but it seems clear that its solution must at least be attempted if increased participation in technology assessment is to become a reality.

A final word must be said on how technology assessment can assist government in its regulation of technology. As brief as it has been, the discussion so far makes it plain that the techniques of technology assessment do not provide government with a panacea for the problems of regulation. Technology assessment, whether embodied in research documents or in the establishment of assessment systems, can — in practice — do little more than enlarge the context in which decisions are taken by increasing the awareness of potential impacts of technological change. Increased awareness of benefits and disbenefits is a necessary, but not sufficient, condition for balanced technological development.

Notes

1. T. Roszak, *Where the Wasteland Ends* (New York, Anchor Books, 1973), ch.3.
2. See, for example, V.T. Coates, *Technology and Public Policy: The Process of Technology Assessment in the Federal Government*, Program of Policy Studies in Science and Technology (Washington, George Washington University Press, 1972), 3 vols.; D. Medford, *Environmental Harassment or Technology Assessment?* (Amsterdam, Elsevier, 1973); F. Hetman, *Society and the Assessment of Technology* (Paris, OECD, 1973).

3. An excellent contemporary exposition of both positions is available in M.J. Cetron and B. Bartocha (eds), *Technology Assessment in a Dynamic Environment* (London, Gordon and Breach Science Publishers, 1973).

4. US House of Representatives, 17046, approved 16 April 1970.

5. See, for example, *A Comparative Analysis of the 1976 ERDA Plan and Program*, United States Congress, Office of Technology Assessment, May 1976; and *Oil Transportation by Tankers: An Analysis of Marine Pollution and Safety Measures*, Congress of the United States, Office of Technology Assessment, July 1975.

6. These comments on the Executive Branch in the USA are taken from *A Technology Assessment System for the Executive Branch*, Report of the National Academy of Public Administration (July 1970), p.2.

7. H.P. Green, 'The Adversary Process in Technology', in R.G. Kasper (ed.), *Technology: Understanding the Social Consequences of Technological Applications* (New York, Praeger, 1972), pp.49-69.

8. This quotation has been attributed to Dr Chauncey Starr by D.M. Kiefer in 'Technology Assessment Aired in Europe', *Chemical and Engineering News* (16 October 1972), p.8.

9. V.T. Coates, 'Technology and Public Policy: The Process of Technology Assessment in the Federal Government', *Program of Policy Studies in Science and Technology* (Washington, George Washington University Press, 1972), vol.1.

10. C.E. Lindblom, *The Policy Making Process* (Englewood Cliffs, N.J., Prentice-Hall, 1968), p.13.

11. C.E. Lindblom, *The Intelligence of Democracy* (New York, Free Press, 1965), pp.137-62.

12. Y. Dror, *Public Policy-making Re-examined* (San Francisco, Chandler, 1968), and A. Etzioni, *The Active Society: A Theory of Society and Political Processes* (New York, Free Press, 1968), *passim.*

13. A. Etzioni, *The Active Society*, p.388.

14. Ibid., p.389.

15. D.G. Howey and W.R. Menchen, *A Technology Assessment of the Transition to Advanced Automotive Propulsion Systems*, Hittman Associates Inc., Columbia, Maryland, USA (HIT-S41), May 1974.

16. R. Bowers and J. Frey, 'Technology Assessment and Microwave Diodes', *Scientific American*, 226 (1972), p.18, and R. Bowers *et al.*, *Communications for a Mobile Society – an assessment of new technology*, mimeo. (Cornell University, Ithaca, New York 14853), 1977.

17. S. Enzer, 'Cross-Impact Techniques in Technology Assessment', *Futures*, 4 (1969), p.30.

18. G. Strasser, 'Methodology for Technology Assessment – Case Study Experience in the United States', in M.J. Cetron and B. Bartocha (eds), *Technology Assessment in a Dynamic Environment*, pp.905-40.

19. See note 3.

20. See, for example, the report of the Science Council Committee on Northern Development, published in *Issues in Canadian Science Policy No.3* (Ottawa, Science Council of Canada, 1976).

21. *Northern Development*, Science Council of Canada discussion paper, prepared by L.E. Auerbach and R.D. Voyer (October 1975). See also *Northward Looking: A Strategy and a Science Policy for Northern Development*, Science Council Report No.26 (August 1977).

22. S. Meyers, 'US experience with national environmental impact legislation', in T. O'Riordan and R.D. Hey (eds), *Environmental Impact Assessment* (Farnborough, Saxon House, 1976), pp.45-52.

23. Ibid., p.48.

24. M. Gibbons and R. Voyer, *A Technology Assessments System: A Case Study of East Coast Offshore Petroleum Exploration*, Science Council of Canada Background Study No.30 (Ottawa, Science Council of Canada, 1974), pp.86-93.

25. B. Wynne, 'The rhetoric of consensus politics: a critical review of technology assessment', *Research Policy*, vol.4 (1975), pp.108-58.

26. G. Vickers, *Value Systems and Social Processes* (London, Tavistock, 1968), *passim.*

10 DIRECTING TECHNOLOGY: A ROLE FOR PARLIAMENTS

John Hartland

In parliamentary democracies governments are expected to be responsive to public opinion. Public opinion, in the last analysis, makes itself felt through parliaments. Or so the theory goes. In fact, and in no small part due to technology, the influence of parliaments on governments has been diminishing. Our societies have become technology-dependent. The technologies on which they depend have become increasingly interdependent. Government legislative proposals and executive action have come to rely on proportionately larger inputs of scientific and technical expertise — of a kind and to a degree which are simply beyond the reach of parliaments. Deteriorating control and scrutiny by parliaments of the Executive is reflected in the multiplicity of 'direct action' movements and initiatives aiming, but rarely with reference to criteria of general policy or national interest, at blocking specific projects (often of high technology content) and at reversing specific central government decisions. If, in accordance with one of the themes of this book, governments are to play stronger or more sophisticated roles in directing the technological evolution of our societies, the question naturally arises — at least in the thirty or so countries trying to operate parliamentary democracies — how the performance of these roles may be rendered sensitive to the concerns of public opinion as expressed through parliamentary channels.

With regard to high technology policy some more or less tentative experiments are under way. They can be classified according to how it is sought to sensitise government to parliamentary influence (making parliaments a more effective counterweight? bringing parliamentarians into the actual decision process?) and according to how directly it is sought to influence technological developments. In illustration of these two axes of classification, let us briefly examine the *Swedish Research Councils Co-ordinating Board*, the *United States Congress Office of Technology Assessment* and the *European Parliamentary Hearings* organised within the framework of the Council of Europe's 'Exercise in Scientific Co-operation'.

The Swedish Research Councils Co-ordinating Board

In a 'mixed economy' technology springs from the interaction of
government and market forces combined with whatever influence is
exerted by its originating mechanisms. These are still far from being
clearly discerned (and adequately researched), but it is generally agreed
that there is some kind of spectrum from technology bred by
technology at one end, to technology bred by science at the other.
There is a sense therefore in which policies for research and science may
be regarded as instruments of high technology policy. In the short to
medium term they are probably rather weak instruments; in the longer
term their influence may – though we don't really know – be decisive.

It is from this angle of vision that the setting-up of the Swedish
Research Councils Co-ordinating Board may be regarded as an instance
of the sensitisation of government high technology policy to
parliamentary influence. Along our axis of classification according to
how directly it is sought to influence technological developments, it is
ultra-tentative. But along the axis of sensitisation of government to
parliamentary influence, it is – at least in the context of traditional
constitutional theory of the separation and independence of powers:
executive, legislative and judicial – startlingly innovatory. The RCCB
(as it will, for the sake of convenience, be referred to hereafter) has a
built-in majority of 'politically elected representatives of the
community, in the first place members of parliament'.[1]

Until just a year or so ago Sweden had five research councils
operating under the Ministry of Education – for natural science,
atomic science, medicine, social science and the humanities. They were
more or less independent agencies with their own grants from the
government budget, closely linked by their composition to the world
of university research, and responsible for promoting basic research in
their respective areas through the allocation of grants to research
projects and other means. Their combined resources, though relatively
small (215 million crowns) in relation to government spending on R & D
(more than 2,000 million crowns for the budget year 1974-5), were
considered 'of very great strategical significance'.[2] In the early 1970s
concern arose as to how the activities of the research councils related
to the vaster world of sectoral research conducted under, by or within
the dozen or so other Swedish ministries. A commission of enquiry was
set up in April 1972 to make a survey of the activities, decision
procedures and composition of the research councils – 'with particular
reference to how representatives of public interests should participate

in their decision making'. The commission reported in April 1975, and submitted proposals for a new organisation of the research councils operating under the Ministry of Education. It noted the increasing dependence of society on research, and the enhanced importance of the role of the universities in producing research and training research workers; it noted a greatly accelerated differentiation and specialisation of research over the last decade; it noted a 'marked academic dominance' in the research councils' composition; it identified as requiring special attention 'the breadth of the councils' scientific evaluation of research projects and its anchorage in current research'; it proposed that all future projects should be judged, and priorities ordered, on the basis of evaluations of 'societal relevance' as well as of 'scientific relevance'; it concluded that evaluations of societal relevance required representation of lay opinion in the research council machinery.

Such were the considerations which formed the background to the commission's proposals to reduce from five to three the number of independent councils operating under the Ministry of Education (by merging the atomic and natural science and by merging the social science and the humanities councils), and to set up 'on an equal footing' with the three new councils a *Research Councils Co-ordinating Board*. In addition to its co-ordinating functions, the RCCB was to have the function of initiating and supporting research 'especially in fields of societal importance'. It was to be independent of the three other councils (with which it would operate in their respective areas on a 'joint financing' basis), to have its own secretariat and to have its own resources for grants to research; it was estimated that these should be about 30 million crowns for the budget year 1979-80. The RCCB was to have a government-appointed chairman and twelve other members: five would be representatives of the three new research councils, the agricultural and forestry research council and the board for technical development; the other seven, appointed by the government, would 'represent politically elected representatives of the community, in the first place members of parliament'; the mandate for all members would be three years.

Through the composition of the RCCB, the commission reckoned that representatives of public interests, and notably parliamentarians, could 'have a dominating influence in a body with great strategic significance for Swedish research'.[3] The report of the commission was approved by the Swedish parliament in 1976, and the new machinery set up and brought into operation in 1977. The commission, meanwhile, practising what it preached, co-opted four parliamentarians to help with its further work on questions relating to the prospects for long-term research planning in general.[4]

It is of course too early to evaluate the performance of the RCCB within the new machinery. Its setting-up needs to be viewed in the context of Swedish institutions, among which the central bank is itself formally an organ of Parliament and has operated since 1964 a research fund (of about 25 million crowns) administered by a Parliament-appointed board having a majority of parliamentarians.

Reservations likely to be expressed with regard to such an innovation in countries with a strong constitutional tradition of the separation of powers might be that it blurs an important distinction between parliamentary and executive responsibilities and functions, and that it represents an encroachment on (opening the gate to politically-inspired interference with) the self-government and independence of the scientific community.

The United States Office of Technology Assessment

An alternative strategy to bringing parliamentarians into the decision process is to restore to parliaments the capability of being effective counterweights to the Executive. In the area of high technology policy one of the most striking moves in this direction has been the setting-up of the United States Congress Office of Technology Assessment (referred to hereafter as OTA).

Congress has a long history of developing its own information capability so as to be able to examine legislative proposals and overall government policy independently of the Executive. The first agency to be set up was the Library of Congress in 1801, and within it, a hundred years later, the Congressional Research Service. After the First World War, to help Congress improve its control over government spending, there was set up the General Accounting Office. With the launching of the first Sputnik in 1957, the Congressional Research Service started to build a staff capability in science and technology in order to service the new standing committees on science, technology and astronautics set up by the House of Representatives and the Senate. It established close relationships with the National Academies of Science and Engineering, which both did studies in the early 1960s on the conceptual basis of an 'office of technology assessment'. The studies were initiated by Emilio Daddario, then a member of Congress, who became OTA's first director when it was finally voted into law in 1973. It quickly built its staff to around 100, and its first tasks were an assessment of the Energy Research and Development Administration's

annual budget (within the two weeks from the time the budget was
made public by President Ford to the start of Congressional
authorisation hearings in June 1975) and the setting up of major
programmes of ocean assessment (directed to the discovery and
production of additional domestic energy resources) and transportation
assessment (directed to energy saving through changes in fuel
consumption patterns). Its areas of study quickly grew to cover energy,
materials, food, health, international trade, and overall research and
development. It conceived its role as to help members and committees
of Congress to take account of the secondary effects of science and
technology on society, before these secondary effects should
accumulate and combine to create unacceptable situations. OTA seeks
to enable Congress to exert direct influence on the technology policy
proposals and decisions of the Executive. It is therefore, on this
particular axis of classification, a far more ambitious venture than the
Swedish RCCB.

Emilio Daddario summed up its philosophy at the Fourth
Parliamentary and Scientific Conference in Florence in 1975:

The aim is for Congress to be a co-equal branch of Government with
respect to information on technological issues. Congress must be
able to ask the right questions. To do this it needs background
information, and it also needs a better understanding of the
secondary and tertiary consequences of technological applications.
To improve policy it needs to be able to debate in a more intelligent
way the alternatives and objectives which are laid before it at any
particular time, and to give that debate wide public visibility. By so
doing, it can improve the democratic process – which itself depends
on a process of public education and choice. The choices society
makes are obviously going to be better if the public itself is better
informed about what is going on: a process whereby the Executive
simply lays before Congress proposals representing predetermined
policies can surely be improved. . .All the legislatures I have been in
touch with over the last twenty years have wanted to be able to
examine more effectively the proposals laid before them by the
executives. These proposals have already undergone rigorous
examination: proponents and opponents within the responsible
departments of the executive branch have had their say; they have
had that say before a final definitive position has been reached, and
scientific and technical advice will have been included in the
decision-making process. In wanting to examine these proposals

legislators want to know what were the arguments which entered into the decision-making process. How was the final decision reached? What alternatives and options were examined? Or why weren't certain options and alternatives examined?[5]

Such then are the needs to which OTA represents an effort to respond. It embodies no new innovatory principle, as does — at least in an Anglo-Saxon context — the Swedish RCCB, but is rather a logical extension of an existing line of institutional development in order to meet the needs of a technology-dependent society. It enables parliamentarians to perform more effectively their traditional roles of controlling and scrutinising the actions of the Executive in the field of technology policy.

OTA's policy is controlled by a 'Technology Assessment Board' consisting of twelve members of Congress — six from the House of Representatives and six from the Senate, with both parties (Republican and Democrat) equally represented and the spectrum of ideology ranging from liberal to strong conservative:

This wide spectrum of ideology assures there is no bias in gathering our data and developing information, since each Board member has to be put in a better position to judge, in the light of his or her philosophy, how he or she would like to approach any particular issue.[6]

The Board operates in conjunction with a 'Technology Assessment Advisory Council', also of twelve members. The heads of the Congressional Research Service and the General Accounting Office are members *ex officio*, and the other ten are chosen to represent the universities, industry, consumer associations and public interest groups. There is a 'public panel' for each field of activity, and the task of the Board is to filter the information flowing to it from the Advisory Council and all OTA panels, to determine what the policy options are, and to consider what action can be recommended to committees of Congress vis-à-vis the Executive.

To David Beckler, former White House science adviser and now director of science, technology and industry at OECD, OTA has the advantage of offering a neutral perspective in relation to the various committees of Congress, which each have their own subject area and special interests:

A White House Science and Technology Office, in similar fashion, has an outlook which cuts across the department/agency structures of the federal government. Now wherever you have a strong department/agency or committee structure incorporating special perspectives on particular problem areas, you need to provide some further way of looking at these areas, which not only puts the pieces together, but provides a general overview — synthesizing the various perspectives. If some kind of 'office of technology assessment' is set up in Europe, I should like to think it will provide a capability for mobilizing the scientific and technological communities of European countries in the same way that OTA promises to be a great source of strength in the processes of the United States Government.[7]

The notion of Europe having its own OTA, touched on by David Beckler in his concluding remarks at the Fourth Parliamentary and Scientific Conference at Florence in 1975, seemed a few years ago a not wholly impracticable proposition — notably in the context of the 'Europe plus Thirty' project of the Commission of the European Communities. But continued and tightening financial stringency — together with the Commission's less than enthusiastic response to the 'Europe plus Thirty' project recommendations — means the idea is no longer on the cards, unless a directly elected European Parliament were to revive it.

Meanwhile, pending the initiatives of a directly elected European Parliament, is there no cheaper way to arrange for an information facility to be at the disposal of European parliamentarians, giving them access to sources of knowledge and expertise independently of the Executive, and enabling them to conduct a proper scrutiny of Executive proposals and decisions in specific areas of high technology policy?

The Parliamentary Hearings of the Council of Europe 'Exercise in Scientific Co-operation'

One such intermediate solution is the object of an institutional experiment at European level, the Council of Europe 'Exercise in Scientific Co-operation'. Its aim has been to induce the voluntary mobilisation of scientific and technical expertise on specific technology policy issues of concern to parliamentarians. Initiated in 1970 and managed by Jean-Pierre Massué, a nuclear physicist,[8] the 'Exercise' consists in the activities of a dozen or so scientific working parties and study groups, manned primarily but not exclusively from the twenty member countries of the Council of Europe, and spanning the whole spectrum of disciplines from mathematics to archaeology. The working parties and study groups are free to open up participation for any specific activity, and they operate according to four criteria:

they must be genuinely interdisciplinary;

they must not overlap with the activities of any other international organisation or programme;

participants must be working scientists: 'elder statesmen' of the European scientific community do indeed figure among the membership but strictly in their capacity as working scientists;

they must try to promote a better understanding among parliamentarians of the spirit, problems and constraints of scientific research.

This last criterion stems from what is the chief institutional originality of the 'Exercise'. It functions under the auspices of a parliamentary body – the Council of Europe's Parliamentary Assembly – and a continuing interface is provided between the worlds of science and politics through the 'European Joint Committee for Scientific Co-operation'. While formally a sub-committee of the Parliamentary Assembly's Committee on Science and Technology (which naturally enough provides the bulk of its parliamentary members), the Joint Committee provides an informal framework for the leaders of the scientific working parties and study groups to meet on an equal footing with parliamentarians to discuss the general directions of scientific co-operation within the 'Exercise', and to consider how the potential of scientific and technical expertise mobilised within it at European level may be focused on problems of concern to parliamentarians.

The 'Exercise' thus constitutes, at European level, a scientific and technological information facility for parliamentarians, on the same principle as (though of course less institutionalised than) OTA. It is also of course a far less expensive operation than OTA, and this is achieved by enlisting the voluntary co-operation of the scientific and technological communities.

The fact that co-operation is voluntary does not mean of course that it is disinterested. As individuals, scientists and technologists have their own reasons for welcoming opportunities to expound their views to parliamentarians on policy issues which affect the future of their research, and to bring influence to bear on the legislation and standard-setting which will govern the introduction of new technologies or the development and diffusion of existing ones.

The mode of focusing expertise on areas of political concern is the 'parliamentary hearing'. Basically, a group of experts bearing responsibility for the field of technology policy in question (drawn, at European level, from the governments, industries and scientific and technological institutions of a large number of different countries and also from international organisations) is subjected to questioning by a group of parliamentarians, the members of which are briefed and advised by scientists working within the 'Exercise' as independent representatives of their own particular discipline and research communities.[9]

The first 'Parliamentary Hearing' on this pattern was organised in Toulouse on 11 March 1978 and had as its focus 'Europe's Specific Needs in the Field of Remote Sensing'. The second, on 4 July 1978 in Paris, focused on coastal pollution from hydrocarbons; the third, in 1979, will examine 'Safety and Security Aspects of the Fast Breeder Nuclear Reactor'.

Reports on the hearings are prepared by the appropriate specialist committee of Parliamentary Assembly – on remote sensing by the committee on science and technology, and on pollution by the regional planning and local authorities committee (which deals with environment questions) – with a view to debate on the floor of the Assembly and the adoption of recommendations to governments and international organisations. At the same time members of the Assembly may put questions and bring pressure to bear in their national parliaments as a result of information generated by and policy positions set forth at the hearings.

Conclusion

The tentative conclusion one comes to is that the experiment in public Parliamentary Hearings within the Council of Europe 'Exercise in Scientific Co-operation' merits further study with a view to establishing comparable arrangements – particularly in countries where steps have been taken to establish regular contact between parliamentarians and the scientific community, along the lines of the 'parliamentary and scientific associations' in Scandinavia and the Parliamentary and Scientific Committee in Britain. Parliamentary hearings organised on this particular pattern and relying on a comparable infrastructure of independent and freely given scientific and technical expertise, certainly offer a means of strengthening parliamentary influence on the high technology policies of the Executive. Unlike the RCCB innovation in

Sweden, they do not break with traditional constitutional principles which are deeply-rooted in many European countries (though, as has been pointed out, the RCCB is a continuation of a principle already accepted in Sweden). Unlike OTA, they are relatively inexpensive — and do not entail the risk of establishing an extra wodge of bureaucracy (though an extra benefit from the OTA model, which could hardly be achieved without the same degree of funding, is its capacity to generate public involvement in the course of its assessments). Furthermore, in addition to providing a means of harnessing for parliamentarians the scientific and technological information potential created within the framework of the 'Exercise', the Hearings have a salutary effect in making scientists and technologists better aware of the motivations and constraints of democratic policies. Few would deny the need for strengthening this awareness at national level in many countries.

Notes

1. Swedish Government Commission on the Organisation of Research Councils, *Research Councils in Sweden: Proposal for New Organisation* (Commission Secretariat Summary, Stockholm, 1975).
2. In 1977 one Swedish crown = approximately US $0.23 or £0.14.
3. Swedish Government Commission, *Research Councils in Sweden.*
4. The Swedish Institute, *Research Planning and Organisation in Sweden* (October 1976).
5. Richter Boulloche and Kenneth Warren, *The Sciences and Democratic Government* (London, Macmillan, 1976), pp.36-57.
6. Ibid.
7. Ibid.
8. Currently Head of the Division for Higher Education and Research at the Council of Europe and Scientific Adviser to the Parliamentary Assembly.

11   BRITISH 'SAFETY POLICY' AND PESTICIDES

Brendan Gillespie

There seems to be little doubt that episodes such as those involving thalidomide, vinyl chloride, the nypro plant at Flixborough, nuclear power and recombinant DNA have heightened public awareness of technological risks and contributed to the demands for more stringent controls. Although few of the hazards are entirely new, the insinuation of technologies into practically all spheres of everyday life has altered the degree and distribution of risk which the populace of advanced industrial nations experience. These technological developments have been accompanied by an improved ability to detect a range of more subtle hazards which has intensified concern and necessitated more complex and sophisticated methods of regulation.

Governments in capitalist countries have employed a number of tools to control technological risks. Cornell *et al.* have listed the following:[1]

(1) no intervention, i.e. reliance on the market;
(2) making more information available;
(3) establishing tort principles;
(4) creating no-fault liability schemes or imposing a tax on injuries;
(5) setting safety standards.

With the increase in the number of issues perceived as requiring regulation, safety policies have come to constitute an aspect of national technology policies. By safety policy we mean the policies which governments follow directly or indirectly in regulating the hazards which accompany the use of technological products or processes.[2]

In Britain, for instance, Lord Zuckerman, former chief scientific adviser to the British government, recently suggested that an Inter-Departmental Hazards Committee be established to co-ordinate the work of existing regulatory bodies.[3] In other countries a variety of agencies has been established concerned specifically with environmental, occupational and consumer safety.[4]

Despite these developments, there has been very little systematic analysis of safety policies by academics or policymakers to elucidate the regulatory tools which governments have employed, the historical evolution of those tools and their operation in practice.[5] The international implications of these policies in an increasingly interdependent world system have received even less attention. Not surprisingly, then, Williams has observed that the control of man-made hazards is generally underlain by a variety of myths and assumptions.[6]

It is clearly time that these myths and assumptions were subject to critical scrutiny. However, even if we confine our discussion to the more recent technological developments for which governments have established regulatory institutions, thereby ignoring older technologies and market-control mechanisms,[7] the analytical task is still substantial.

In this chapter we will focus on pesticide technology which poses a number of chemically-related hazards in the occupational, consumer and general environments. We shall do this by analysing the British system for controlling the hazards associated with pesticides — the Pesticides Safety Precautions Scheme (PSPS). The Scheme will be considered in terms of three principles which have guided the operation of British safety institutions: these are flexibility, co-operation and closedness. These principles have been drawn from a variety of primary and secondary sources which were, as far as possible, independent of literature on PSPS.[8] They would clearly benefit from refinement and development but, in the present state of knowledge, they are useful means for relating the regulation of technology to the political context in which it is conducted. Moreover, this approach has three other important features. First, it provides a framework which will be of use in analysing other British regulatory systems and comparing those of other nations. Second, it illustrates the way in which the control of technology is shaped by existing political traditions and structures. Finally, it demonstrates the need for detailed analyses of the regulatory process which penetrate the self-serving myths associated with it.

The Control of Hazards Associated with Pesticides

Since we shall limit our discussion to chemicals used in agriculture, we may define pesticides as substances which maximise the food supply to human populations by eliminating 'pests' such as insects, fungi and weeds.[9] Given the variety of pests and crops that exist, it is not surprising that pesticides constitute a highly diverse set of products. As a class, they exhibit considerable variation in their physical, chemical and toxicological properties and this needs to be constantly borne in mind when discussing the hazards associated with their use. Although pesticides are developed to poison target pests, their variety prohibits any simple characterisation of their hazardous properties.

What risks accompany the use of pesticides? Essentially they stem from their acute (short-term) and chronic (long-term) toxic properties. There is no simple relation, however, between these properties and the degree of risk; the physical and chemical interaction of the substances with their human and natural 'environments' vitiates any simple extrapolation. We may nevertheless specify the types of risk which accompany the use of pesticides. For our purposes we may define them as befalling.[10]

(a) workers involved in the manufacture, formulation and application of pesticides. They are exposed to acute and chronic toxic hazards;
(b) consumers exposed to a chronic hazard from ingesting residues of pesticides on treated crops;
(c) wildlife subject to acute and chronic hazards.

Immediately after the War, it was the concern with the hazards to consumers and workers which initiated government action. In response to a government request, the Advisory Council on Scientific Policy appointed a Committee on Toxic Substances in Consumer Goods (CTSCG) to investigate the threat to consumers from a number of new, chemically-based products.[11] At the same time, there had been growing concern following the deaths of seven agricultural workers due to pesticide poisoning in the period 1946-50. Consequently, the Ministry of Agriculture and Fisheries (MAF) asked Professor (later Lord) Zuckerman, who had chaired the CTSCG, to chair an investigation into the occupational hazards of the agricultural use of pesticides. The working party which conducted this investigation was twice reappointed to consider the consumer and environmental hazards associated with pesticide use.[12] The three reports, published in 1951, 1953 and 1955 respectively, laid the basis for the British control of pesticide technology.

Following a recommendation in the second report, discussions were held to establish a regulatory scheme and PSPS was formally set up in 1957.[13] It was agreed that:

distributors. . .undertake:
    a. to notify such new pesticides, or new uses of pesticides, to Departments before they are introduced;
    b. to ascertain and disclose to Departments all information needed to enable Departments to advise on the precautionary

measures which should be taken when products containing these pesticides are used;

c. not to introduce such products until agreement has been reached on the appropriate precautionary measures;

d. to include the agreed precautions and the BSI common name (or in its absence, the chemical name) of the active ingredients on the label of every container of the product offered for sale and to take all reasonable measures to ensure that others concerned are aware of and in so far as it lies in their power, observe the precautionary measures advised by Departments;

e. to notify any substantial change in the text or layout of a label/instruction leaflet of a product previously cleared under the Scheme;

f. to withdraw a product from the market if recommended to do so by Departments, on the advice of the Advisory Committee on Pesticides and Other Toxic Chemicals, following a review of the safe use of its active ingredient, provided that the distributor has been given every opportunity to make representations to Departments about their recommendations.[14]

We will now examine the operation of the Scheme in terms of the three principles which we have identified as guiding British safety policy.

Flexibility

In so far as flexibility is defined in contradistinction to rigidity, it appears to be a virtually unarguable principle on which to base a safety policy; it suggests speed, pragmatism and a case-by-case approach, which are probably essential when controlling the hazards associated with such a diverse technology as pesticides. Both the standards themselves and the procedures for determining them are guided by the principle of flexibility in the British context. This involves granting considerable discretion to government officials and often some measure of industrial self-regulation.[15]

Most other industrialised countries have a preference for explicit and uniform standards, which generally carry the force of law, and this indicates the special importance which is attached to flexibility in British safety institutions. The legal status of PSPS helps to illustrate this difference. In contrast to other schemes for regulating pesticides,[16] PSPS is a voluntary, i.e. non-statutory, scheme. This is quite puzzling to foreign observers and it seems that some governments place no confidence in the British scheme partly for this reason, and will not accept registration of a pesticide in Britain as proof of safety.[17] However, within the British political context this is not so unusual; legislation is seen as generating rigidity and therefore to be avoided if possible.

We may appreciate the importance which is attached to this principle in British safety institutions by considering the flexibility inherent in the notification procedure outlined in Figure 11.1. At every stage of the process, the notifier has an opportunity to negotiate with PSPS officials and advisers. Thus, even in the initial stages there are no fixed data requirements which firms must supply. Rather there are a set of detailed guidelines which form the starting point of negotiation between the firm and PSPS. Once the data have been produced for a new pesticide they are examined by the Advisory Committee on Pesticides and its Scientific Sub-committee [18] — the 'Committee Procedure'. Notifications involving minor changes or well-established precedents may be processed by the technical secretaries in consultation with an official toxicologist — the 'Quick Procedure'.

Once the safety data have been processed in either of these channels, advice on safe use is proffered to the government departments participating in PSPS. Their views are then correlated by the Ministry of Agriculture, Fisheries and Food's (MAFF) Pesticides Branch. The latter may then negotiate, if necessary, over the precise wording of recommendations which appear on the labels and information sheets once the products have been cleared.

If we consider the statistics of notifications 1964-75 at least two features are apparent. First, clearances by the Quick Procedure have increased to such an extent (75 per cent of 172 in 1964 to 92 per cent of 538 in 1975) that by the end of the period they accounted for more than ten times the clearances by the Committee Procedure. This accords well with the emphasis put on speed and informality in PSPS — attributes which are much appreciated by the agrochemical manufacturers.[19]

The second significant feature is the very low rate of refused clearances. The ratio of notifications cleared to those received has been consistently above 95 per cent in the period for which figures are available. This fact may be accounted for in terms of the close discussions that take place between notifiers and PSPS officials from the start of the notification process; the result is that firms rarely submit a notification that will fail. Thus, the high success rate together

Figure 11.1: Notification Procedure Under PSPS

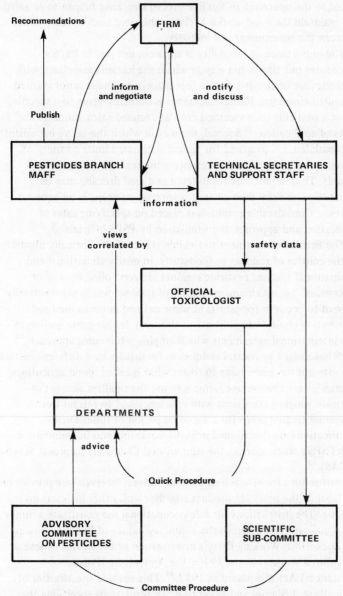

Source: I am grateful to Mr J.A.R. Bates, PSPS Technical Secretary, Plant Pathology Laboratory for providing a similar diagram which I subsequently modified to its present form.

with the speed of the notification process, both of which are intimately linked to the operation of flexible procedures, have helped to establish and maintain the good working relationship that undoubtedly exists between the government and industry.

The importance of flexibility is apparent not just in PSPS's procedures but also in the way in which the hazards associated with pesticides are controlled. In the first place, a pesticide is not granted unlimited clearance. Rather 'clearance is normally given to a specified use of a pesticide on a specified crop at declared rates, numbers and times of application'.[20] Second, the way in which the active ingredient is formulated, i.e. prepared for agricultural use, admits a variety of options which may assist in preventing the realisation of potential hazards. Thus, a pesticide formulated as a seed dressing may be inherently less risky than when it is sprayed on crops in an aqueous solution. Considerable emphasis is placed on specifying rates of application and appropriate formulation by PSPS officials.

The British commitment to flexible standards is classically illustrated by the control of residues in foodstuffs. In nearly all national and international systems pesticide residues are controlled by way of 'tolerances', i.e. maximum quantities of residues which are statutorily allowed to occur in foodstuffs at some defined point in the food distribution chain.[21] In contrast to this, and despite participation in two international agreements which employ a tolerance approach,[22] PSPS has sought to control residues in foodstuffs by a different method. The attempt has been made to foster what is called 'good agricultural practice', i.e. to encourage farmers to use the smallest amount of pesticide which is consistent with efficiency and to refrain from harvesting treated crops for a specified period of time. These specifications are determined prior to marketing and in conjunction with PSPS's sister scheme, the Agricultural Chemicals Approval Scheme (ACAS).[23]

Instructions for efficacious use and 'harvest intervals' are printed on the label of the pesticide product together with other instructions for safe use. The instructions for safe occupational use constitute a minor but significant exception to the voluntary nature of PSPS. Following the Zuckerman Working Party's investigation of the deaths of several agricultural workers in the 1940s, the Agriculture (Poisonous Substances) Act was passed in 1952.[24] This enabled the Minister of Agriculture, Fisheries and Food to make regulations specifying the precautions which farmers and farmworkers must take before using certain highly toxic pesticides. Currently, regulations have been passed for about a quarter of the 250 available pesticides.[25] This 'deviation' from normal practice is explicable in terms of the perceived need for stringent controls following the deaths of seven agricultural workers. As such it seems to be the 'rigid' exception which proves the flexible rule.

Quite apart from ensuring operational efficiency and the development of a good working relationship between regulators and regulatees, the stress on flexibility serves another important function. If PSPS were too restrictive – 'rigid' – the larger manufacturers could threaten not to market their products in Britain. Following her recent survey of agrochemical manufacturers, Tait reported that

> As most manufacturers are operating in the international market, and as the British market is so small as to be irrelevant, they are not particularly concerned with the system in operation in this country. The United States system is the most important as many small countries which do not operate their own Schemes will base acceptance on it.[26]

These findings help to explain why the

> manufacturers interviewed did not consider that any pressure was exerted on them by the PSPS, and were in fact carrying out more tests than the required minimum.[27]

These interviewees were predominantly from the larger companies with international sales. This suggests that PSPS's flexibility is an institutional means for ensuring that there are no obstacles to prevent these manufacturers marketing their products in Britain. At the same time, it ensures that the products of smaller companies which are parties to the Scheme are examined before marketing and in a way which does not overly constrain them.

Co-operation: I – Manufacturers and Farmers

As indicated in the previous section, the stress on flexibility in British safety policy is closely related to the co-operative nature of the relationships established between regulator and regulatee. In view of the importance of negotiation and compromise in the British style of government, it is crucial for the success of the process that some basis of mutual trust and understanding be established amongst participants. As a corollary, it is important that the groups participating in the policy process have a direct commitment to securing an agreement within the negotiable but nevertheless constrained, rules of the game. An important means of achieving an 'appropriate' consensus has been to limit access to the policy process to 'serious and legitimate' interests.[28]

In this section we will consider the types of relationship that have been developed between British regulators and regulatees by examining those which the Ministry of Agriculture, Fisheries and Food (MAFF) has established with the agrochemical and farming industries respectively.

During and after the War, the British state intervened massively in the agricultural sector through the agency of MAFF and its predecessor.[29] Although several government departments are party to PSPS, there is little doubt that MAFF plays the leading role: 80 per cent of pesticides are used for agricultural purposes, the Minister of Agriculture, Fisheries and Food answers parliamentary questions about pesticides and PSPS, most of the supporting staff are MAFF officials and it is MAFF's Pesticides Branch which co-ordinates the views of other government departments. Indeed, it is worth emphasising that the problem of controlling the hazards associated with pesticides has been perceived as unquestionably falling within MAFF's jurisdiction. Thus it was MAFF's predecessor, MAF, which appointed the Zuckerman Working Party [30] and whose officials co-operated with the pesticide industry in establishing ACAS and PSPS.

The location of a pesticide regulatory institution within an agricultural department is clearly not inevitable as the evidence from other countries indicates.[31] In some cases, these institutions have been located within health and environmental departments precisely to avoid the conflict of interest which accompanies the dual responsibilities of promoting and controlling agricultural technologies.[32] However, in the case of PSPS, it is not just that it is located within MAFF; rather, the important point is that it is also located in the same laboratory as ACAS, and that the officials of both schemes are employed in the Agricultural Development Advisory Service (ADAS). Since this is the part of MAFF responsible for the dissemination of the latest technical advances to the agricultural community, the control of pesticide-related hazards appears to be at least institutionally subordinate to the Ministry's responsibilities for the promotion of agricultural technologies. Moreover, there is empirical evidence to suggest that this is the case in practice. After examining the activities of ADAS officials, Tait concluded that they 'do not give the kind of advice which would lead to the reduction of pesticide usage'.[33]

To appreciate why this is an unsurprising conclusion, we need to consider the relationship of MAFF to its regulatees in the agricultural sector. The pesticide industry has been represented in its dealings with MAFF by a succession of trade associations, the most recent of which is the British Agrochemicals Association (BAA). Currently there are 46 members of BAA which account for over 90 per cent of domestic and overseas sales.[34] The membership includes some of the world's largest multinational companies – ICI and Shell for example – and smaller firms which do not manufacture their own products. The Association is recognised by the government as the sole representative of the industry and, in return, it has agreed to maintain the industry side of the bargain, in so far as it is able. Thus all firms which are members must submit their products to the PSPS notification procedure.

The industry's history of co-operation with government extends beyond 1957, the date when PSPS was formally established. BAA's predecessor had participated fully in the establishment of the Scheme to test the efficiency of pesticides in farming use – that became ACAS – in 1942, a full fifteen years before the establishment of PSPS.[35] It is clearly important to locate the origins and subsequent development of PSPS within this evolving relationship.

Farmers' leaders were closely involved in the postwar transformation of British agriculture and they have been ably represented in this regard by the National Farmers' Union (NFU). Self and Storing's analysis of these developments has revealed just how important the co-operative relationship between MAFF and the NFU has been:

> It would be misleading to suggest that the Ministry simply succumbed to Union pressure, or developed anything like the dependent relationship upon a specialised clientele which characterises, for example, some American government agencies. . . what is true is that continuous contact with one powerful organisation induced a defensive posture in the Ministry which allowed the Union to set the pace or hold it back. The Union's views were not opposed by any other organised interest of comparable strength and access to a government department.[36]

While farmers have been far from uncritical of pesticides – witness the existence of a scheme such as ACAS – they have nevertheless recognised the important contribution which these chemicals have made to profitable farming.

As we shall see in the following section, the relationships which MAFF has established with the BAA and NFU are critical to any understanding of PSPS's structure and operation. At the same time, these relationships illustrate the importance which is attached to co-operation with regulatees in British safety policy. Officials have traditionally preferred to stress their consultancy and advisory roles and to encourage compliance by means of persuasion rather than legal sanction. In this way they maintain professionally satisfying relationships which assist the negotiation of safety with their regulatees. This contrasts with the situation in many other countries where an adversarial, police-type of relationship exists between regulators and regulatees.

For obvious reasons, industrial regulatees have tended to prefer the British approach which allows them to present their individual cases in detail to co-operative regulators. This is not to cast doubt on the integrity of officials; some of the most perceptive critics have stressed that British safety institutions are competent, efficient and by no means corrupt.[37] Nevertheless, the close and continuous contact between the sides, and the absence of any other organised interests, has tended to produce a professional and ideological identification between regulator and regulatee. This becomes most apparent when regulatees or their technologies are subject to criticism. Although these attacks assist the regulators' bargaining position, they are also aimed, by implication at least, at the way in which they have discharged their duties. Consequently regulators have tended to defend regulatees under attack.[38]

Co-operation: II – Structure and Operation

There has been a tendency within British government to perceive safety issues as essentially technical in character and this has affected the way in which schemes like PSPS have been organised, operated and justified. Given a consensus on the desire for 'safe' products and processes, the further assumption has been made that this can be unproblematically achieved by the experts most familiar with the problems – usually government and industrial scientists. The considerable discretion granted to safety institutions and their location within the more technically-oriented executive ministries and departments has reinforced this tendency.

The importance of this 'technicalisation' of safety is illustrated by the fact that the two key assessment forums – the Advisory Committee on Pesticides and its Scientific Sub-Committee – are constituted on the basis of their expertise rather than representativeness. Moreover, the self-image of their division of labour is revealing. The Scientific Sub-Committee is presented as considering the evidence from the scientific point of view while the Advisory Committee considers the evidence in ways other than purely scientific.[39] However, if one examines their work more closely it transpires that this does not represent a division between technical risk determination and a normative assessment of acceptability – the two processes inevitably involved in this type of activity.[40] Rather the Sub-Committee performs the bulk of both types of work, i.e. determining risk and judging its acceptability,[41] yet this is presented as a purely technical exercise. Moreover, the Advisory Committee appears to have a correspondingly impoverished view of what 'other than purely scientific' means. Their definition seems largely confined to the administrative implications of decisions rather than the moral and political dimensions of 'acceptable risk'.

The only interests which are formally represented on the two committees are the government departments which are party to PSPS. In keeping with the expert nature of these advisory bodies, and in an attempt to reinforce the neutral image of PSPS, there are no industrial representatives on either committee. However, this should not be allowed to conceal the close co-operation and negotiation which actually takes place between industrial representatives and the two committees. Whenever a company's product is being considered by either committee, a representative may attend to put the company's case. Such an arrangement has two advantages from the notifier's point of view: it ensures that commercial competitors do not obtain potentially useful information and that the interests of the notifier are defended at the most critical phases of the notification process. Finally, the BAA and the Scientific Sub-Committee have established a number of Joint Panels, to consider specialist issues of importance.[42]

This example clearly shows the need critically to probe the categories which regulators use to describe their activities. Failure to do so contributes to the perpetuation of self-serving myths. The importance of this argument is underlined if we examine the implications of the technical perception of safety issues more fully.[43]

If safety is essentially technical, the location of safety institutions such as PSPS within ministries which are primarily concerned with the promotion of technologies becomes 'obvious', and any conflict of interest which it entails, secondary.[44] Furthermore, this perception has provided further justification for the exclusion from the policy process of interests not thought to be sufficiently 'serious and legitimate'. Thus consumers, environmentalists[45] and trade unionists[46] have generally found it difficult to play an effective role in the safety policy process even when their organisations and resources have permitted them to do so.

In the case of PSPS there is no opportunity for the representation of the interests of farmworkers and consumers[47] — the two principal human groups at risk. Paradoxically environmental interests are effectively represented in the persons of experts from the Nature Conservancy Council, a governmental body with management and advisory responsibilities for conservation. These scientists are therefore the only members of either committee with a direct and immediate interest in the control of the hazards associated with the use of pesticides.

Turning now to the operation of PSPS, we should note that prior to the marketing of a product, responsibility for the provision of safety data lies with the notifier. While this is generally regarded as an equitable arrangement, it does tend to induce a dependence of regulators on their regulatees. Indeed Tait found that

> the manufacturers interviewed were very disparaging about the quality of toxicological work carried out by universities and governmental research establishments, implying that their own expertise was much greater in this field.[48]

Moreover, this arrangement poses the problem of the impartiality of the data. There is recent evidence demonstrating that data supporting the notification of certain products have been of poor quality and even fraudulent.[49] It was no accident that these inadequacies were first identified in autonomous safety institutions in the US.

PSPS officials place considerable emphasis upon encouraging 'good agricultural practice' amongst farmers. Essentially, this is an attempt to establish a preventive rather than retroactive system of control. The conditions under which pesticide products may be used 'safely' are determined, printed on the label and farmers encouraged to comply with them. In principle it seems a reasonable approach and one well-suited to PSPS's location within ADAS. However Tait's[50] recent study of pesticide usage has revealed that label instructions were frequently not obeyed.

This failure indicates a crucial weakness in PSPS. With the exception of some occupational health and safety provisions, farmers are under no obligation to follow any recommendations which PSPS makes concerning the use of pesticides, yet the effectiveness of control measures depends critically on their doing just that. Moreover, in this situation, the absence of an adequate monitoring system means that the often-made claim that PSPS is working well takes on an irrefutable and self-congratulatory ring.

Closedness

Despite the tendency in British politics to treat safety issues as technical and the questionable reliability of some notification data, there are no mechanisms whereby scientists, or anyone else unconnected with PSPS, could review PSPS's decision making. The closed nature of safety institutions, however, must be seen within the context of the British government's traditional preoccupation with secrecy. Thus the Official Secrets Act draws a line around a staggering amount of information and is quite different in principle to the US Freedom of Information Act, say, which requires secrecy to be justified.[51]

There are several other considerations which are relevant to the closedness of British safety policy. The first is commercial secrecy which has been used to justify the non-disclosure of data collected by regulatory institutions. The validity of this justification has been seriously questioned, however, by two royal commissions[52] in the case of industrial effluents and emissions, and some firms, at least, have been willing to release such data.[53] The second is the stress on the importance of an efficient and rational decision-making process. One way of achieving this has been to limit relevant information to a carefully defined set of decision makers and advisers. Related to this has been the fear in government and industry circles that making information more widely available would provide materials with which politically-motivated groups could mobilise an 'irrational' public and force the government to take 'unnecessary' measures. This view has been clearly articulated by, amongst others, a former Chief Alkali Inspector:

> I am a great believer in informing the public but not in giving them figures they cannot interpret. You would get amateur environment experts and university scientists playing around with them. People can become scared of figures, they can get the wind up. . .What evidence have you got for public concern? A lot of this trouble is caused by one or two militants and agitators. The general public doesn't give a damn about figures.[54]

Government and industry officials have generally preferred to adopt a low profile rather than engage in activities which would draw public attention to their activities. In the case of pesticides, the government publishes no details of its decisions or their underlying rationales, other than the information sheets issued by MAFF which state the recommended uses of cleared pesticides. The notifiers have been reluctant to publish information which may be used by competitors when their patent expires. The result is that the data used to assess risks have generally not been made publicly available.

In its twenty-year history, the Advisory Committee has issued five reports.[55] Three examined the problem of organochlorine pesticides, one took up the issue of collecting residue data and the fifth considered the possible enactment of legislation and its implications for PSPS. While these are a valuable source of information, their style of presentation indicates a concern to reassure the public and to justify existing arrangements, of which the Advisory Committee is a central part.

In the same period, there have been four independent investigations. The first was by a Research Study Group whose report in 1961 seemed to be directed to a defence of pesticides against increasing environmental criticism.[56] The second investigation, by a parliamentary committee, went the other way and was essentially an attempt by some MPs to apply pressure to MAFF in the cause of an environmental issue which was current at the time.[57] The final two studies were part of the Royal Commission on Environmental Pollution's general reviews of pollution control in Britain. As such they were confined to the environmental effects of pesticides and were quite limited in depth.[58] It is not stretching the point, then, to argue that there has been no detailed, independent evaluation of PSPS in its twenty-year history.

The defence of closed schemes such as PSPS has traditionally been made in terms of representative government. Although they are somewhat secretive, the argument runs, they are nevertheless accountable to elected representatives in Parliament. In view of the unrepresentative character of PSPS and its closed mode of operation, this mechanism is particularly significant in terms of PSPS's continued legitimacy. However, Members of Parliament receive little technical assistance for this purpose, and Parliament performs a very limited 'oversight and appropriations' role. There have been a number of important parliamentary debates and questions[59] since the War, but analysis of these reveals that only the most persistent, informed and well-organised MPs succeeded in obtaining more than minimal information. Moreover, as pesticides have slipped down the political agenda there have been virtually no MPs with sufficient motivation to probe PSPS's activities effectively.

The only remaining institution which could conceivably play a significant role in British safety policy is the judiciary. As Enloe has argued though:

> Confrontation and irrationality are anathema to British political actors. Better set up a new quasi-government board or create a Royal Commission than to trust national policy to the heat of the courtroom.[60]

In other words, the courts have been regarded as inappropriate institutions for dealing with safety issues[61] and this is reflected in the very narrow definition of legal standing employed and the system of legal costs.[62] Safety issues, it is thought, are better dealt with by experts using the principles of science than by lawyers debating the interpretation of rigidly defined laws. The result has been that, with the possible exception of workers' compensation cases, the courts have played even less of a role than Parliament in controlling the hazards associated with pesticides. In view of the foregoing, it seems impossible not to conclude that, in any substantive sense, PSPS has been virtually closed and unaccountable.

Discussion

In this chapter we have examined the way in which technological change and the risks associated with it pose political problems for contemporary governments. The way in which they manage those problems, it should be clear, is closely related to the traditions and structures within which they operate. This means that the significance assigned to technological risk will vary in different political contexts.[63] At the same time, the similarities that exist between advanced capitalist countries, and the international character of technology and the risks associated with it, ensure that many of the political problems posed by technological change are common ones. With this in mind, we will conclude by examining some of the issues raised by the British response to the problem.

Perhaps the most striking lesson to emerge from this case study is that the images and descriptions of the regulatory process employed by the participants require careful scrutiny. Nowhere is this more true than in the tendency to characterise safety policy as a technical process.

We saw how this description legitimised the organisation, operation and location of PSPS in government. This form of scientism is quite pervasive in advanced industrial countries, so that its limitations are worth emphasising.

The assessment of risks associated with technologies such as pesticides undoubtedly requires expertise from a number of fields — toxicology, biochemistry, chemistry, entomology and others. However, the point which is missed in PSPS and similar institutions is that the determination of 'safe' or acceptable uses of pesticides is not *just* a factual activity. Normative judgements are inevitably involved in two distinct ways.[64] First, when the extent and nature of the risks have been determined, the problem of how acceptable they are, or how they should be balanced against benefits, remains. Second, since the specification of risk is often such an uncertain process, extra-scientific considerations are generally required to guide the interpretation of data.[65] Thus it is crucial that analyses of safety regulation subject even the most apparently technical aspects of the process to critical scrutiny[66] as they are intimately tied up with such questions as: What constitutes acceptable risk? Under what conditions, if any, should someone be entitled to impose a risk on someone else so as to benefit yet another? What constitutes a 'fair' balancing of risks and benefits? Where, and how, should the balance of doubt be awarded in uncertain assessments?

The juxtaposition of the inescapably moral and political dimensions of safety regulation with the inadequacies of traditional mechanisms in dealing with problems posed by technological risk, has helped generate what Nelkin has called the ideology of participation.[67] While demands for increased participation have created considerable problems for a number of states, they have been particularly difficult for British politicians to come to terms with in the context of the traditional approach to these issues. From the government's point of view, increased participation in decision making by groups exposed to technological risk would involve a redefinition of what constitutes a 'serious and legitimate' interest, and in many cases it is unclear how this may be achieved.[68] An expanded number of participants would also have implications for regulator-regulatee relationships and the negotiation of flexible policies. The inclusion of groups with opposed interests in the decision-making process suggests that British officials would have to contemplate the possibility of (irreconcilable) conflict, in opposition to the traditional stress on consensus, together with all the delays, uncertainties and inconsistencies which participatory decision making entails.

Would-be participants need to be aware of the implications of their demands for the traditional conduct of British government. Furthermore, they should recognise that participation in decision making may be largely symbolic while existing structural inequalities and imperatives persist.[69] In view of these problems, defenders of the present system might argue that although forums such as PSPS are less than ideal, they nevertheless make decisions which ensure the safe use of pesticides and so there is little point in replacing them with different systems which cannot guarantee 'better' policy.

There are a number of serious objections to the 'do nothing' argument. In the first place, substantive decisions on issues such as safety which involve a significant equity component are inseparably tied to the procedures which determine them: the product cannot be neatly separated from the process that achieves it.[70] Second, the limited evidence which is available indicates that PSPS decision making reflects the way in which agricultural and industrial interests dominate the decision-making process.[71]

This leads to the further point that the scientistic depiction of safety generally conceals the way in which various interests actually operate. The conflicting demands on government to both promote and control technologies clearly underlies this mystification: describing existing decision-making procedures as 'rational', 'efficient', 'technical' and even 'flexible' provides a convenient means for glossing over the issues and of tacitly securing consensus around a particular set of interests, namely those promoting, and gaining most directly from, economic development through technological change. By definition, views which are critical or opposed to these interests are 'irrational'.[72]

For countries such as Britain with sluggish rates of economic growth there are particularly strong pressures not to hinder technological innovation and economic development. One response to the problems of technological change has therefore been so to locate the control function in government that it is institutionally subordinate to promotion. There is nothing intrinsically problematic about such a practice as long as it is recognised as a political act with important implications for the way in which control is exercised. Safety issues will clearly be perceived differently in ministries charged with the promotion of economic development and safety respectively.[73] In the case of PSPS we saw how its location and organisation was informed by a desire not to impose obstacles which might prevent manufacturers from marketing their products in Britain. It would be of considerable interest to explore more fully the relation of a country's market size to the form of technological regulation it employs.

Next, the secretive nature of British safety policy has a number of serious drawbacks. In the first place, it is difficult to see how the failure to provide the British population with information about the risks they face can be morally or politically justified without reference to highly elitist and paternalistic arguments. More substantively, Wynne's point about nuclear power has a general validity:

> When research is dominated by scientists within policy-related institutions as is the case with radiation ecology and biology, there is an especially strong danger that the demands of policy will gradually suppress the scientists' critical role and that areas of uncertainty, error, or alternative practices will be ignored. This is more or less the case in Britain: there (are) no flourishing traditions of independent university research in nuclear safety to cut across and enliven the policy-oriented scientific bodies in their inevitable tendency to settle into a particular paradigm. It is precisely the differentiated nature of scientific research communities, and the interactions between different sub-units within communities, which maintains scientific openness and innovation and avoids the tendency to degenerate into a 'closed' framework of knowledge.[74]

Finally, if the groups which have traditionally been excluded from decision making are to make any meaningful contribution to that process in the future, an essential prerequisite is that they have access to that information.

Once again, the way in which the traditional British approach to these issues impedes such a reform should not be underestimated. Quite apart from concerns about 'rational' and 'efficient' decision making, it is difficult to see how there can be any genuine attempt made to open up decision making as long as the public continues to be regarded as easy prey for 'trouble-makers' in the press and universities to incite to 'irrational' and unnecessary safety demands. Moreover, the repudiation of this attitude is hindered by the vicious circle which the attitude itself engenders. The very secrecy of safety institutions causes mistrust and suspicion amongst 'outsiders' which, when expressed, unites 'insiders' more closely against the critics who 'do not really understand them'. Thus, the need for secrecy is reinforced amongst decision makers and advisers.[75]

It is clear, then, that the British style of government imposes important constraints on the way it can respond to problems of technological change. In contrast, the US style of government, with its emphasis on open and adversarial processes, has fostered more varied and creative responses to the same problems. Without a more detailed analysis of the US system, it is difficult to ascertain precisely their relative strengths and weaknesses. Tinker's rather facetious characterisation of the British approach as being 'more suited to an Edwardian girls' school than to an advanced industrial society'[76] has, however, retained more than a grain of truth.

Notes

1. N.W. Cornell *et al.*, 'Safety Regulation', in Henry Owen and Charles Schultze (eds), *Setting National Priorities: the Next Ten Years* (Washington, DC, Brookings Institution, 1976).

2. Cornell *et al.*, ibid., define 'safety regulation' as 'policies that seek to prevent parties to private market transactions from taking certain risks that they would otherwise assume'.

3. Lord Zuckerman, 'Risks of a No-Risk Society', *Observer*, 30 April 1978.

4. For instance, in the United States, the most safety-conscious of the advanced industrial countries, consumer product safety, occupational health and safety and environmental protection agencies have been established in the last ten years. See Judith Reppy, in this volume, and Paul H. Weaver, 'Regulation, Social Policy and Class Conflict', *Public Interest*, vol.50 (1977), pp.45-63.

5. Roger Williams, (a) 'Government Response to Man-made Hazards', *Government and Opposition*, vol.12 (1, 1977), pp3-19, and (b) *Government Regulation of the Occupational and General Environments in the UK, USA and Sweden* (Science Council of Canada, Background Study No.40, 1977) are the most useful reviews available.

6. Ibid., 1977 (a).

7. For a recent examination of some of these mechanisms in the British context see *Report of the (Pearson) Committee on Civil Liability* (London, HMSO, 1978).

8. These include Cynthia Enloe, *The Politics of Pollution in a Comparative Perspective* (New York, David McKay Co., 1975); H.F. Steward, *Food Additives – Their Utilisation and Control with Specific Reference to the Case of Cyclamates* (University of Manchester, unpublished MSc thesis, 1971); Jon Tinker, 'Britain's Environment – Nanny Knows Best', *New Scientist*, 9 March 1972, pp.530-4; T. Vickers, 'Flexible DNA Regulation: the British Model', *Bulletin of the Atomic Scientists*, vol.39, pp.4-5; Williams, 1977a and 1977b; Brian Wynne, 'The Politics of Nuclear Safety', *New Scientist*, 26 January 1978, pp.208-11. More official sources include the six reports of the Royal Commission on Environmental Pollution and the Report of the (Robens) Safety and Health at Work Committee, Cmnd.5034 (London, HMSO, 1972).

9. We focus on the agricultural usage of pesticides because they account for the most significant proportion by far. See *The Industry's Statistics 1975* (London, British Agrochemicals Association, 1976). Probably the best general discussion of pesticides is to be found in National Academy of Sciences, *Pest Control Volume 1. Contemporary Pest Control Practices and Prospects*

(Washington, DC, NAS, 1975).

10. Others put at risk by pesticides include users of treated produce, livestock, domestic animals, and passers-by inadvertently present at the time of crop treatment.

11. *Fourth Annual Report of the Advisory Council on Scientific Policy* (London, HMSO, Cmnd.8299, 1951).

12. *Report to the Minister of Agriculture and Fisheries of the Working Party on Precautionary Measures against Toxic Chemicals used in Agriculture* (London, HMSO, 1951); *Report to the Ministers of Agriculture and Fisheries, Health, and Food, and to the Secretary of State for Scotland of the Working Party on Precautionary Measures against Toxic Chemicals used in Agriculture. Residues in Food* (London, HMSO, 1953); ibid., *Risks to Wildlife* (London, HMSO, 1955).

13. Ministry of Agriculture, Fisheries and Food (MAFF), *Pesticides Safety Precautions Scheme Agreed Between Government Departments and Industry* (London, Pesticides Branch, revised March 1971), para.1.

14. Ibid., para.6.

15. Robens Committee (Safety and Health at Work), ch.9.

16. S. Hahn, 'Regulatory Schemes of Current Members of the EEC', *Proc. 11th British Weed Control Conference* (1972); 'WHO Control of Pesticides – A Survey of Existing Legislation', *International Digest of Health Legislation*, vol.20 (1969), pp.579-726.

17. Elizabeth J. Tait, 'Factors Affecting the Production and Usage of Pesticides in the UK' (unpublished PhD thesis, Cambridge University, 1976), p.15.

18. This Committee was previously known as the Advisory Committee on Pesticide and Other Toxic Chemicals and, before that, as the Advisory Committee on Poisonous Substances used in Agriculture and Food Storage. See B.F. Gillespie, 'British Control of Pesticide Technology' (unpublished PhD thesis, University of Manchester 1977), pp.110-11.

19. Tait, 'Production and Usage of Pesticides', p.15.

20. J.A.R. Bates, *The Control of Pesticides in the United Kingdom*, paper presented to the South-East Asia Workshop on Pesticide Management, Bangkok, 14-16 March 1977, p.7.

21. Gillespie, 'Control of Pesticide Technology', ch.7 and D. Kay, *The International Regulation of Pesticide Residues in Food* (Washington, DC, American Society of International Law, 1976).

22. The European Economic Community and the United Nations' Codex Alimentarius Commission; see Gillespie and Kay, ibid.

23. Bates, *Control of Pesticides*, p.6.

24. Gillespie, 'Control of Pesticide Technology', pp.139-44. For a review of other laws with potential relevance for pesticides, see J.A.R. Bates, 'Legislation Regarding the Use of Chemicals in Agriculture', in D. Irvine and B. Knights, *Pollution and the Use of Chemicals in Agriculture* (London, Butterworth, 1974).

25. Bates, *Control of Pesticides*, p.4.

26. Tait, 'Production and Use of Pesticides', p.17.

27. Ibid., p.16.

28. Enloe, *Politics of Pollution*, p.285.

29. P. Self and H. Storing, *The State and the Farmer* (London, Allen and Unwin, 1971) and B. Davey, 'Postwar Development of British Agricultural Policy', in Davey *et al.* (eds), *Agriculture and the State* (London, Macmillan, 1976).

30. The Ministry of Agriculture and Fisheries was amalgamated with the Ministry of Food to form the Ministry of Agriculture, Fisheries and Food in 1956. See Sir John Winnifrith, *The Ministry of Agriculture, Fisheries and Food* (London, Allen and Unwin, 1962).

31. See the references in note 16.

32. This was the case in the US for instance. See John Blodgett, 'Pesticides and Evolving Technology', in Samuel Epstein and Richard Grundy (eds), *The Legislation of Product Safety*, 2 vols. (Cambridge, Mass., MIT, 1974).

33. Tait, 'Production and Usage of Pesticides', p.152, and *Proposed Changes in the Work of the Ministry of Agriculture, Fisheries and Food* (London, HMSO, Cmnd.4564, 1971).

34. 'British Agrochemicals' Association – Spirit of Togetherness', *Farm Chemicals*, vol.139, no.9, p.40.

35. BAA, *History 1926-76* (London, BAA, 1976).

36. Self and Storing, *State and the Farmer*, p.323; R. Kimber and J. Richardson (eds), *Pressure Groups in Britain* (London, Dent, 1974), p.23, have argued that the relationship has grown even closer since the completion of Self and Storing's study in 1961.

37. Tinker, 'Britain's Environment', p.530.

38. This was the case when pesticides were under attack by environmentalists in the early 1960s. See Gillespie, 'Control of Pesticide Technology', pp.186-208.

39. MAFF, *Pesticides Safety Scheme*, para.7.

40. Council for Science and Society, *The Acceptability of Risks* (London, Barry Rose, 1977), and William Lowrance, *Of Acceptable Risk* (Los Altos, Calif., William Kaufman, 1976).

41. Personal Communication, PSPS Technical Secretariat, 28 April 1977.

42. Currently there are three in operation on toxicology, wildlife and labelling. Personal Communication, PSPS Technical Secretariat, 28 April 1977.

43. One important aspect of the technicalisation of safety which cannot be dealt with any detail here is the increasing importance attached to quantitative approaches to risk assessment. See Zuckerman, 'No-Risk Society', and Wynne, 'Nuclear Safety', for contrasting views of this development.

44. L. Tivey, 'The Politics of the Consumer', in R. Kimber and J. Richardson (eds), *Campaigning for the Environment* (London, Routledge and Kegan Paul, 1974).

45. Kimber and Richardson (eds), *Campaigning for the Environment* (London, Routledge and Kegan Paul, 1974), and Philip Lowe, 'The Environmental Lobby: Political Resources', *Built Environment Quarterly*, 1, pp.73-6.

46. J. Grayson and C. Goddard, *Studies for Trade Unionists* (Workers' Educational Association, 1975), and the Robens Report (Safety and Health at Work).

47. To be fair, they have not asked to be included. But as we shall argue below, the approach of the British government to safety issues is, in part, responsible for this.

48. Tait, 'Production and Usage of Pesticides', p.24.

49. In discussing the particularly flagrant misrepresentation of data by Industrial Bio-Test (IBT) Laboratories, Smith writes: 'IBT data also were relied upon by the EPA and ultimately the corresponding agencies in several foreign countries, in setting the accepted levels of tolerance in foodstuffs for 160 pesticide products.' See R. Jeffrey Smith, 'Creative Penmanship in Animal Testing Prompts FDA Controls', *Science*, vol.198 (23 December 1977), p.1227; and Melvin D. Reuber, 'Review of Toxicity Test Results Submitted in Support of Pesticide Tolerance Petitions', *The Science of the Total Environment*, 9, pp.135-48.

50. Tait, 'Production and Usage of Pesticides', p.103.

51. Dan Greenberg, 'Let the Sun Shine In', *New Scientist* (11 August 1977), pp.344-5.

52. The Second (Cmnd.4894) and the Fourth (Cmnd.5780) Reports.

53. Tinker, 'Britain's Environment', p.533.

54. Ibid.

55. These were *Review of the Persistent Organochlorine Pesticides. Report by the Advisory Committee on Poisonous Substances used in Agriculture and Food Storage* (London, HMSO, 1964); *Supplementary Report* (London, HMSO, 1974); *Review of the Present Safety Arrangements for the Use of Toxic Chemicals in Agriculture and Food Storage. Report by the Advisory Committee on Pesticides and other Toxic Chemicals* (London, HMSO, 1967); *The Collection of Residue Data. A Report by the Advisory Committee on Pesticides and other Toxic Chemicals Covering a Report by its Working Party on the Collection of Residue Data* (London, HMSO, 1969); *Further Review of Certain Persistent Organochlorine Pesticides Used in Great Britain. Report by the Advisory Committee on Pesticides and other Toxic Chemicals* (London, HMSO, 1969).

56. (Sanders) Research Study Group.

57. Sixth Report of the Estimates Committee, Session 1960-61. *Ministry of Agriculture, Fisheries and Food, Parliamentary Papers*, vol.5 (London, HMSO, 1961).

58. The Second and Fourth Reports.

59. Gillespie, 'Control of Pesticide Technology', pp.120 and 202.

60. Enloe, *Politics of Pollution*, p.283. The British tendency to appoint *ad hoc* bodies is also noted by Pearce *et al.*, 'Energy: How to Decide', *Nature*, vol.272 (9 March 1978), pp.115-16.

61. Compensation for industrial injury is an exception to this rule. See the Robens (Safety and Health at Work) and Pearson (Civil Liability) Reports.

62. D.A. Bingham, *The Law and Administration Relating to Protection of the Environment* (London, Oyez, 1973).

63. B. Gillespie, D. Eva and R. Johnston, 'National Styles of Risk Assessment: the Role of Science and Politics in the Evaluation of Carcinogenicity', in press.

64. Council for Science and Society, *Acceptability of Risks*, and Lowrance, *Of Acceptable Risk*.

65. Jeff Masten, 'Epistemic Ambiguity and the Calculus of Risk', *South Dakota Law Review*, vol.21 (Spring 1976), pp.423-51.

66. One detailed study which clearly demonstrates the value of such an approach is Ackerman *et al.*, *The Uncertain Search for Environmental Quality* (New York, Free Press, 1974).

67. Dorothy Nelkin, *Democratizing Technical Decisions* (Beverly Hills, Calif., Sage, 1977), ch.1.

68. The case of consumer representation, for example, is particularly problematic. See Tivey, 'Politics of the Consumer', and Council for Science and Society, *Acceptability of Risks*, Appendix 6, for one proposed solution.

69. The experience of the conservationists with PSPS is quite instructive in this respect. See Gillespie, 'Pesticide Technology', ch.6.

70. Jerome E. Milch, 'Technical Advice and the Democratic Process', paper presented to AAAS meeting, Washington, DC, 12-17 February 1978, p.12.

71. Gillespie, 'Pesticide Technology', chs.6, 8 and 9.

72. See Brian Wynne, 'The Rhetoric of Consensus Politics', *Research Policy* (1975), pp.108-58.

73. A relevant illustration of this is the intense political conflict which took place over which part of government should be responsible for the agricultural provisions in the HASAW Act. See Gillespie, 'Pesticide Technology', pp.159-70.

74. Wynne, 'Nuclear Safety', p.211. The tremendous opposition which ecologists encountered when they presented their views to PSPS in the early 1960s illustrates this point well. See Gillespie, 'Pesticide Technology', ch.6.

75. Wynne, ibid.

76. Tinker, 'Britain's Environment', p.530.

12 REGULATING THE EXPLOITATION OF RECOMBINANT GENETICS

Edward Yoxen

In July 1974, a group of leading American molecular biologists announced that in their view a moratorium should be imposed on a rapidly expanding area of research known as recombinant genetics. Their concern was that the hazards of doing this work were essentially unknown, but potentially serious.[1] Their proposals were immediately endorsed by national biomedical research agencies, and much of the work in this area was therefore delayed for about two years. Since 1974, there has been an important debate, particularly in the United States, about the safety and desirability of proceeding into this area. After four years, there is now a consensus amongst many, but not all, molecular biologists that any hazards can be contained.[2] There are regulatory agencies specifically for recombinant genetics in most countries where it is being undertaken[3] and a rapid increase in industrial investment in its applications is now occurring.[4]

Partly because of the strenuous debate over what may come of these new scientific techniques, a powerful rhetoric has been developed suggesting that we stand at the threshold of a 'new technological age'. This may well be true. It is quite easy in principle to see how new micro-organisms could be engineered, which for example, could synthesise hormones or proteins cheaply and reliably for use in medicine or which could rapidly digest industrial or urban waste. In practice, this may prove very difficult to achieve. Similarly in agriculture, it may be possible one day to produce cereal crops by genetic manipulation which themselves fix atmospheric nitrogen.[5]

All these things are only possibilities at present. However, the problem of potential hazards remains, and henceforth the issues of promotion and control will go – or most certainly should go – together. We want to ensure that applied recombinant DNA research is environmentally and medically safe, and we also need to consider much more carefully than has yet been done the nature of the resulting technologies and how such goals are to be attained.

My argument falls into three sections. The first is a rapid review of developments and decisions up to the time of writing. The second section is a consideration of some of the policy questions that have yet to be seriously confronted. In the third section, I try to evaluate the capability of some existing institutions for dealing with these issues and conclude that in Britain at least, trade unions for technical personnel with members in hospitals, universities and industry, are well placed to call upon the practical experience, technical knowledge and political understanding necessary to tackle the problems which lie ahead. Almost certainly they are uniquely qualified in that respect.

In what follows, I shall concentrate very largely upon Britain, for several reasons. The British situation makes an interesting case study, first because it is one of the two countries that has produced an important set of guidelines for the practice of recombinant genetics, and these have been promoted by the European Science Foundation and to some extent within the European Molecular Biology Organisation.[6] Second, the regulatory agency in Britain, the Genetic Manipulation Advisory Group, is an innovation, that has emerged from a particular political context, within which a number of interest groups confront one another.

The Governmental and Scientific Response to the Emergence of Recombinant Genetics since 1974

The history of the more public events of the last four years concerning recombinant genetics has been rehearsed many times by now.[7] In this section, I shall present a very partial and schematic account of the recombinant DNA debate, and make some observations on the context and spirit of policy making so far.[8] I shall not consider the medical policy implications of current work, although they are certainly equally important.[9]

The Changing Consensus about Hazards

Seemingly the first concerned discussions of the power and potential hazards of recombinant DNA research took place in June 1973, at a colloquium for biochemists and molecular biologists in New England.[10] This meeting set in train the deliberations organised by Professor Paul Berg of Stanford University that led to the much publicised, worldwide moratorium on certain categories of research in this area which began in July 1974. At this stage, no one seems to have concerned himself with questions of social impact, and certainly no professional or governmental institution thought it necessary to raise these issues.

In some of the rhetoric generated by the moratorium, there were echoes of the nuclear physicists' dilemma of 1939. There can be no doubt that in addition to its ostensible, practical function, as a gesture, it was intended to create an impression of social responsibility.[11] Several of the signatories of the Berg letter have recently repudiated their erstwhile manifestations of concern.[12]

Clearly, the moratorium required more or less universal compliance; its proponents were however assured of its success, since they were the world leaders in the field. Similarly, it only succeeded, one suspects, because in 1974 significant capital investment by industry had yet to occur. It was a measure based on the powers of professional censure, the continuing shared realisation that the possible hazards had to be considered, the possibility of powerful public reaction, and effective control by one group of the financial support for research projects in this area.

That a consensus among molecular biologists about the need for caution has survived, in one form or another, through several critical moments, under the strains of intense, intraprofessional competition, nationalistic pride and possible financial gain, is rather significant. Two comments are in order. First, the consensus about the problems arising has been related almost entirely to questions of risk, and not, for example, to the need for discussion of the technological and social consequences. Second, the known existence of collective concern amongst molecular biologists has been a precondition for a continuing degree of autonomy and self-regulation. Without it, and this point has been made by the more politically astute molecular biologists, control of experimentation could well have passed to an 'external', non-scientific agency, with different views about the ways in which and the goals towards which fundamental research should be organised.[13] This issue, which is both symbolic and substantive, underlies the continuing struggle over the legislative control of recombinant DNA research.[14]

Moreover, this consensus has survived a major transformation. In 1974, the vast majority of molecular biologists were prepared to accept a temporary halt in their research, in order that the potential hazards could be examined. This prudential view was reinforced by government support. By 1978, the consensus has shifted to the view that the hazards of recombinant DNA research have been adequately considered, and that the regulatory system imposed by government is almost certainly too strict, although this can be borne for the time being. This effective unanimity is a powerful influence on government policy and serves to inhibit public debate, since there is no evidence of controversy and therefore no point of access for public interest.

The Shortcomings of the Ashby Committee in Britain

The announcement of a moratorium was not entirely a surprise to leading molecular biologists and government scientific agencies in Britain. On 26 July 1974, very soon after the public statement in America, the Advisory Board for the Research Councils established a Working Party 'to assess the potential benefits and potential hazards of techniques which allow the experimental manipulation of the genetic composition of micro-organisms'.[15] Moreover, the Board decided 'that the membership of the Working Party should, as far as possible, not include those who were using the techniques and who might therefore, be directly affected by its conclusions'.[16]

The very narrow spectrum of scientific expertise and experience represented on the Ashby committee has already been criticised.[17] It is interesting to note that, for all their supposed independence in 1974, within three years six members of the committee were directing laboratories in which research on recombinant genetics was being carried out, and three of them have been directly involved in strategic planning by the British Agricultural Research Council (ARC) of programmes using recombinant DNA research. Susan Wright has argued that the deliberations of the Ashby committee represented policy making by default, based on the implicit belief that in some form the research would continue.[18] One can also make a related criticism concerning technological or industrial planning to which Ashby's committee seems to have given very little thought. No industrial scientists sat on the committee, nor indeed were any invited to give evidence. This is certainly surprising, if one reflects upon the very considerable optimism in the report about the potential benefits in the fields of drug manufacture and agricultural production.

Moreover in September 1974, there was an announcement from ICI, publicised in two articles in the *Financial Times*, that it was assisting the development of recombinant genetics techniques.[19] Certainly one looks in vain in the report for any indication that Lord Ashby and his colleagues had tried to define in concrete terms how the potential benefits of which they spoke so enthusiastically could be realised by the British, or indeed by any other economic and industrial system.

To say that such issues fell outside the remit of the working party, which was undoubtedly the case formally speaking, is largely to avoid the issue. For it ignores the fact that academic scientists and civil servants of the background and experience represented there are seldom motivated to ask such questions or to ensure that anybody else does so

either. In no obvious way did they raise for public discussion the
question of what sort of technology or medical policy would be
appropriate in Britain, given its particular economic needs.

   Lord Ashby and his distinguished colleagues were brought together
to provide a comprehensive and informed analysis of the policy issues
raised by recombinant DNA research, at a pivotal moment in the
emergent debate. Had they, for example, commissioned from a series
of widely recruited sub-committees studies of the technical feasibility
of applying these new techniques, the potential hazards, current lab
practice in molecular biology, criteria for judging socially acceptable
risks in applied biology, investment strategies of large industrial
corporations in, say, the drug industry, and social priorities in
biomedical research, and had they on this basis reported that no firm
conclusions could yet be reached, then the subsequent debate in
America and elsewhere would have been very different. As it was, they
felt themselves required to report as soon as possible. Their report came
out in January 1975, with the important recommendation that research
should continue, based on the idea of enfeebled strains of bacteria,
which could be devised so that they would only live in highly artificial
environments. This notion of biological containment, which has proved
much harder to arrange than was supposed in 1975, was enthusiastically
taken up again at the international conference at Asilomar in California
in March 1975, attended by some 140 molecular biologists from all
over the world.

*From the Asilomar Conference to the Genetic Manipulation Advisory
Group: the Problems of Establishing and Implementing Guidelines*

The Asilomar conference, which was convened to debate the potential
safety problems described in the original statement of the moratorium
proposal, has been cogently criticised for its exclusiveness, and for a
very narrow selection of expertise amongst those present.[20] During the
meeting, the distinguished scientists present were made to feel their lack
of legal competence,[21] and several leading participants have
subsequently admitted that they should at least have invited specialists
from other fields, such as epidemiology, microbial ecology and
occupational health.[22] This restriction of discussion about the hazards
of recombinant DNA research can be interpreted as a tactic by
molecular biologists to retain professional control of the assessment of
risk. Indeed, much of the debate can be regarded as an extended
negotiation with other professional or interest groups over their
exclusive claim to competence in this area, and thus to regulate their

own practice. This shortcoming was exacerbated in the composition of the committee established under the aegis of the principal funding agency in the United States, the National Institutes of Health (NIH), to draw up guidelines for the safe practice of research. Indeed, this self-interested selectiveness or political ineptitude, whatever one wishes to call it, rebounded upon the molecular biologists and the directorate of the NIH in the subsequent, often quite heated debate in America.[23] Moreover, it seems only to have been in the public debate that any serious consideration was given to the question of the social impact and social utility of the continuing rapid development of this field.[24]

Just as the preparation of guidelines began in America in 1975, so too in Britain a further governmental committee was established in that year

> to draft a central code of practice and to make recommendations for the establishment of a central advisory service for laboratories using the techniques available for such genetic manipulation, and for the provision of necessary facilities.[25]

This body was appointed by the Secretary of State for Education and Science, and worked under the chairmanship of Professor Sir Robert Williams, Director of the Public Health Laboratory Service. Notably it included several people with an active research interest in recombinant genetics, who had also been closely involved with the politics of the debate up to that point, in particular Dr Sydney Brenner of the Medical Research Council Laboratory of Molecular Biology in Cambridge. It also included people with considerable experience in the direction of laboratories where dangerous pathogens were handled, and one representative from the field of industrial health and safety, Dr Owen, Director of Medical Services for the newly formed governmental Health and Safety Executive (HSE).[26] The Williams committee took evidence from a much wider range of individuals and organisations than had been allowed to approach the Ashby committee, although in a sense, its task was rather more specialised.

The ensuing report concerned itself with the categorisation of experiments according to the degree of risk which they posed, with corresponding codes of practice. It recommended that there should be more training in laboratory safety, more health monitoring in recombinant DNA labs, more supplementary research on containment and risk assessment and more consideration given to appropriate modes of enforcing safety regulations. This last issue was complicated by the passing into law of the Health and Safety at Work Act in 1974, which encompassed laboratory investigation in recombinant genetics. The Williams report was accompanied by a consultative document from the HSE that led to a vigorous controversy in late 1975, ostensibly over the definition of genetic manipulation that regulatory bodies should use, although undoubtedly the right of scientists to define safety standards for their research was being contested as well.[27]

The Williams report also recommended the establishment of an advisory group to monitor the practice of genetic manipulation. Such a body, the Genetic Manipulation Advisory Group (GMAG), came into operation at the beginning of 1977, tendering advice to the HSE, although funded by the Department of Education and Science. Initially proposed experiments in genetic manipulation were notified to GMAG on a voluntary basis, although from 1 August 1978 this is a statutory requirement. At present, it is a precondition for research council support. Indeed, the HSE regards the failure to obtain approval for such experiments as a *prima facie* breach of the Health and Safety at Work Act, which would enable the Executive to bring considerable powers to bear on anyone attempting to work outside the regulatory system. In practice, the situation could easily become more complicated, since the legal force of GMAG recommendations has yet to be tested in a court of law, and it is not clear how the issue would be resolved, if an influential defendant, with long-term financial interests at stake, sought to contest the GMAG recommendations. In some cases, the HSE might very well decide not to take action.[28]

GMAG: Advice Without a Strategy

GMAG is a very interesting institutional innovation. It is made up of some twenty-five people, including eight biologists nominated as experts on various aspects of DNA work, four trade union representatives and four people thought 'able to take account of the interests. . .of the general public'. In fact, the structure of interests within the Group is rather complex, with several of the academic biologists having financial interests in the expansion of the field, and two of the trade unionists being concerned with recombinant genetics as a research topic; one of the public interest representatives is the Director of the Nuffield Foundation which is currently supporting recombinant genetics research, and has used his position as a noted broadcaster and science journalist to campaign surreptitiously for the relaxation of controls in Britain.[29]

The group meets monthly to consider proposed experiments and to discuss the longer-term issues and problems which attend its operation. After sixteen months' existence, its first report was published in May 1978, and makes informative reading.[30] Although GMAG is essentially an advisory body to the regulatory agency — and most of its members regard their role thus — its procedures and decisions do impinge directly and indirectly on other areas of concern and issues of policy. This is well illustrated by the crisis within GMAG in the autumn of 1977 concerning confidentiality. Many of the members of the group are in Civil Service terms lay people; they are involved specifically as representatives of non-governmental organisations, which require them to report back. They are not therefore as directly controlled by the Official Secrets Act, which cloaks the activities of all state institutions in Britain, as someone whose continuing employment depends upon its observance, and they have not been socialised into the obsessive secrecy characteristic of these bodies. Under existing patent law products can only be patented if there has been no 'prior disclosure', a term which excludes the submission of information to official bodies that operate in strict confidentiality.[31] The problem has arisen as to whether GMAG, with its public interest and trade union representatives, would be so regarded in a patent application. Various pharmaceutical and chemical companies have required assurance on this point before submitting information to GMAG, while at the same time most of the lay members have insisted on their right to report back on matters of general policy. A compromise has now been arranged, although it remains to be seen whether it will prove adequate.[32] The incident does however reveal some of the connections between the type of regulatory agency that is established, and allowed to remain in existence, and patterns of investment and technological development. Clearly in insisting on a certain freedom of manoeuvre, the lay representatives on GMAG were placing in jeopardy the whole rather unusual participatory exercise with which they were involved. This highlights the real issue which is the need to accommodate patent legislation to public participation, and not the other way round.

Institutions Involved with the Promotion of Recombinant Genetics in Britain

To conclude the first section, I want to list those bodies which are concerned with the support of this research in Britain. Three of the research councils, the Medical Research Council, the Agricultural Research Council and the Science Research Council, are funding work in various places,[33] as are three private foundations, the Muscular

Dystrophy Group, the Imperial Cancer Research Fund and the Nuffield Foundation. The last of these is doing so jointly with the MRC and the Wellcome Drug Company.[34] Recombinant genetics has now reached the stage at which money is being made available for development work, for example, by the state-controlled National Research Development Corporation (NRDC) in Britain.[35] If a coherent technology policy is to be created for recombinant genetics, assuming that it makes sense to base such a policy on a set of techniques which may have rather disparate applications, then the role of the NRDC seems very important, to create some degree of strategic co-ordination of effort. If this possibility were not taken up, DNA research might well pass to multinational corporations, with different economic interests, and far less under social control.

A number of such companies have openly declared an interest in this field, notable ICI, G.D. Searle, and Unilever. Several companies have an undeclared interest, amongst them Pfizer, Glaxo, Wellcome, BP, Shell and Beechams, and the plans of foreign-owned multinationals outside Britain like General Electric, Hoechst, and Hoffman-LaRoche may also affect the British industrial situation.[36]

The situation at the time of writing (June 1978) is that recombinant DNA research is being pushed vigorously by a number of scientific and industrial groups, operating within the constraints of a regulatory system, established over a four-year period. The system has been constructed on four basic assumptions: (1) that significant scientific, medical and technological benefits are likely to accrue from the development of this field, so that it makes sense to carry on with research and development in the face of possible problems; (2) that the potential hazards are sufficiently serious for some sort of regulatory measures to be implemented; (3) that an adequate scientific basis can be provided for the analysis of such hazards; and (4) that the institutions which have been brought into the field have the power to contain the possible risks to health and the environment. My suggestion is that in Britain and elsewhere the first, third and fourth assumptions have been accepted rather uncritically, in a period when policies for promotion and control have been powerfully influenced by scientific pressure groups. These issues I want to explore in more detail in the next section by considering first existing methods of risk assessment and second corresponding policies for the realisation of the possible benefits.

Technology Policy and Risk Assessment

One of the basic principles of risk assessment in this area has been the categorisation of experiments, according to estimated hazard. This classificatory procedure emerged in the course of the policy discussions, and was first publicly announced with the proposal of the moratorium; more importantly, the principles of classification are not universal at present, they have mutated and diverged in the course of the debate.

Berg and his colleagues provisionally classified possible experiments in 1974, separating work with antibiotic resistance factors, bacterial toxin systems and animal virus material from the linkage of animal DNA to plasmid or viral DNA.[37] Lord Ashby's committee took the analysis a stage further, by talking of predictably hazardous work, such as that involving the transmission of drug resistance, and that of which the dangers were unpredictable; they wrote of a need 'to match the scale of the precaution to the estimate of risk'.[38] In their view, this could best be derived from existing microbiological expertise. The emphasis was on self-regulation by experienced research workers, advised if necessary by biological safety officers in each centre. *'As an initial step* (author's emphasis), a widely publicised advisory service, perhaps offered by the public health laboratories, would help to safeguard the interests of the public and those engaged in the experiments.'[39]

Eighteen months later, the Williams committee organised its report around a suggested categorisation of experiments that would be considered by the Genetic Manipulation Advisory Group. The intention was to set up a comprehensive framework, which would allow a flexible response to the changing problems of regulation, based on a 'case-law' approach.[40] This is in marked contrast with the principles employed by the analogous body in America, which in the same period came up with a more rigid system that involved the specification of all conceivable types of experiment. The Williams report proposes a system of categorisation to locate experiments on a continuous spectrum of hazard, using factors such as the source and purity of DNA sequences, the vector-host system and the manipulative procedures to be employed.[41]

It is an interesting and persuasive exercise, designed to cope with a situation of uncertainty. But for all its ingeniousness, it is only a set of conventions or rules, with a certain plausibility and without very much quantitative data to support it. There are indeed other ways of approaching the same problem, or related problems, as for example that employed by an ICI team in a study of a proposed containment facility for recombinant DNA work.[42] They attempted to specify hypothetically all possible failures of the safety systems, and to attach probability estimates to each outcome in connected chains of events, in order (1) to see what might go wrong, and (2) to assess the seriousness of the most likely accident. Again the exercise is persuasive, although trenchant criticisms have been made of this approach, because of its unreliability.[43]

This leads to a serious problem, that the procedures for hazard analysis in this new field are relatively undeveloped and untested, and have not been subjected to critical scrutiny by those who are professionally best able to judge them. This is compounded by the fact that an institution has already been created around these principles. Thus, not only GMAG and its licensing activity, but also its sub-committees on safe vectors and the risks of scale-up, are based upon the belief that current procedures are adequate for the assessment of risk. Interestingly, the deliberations of the safe vectors sub-committee have already called into question one of the main principles of categorisation, that in higher organisms 'hazards are related to the closeness of the evolutionary relationship between the organisms constituting the source of the excised nucleic acid and the organisms at risk.'[44]

We have to face, therefore, the problem of assessing risk assessment in this area. This implies an urgent need for independent scrutiny of the assumptions and procedures used in classifying hazards, by an informed group separate from the regulatory agencies, or at least independent of GMAG. This may be difficult to arrange given the dispersion of risk assessment studies — in so far as they yet constitute a unified body of knowledge — amongst various professional groups. This might even be an advantage however, if the practical problems of creating a technical debate could be solved, just because of the disparate approaches to the problem of defining socially acceptable risks of fundamental and applied recombinant genetics that could be brought together. In particular, there is an urgent need for comparative studies of, say, the handling of laboratory pathogens, enzyme engineering, vaccine production, plant virus research and the use of antibiotics in agricultural production, as part of a strategic programme for policy-related risk assessment. It is therefore, rather disturbing that GMAG has shown some indication of having put these questions a long way down its list of priorities, and that no agency in this area has done very much to promote the discussion of risks. A very serious danger is that much of this analysis of hazards, and the quantitative data relevant to it, will be confined within government agencies and not tested in professional or public debate.

Elements of a Technology Policy for Recombinant Genetics

Some sort of policy framework is needed for the development and application of these new techniques. Clearly by establishing regulatory systems of particular types, funding policy-oriented research or not doing so, and by providing support for fundamental studies and development work, governments have committed themselves to specific policies in this area. Thus for example, the failure of the American regulatory agencies and legislature to produce a system for the effective regulation of industry, although massive investment in recombinant DNA work is now going on, is effectively a policy decision.

In this section, I want to present four principles that, in my view, should inform the creation of a technology policy for recombinant genetics; they are flexible regulations, compatibility of promotion and control, social utility and public discussion (chapter 11). Clearly, the scientific basis on which judgements are made about hazards and benefits is going to change continually. Any system of controls should therefore be institutionally and legally flexible, so that new powers are readily available, as the object of regulation changes. The question should be asked at each stage, 'Are there types of research, development or production — and by extension, any related hazards — with which the regulatory system cannot cope?' Currently, this seems to mean that risks have to be reduced to the accepted levels in any biology laboratory, although this is not an ideal criterion. Looking to the future, there are already serious problems in view: (1) controlling use of the *products* of recombinant DNA research;[45] (2) the use of much less feeble micro-organisms in industrial production on a very large scale; and (3) international parity of standards and regulatory co-ordination. This prospect is not an argument for relaxing controls; rather it highlights the need for international liaison and more policy-oriented research on hazards.

In addition to flexibility and international coverage, it is clearly desirable that policies for promotion and control should be consistent. For it makes little sense to create the economic conditions under which very powerful producers, like multinational corporations, are given special encouragement to exploit recombinant genetics, if that enhanced power will be used when necessary to evade the legal controls.

There are five main ways in which gene-splicing is being developed industrially. First, leading molecular biologists are being retained as consultants to industrial corporations. Second, there is joint university-industry collaboration, which could become a powerful influence on university biological research;[46] for example, a Department of Applied Molecular Biology is being planned at the University of Manchester Institute of Science and Technology with this in mind.[47] The third possibility is of intramural research by large corporations, such as that by ICI in Britain and General Electric in America. Fourth, there are small, highly-specialised, research-based companies, close to, but formally separate from, university departments, such as GenenTech Inc. in America, which is already manufacturing somatostatin using bacteria.[48] Conventionally, these companies rely on the entrepreneurial skill of their proprietors to exploit a small number of daring innovations. There is no reason however, why they should not serve as the model for community-based, self-managed co-operatives, producing biological or medical goods for markets ignored by the large corporations. Fifth, large state-supported research institutes might supplement their income by the licence fees on patented research.[49]

Much more thought is needed on the question of which forms of economic and industrial organisation will lead to socially useful products and reasonably safe production. For health and safety at work is best ensured by a unionised work force that can rely on the support of a powerful external agency and legal controls over hazards. This is more common in large-scale private industry than in small concerns and state research institutes, where experience of safety bargaining is less developed and the conflict of interests between employers and employees less obvious. Yet to assert the primacy of real social utility over profit, it is probably easier to rely on smaller-scale, more flexible, research-intensive concerns linked to state-supported institutes.

I want to discuss the third element of my policy framework, social utility and economic power, using the often-mentioned example of applying recombinant genetics to antibiotic production. The manufacture and sale of pharmaceuticals is currently dominated by a relatively small number of multinational companies, which rely on large sales to recoup their development costs, but which have considerable control over pricing because of the market structure for specific drugs.[50] This has several consequences. First, there is a relative neglect of uncommon medical conditions; second, drug companies resist systematic assessment of their products, since they are sold by their appeal rather than their efficacy; third, products thought to be dangerous may continue to be sold, since a large outlay has to be recouped. Fourth, the industry argues strenuously for continuing autonomy, high profits and private ownership, on grounds of efficiency and innovative ability. Finally, it does a great deal to promote the continuing importance of drugs in modern medicine, in the face of over-prescribing and dependence.

Now recombinant genetics may offer one way of reducing the manufacturing costs of drugs, but this is only one factor in drug pricing, and the putative economic benefits may not be passed on to the consumer, since price competition is often very attenuated. Equally, these new techniques may indeed confer economic advantages on any producer with the resources to exploit them. It might also be that it rapidly became very expensive to acquire this new expertise in production, so that the structure of markets would shift even further towards monopoly, with unfortunate consequences for the consumer. These are only speculations, but they demonstrate that cheaper drugs are by no means guaranteed by recombinant genetics, and that much more discussion is needed.

From this 'illustration' follows the fourth element of the policy framework, which is that these issues are so complex and so important that they require the fullest public discussion. This, in my view, should be an active principle of governmental policy, which is to say that the agencies responsible for the regulation of recombinant genetics should be required to make explicit and to submit to public scrutiny the bases and assumptions of their policy deliberations, and to initiate and support public debate about them.

Institutions for the Assessment of Regulatory Policy

Behind much of the foregoing analysis lies the tacit suggestion of the need for continuing, critical scrutiny of the ways of assessing socially acceptable risks and suggested benefits, by an independent body, outside the regulatory system and, particularly within Britain, outside central government. The problem is to see how this might be done, by a group or institution, with some formal status and some power. Clearly such critiques of existing policy and practice have to be technically informed, but not exclusively technical. The points at issue will concern the significance of particular sets of data, within the prevailing structures of economic and political power, and any group with this role must be aware of and seek to describe the complex interactions between the technical potential of biology, policy judgements, economic priorities and political institutions.

At present, recombinant genetics is expanding very rapidly, and its social relations are continually changing. Any group monitoring, planning or controlling the field will certainly be forced to evolve, and must therefore, operate with a clearly defined strategy. Lord Ashby's committee neither espoused nor suggested any such plan, and it is also rather disturbing that GMAG, despite its apparently greater performance and flexibility, also seems to operate in a rather pragmatic way, in response to changing external circumstances. Certainly there is no sign of a collectively agreed strategy in its report.

None the less, GMAG is the body in Britain that has given the most careful, informed and imaginative consideration to recombinant genetics. However, many of the problems fall outside its present terms of reference, such as the control of the products of research or the technology policy issues considered above. There is possibly a place for an inter-agency commission to consider these issues, which would include representatives from GMAG, the HSE, the Research Councils, scientific interest groups, private foundations, government departments, various sectors of industry, trade unions and public interest groups.[51] It would allow the generalisation of the successful participatory form of GMAG to strategic economic and technological planning. The problem is whether such an institution could exert any power.

Amongst the bodies formally charged with the creation and co-ordination of science and technology policy in Britain, the Research Councils and their Advisory Board (*pace* Ashby) show no sign of instituting a debate or of taking the initiative in analysing the policy questions. As Grobstein has said, it is by no means clear which lines of development should be pursued, and both public and scientists have a right to know how particular goals are being selected.[52] Nor has the recently created Advisory Committee on Applied Research and Development made any statement on these issues.

In the international agencies, there has been some activity. The European Science Foundation, the Commission of the European Community, the World Health Organisation and the International Council of Scientific Unions have convened meetings about the control of hazards and the possible benefits.[53] But discussion at this level is almost certain to be sporadic, very general and only tenuously related to particular national research programmes. More intensive analysis than this is required.

As one moves away from the formal, governmental institutions for the direction of research, several other possibilities emerge. It is a remarkable illustration of the aloofness of the Royal Society, that although it has on several occasions presented its views to policy-making bodies, such as the Williams committee and the HSE, it certainly has

not done so publicly. Nor has this elite academy followed the example
of its American counterpart in organising any sort of convention, such
as the NAS Forum on Recombinant DNA Research in March 1977.[54]
At a less exalted level, the British Association for the Advancement of
Science could also have followed the example of its American
descendant in arranging workshops at its annual meetings. That it has
not done so in a period when Sir John Kendrew, one of the more
important figures in the development of biomedical research in Britain
in recent years, was president of the association, seems a remarkable
illustration of the desire of the molecular biological elite in Britain to
restrict public debate and of the sterility of 'The British Ass.'[55]

In recent years, leading British scientists have come to realise that
the social impact of science and technology are topics that cannot be
totally ignored, and as a result, in 1973, the Council for Science and
Society was established, with the support of the Royal Society, and
several reports have been produced by working parties on topics like
'risk assessment'. No doubt a few individuals could be mobilised by the
Council for an examination of recombinant genetics, but it is doubtful
whether an isolated report from such a marginal institution could have
any lasting effect.

Moving even further from the corridors of power and the
professional fora of science, one encounters the British Society for
Social Responsibility in Science, which has recently formed a Genetic
Engineering Group, along the lines of the radical groups in America,
and which can draw upon the conceptual and ideological resources of
the radical science movement of recent years. But for all its novelty and
clarity of vision, it is very unlikely that such a group could wield any
influence, unless as part of a broader coalition, which could capture
public attention.[56]

Greater public interest may be aroused in Britain by the proposed
hearings of the Parliamentary Select Committee on Science and
Technology, which are scheduled for autumn 1978. This all-party group
of MPs has a certain reputation for asking novel questions about
scientific and technological issues, largely because of its independence
from the scientific establishment and the civil service. But the strength
and independence of such a body is also its weakness, and the reports
of the Select Committee have a regrettably ephemeral character and
are seldom backed up by a subsequent return to the same issues. There
are very definite limits on the performance of such a group with no
supporting staff of researchers.

What is needed, therefore, is a more permanent institution capable of acting independently of the corporations and the state, with financial resources and access to information, and with some power. One very interesting possibility is the trade union, the Association of Scientific, Technical and Managerial Staffs (ASTMS), which is represented on GMAG. Two national conferences have already been held by it on recombinant DNA research, and another is planned for the autumn of 1978. Indeed, ASTMS has made it its business to recruit and organise precisely that sector of technical labour that is the first to be affected by recombinant DNA research, in universities and industry. Perhaps most importantly the union has a developed interest in the planning of technological development for socially useful ends, within the framework of the mixed economy.[57] A group of highly qualified research workers belonging to ASTMS in various centres of activity in Britain, working with the union research department and the central executive, could be very well placed to analyse many of the policy issues mentioned above. Such a group could have considerable influence, both in its own right and working with the trade union movement. If a parliamentary enquiry takes place, and, in the longer term, if an inter-agency commission on genetic manipulation is established, or even if the restriction of debate continues, such a group could have a significant and valuable impact on policy formation.

Notes

1. P. Berg *et al.*, 'Potential Biohazards of Recombinant DNA Molecules', *Science*, vol.185 (26 July 1974), p.303.

2. An important step in the formation of this consensus was the Workshop on Studies for Assessment of Potential Risks Associated with Recombinant DNA Experimentation, held in Falmouth, Massachusetts on 20-21 June 1977. For a report, see S. Gorbach, *Recombinant DNA Technical Bulletin*, vol.1 (1, Fall 1977), pp.19-23; for dissenting views of the meeting, see J. King and R. Goldstein, ibid., pp.24-5; B. Levin, ibid., pp.25-7.

3. For a review, see D. Kamely and R.B. Curtin, 'International Activities in Recombinant DNA Research', *Recombinant DNA Technical Bulletin*, vol.1 (1, Fall 1977), pp.28-36.

4. J. Campbell, 'All aboard the gene machine', *Evening Standard* (14 December 1977), p.10.

5. R. Dixon, 'Genetic engineering in the fields', *New Scientist*, vol.78 (8 June 1978), pp.684-7.

6. European Science Foundation, *Report 1977*, para.2, pp.10-16.

7. For differing views see N. Wade, *The Ultimate Experiment: Man-made Evolution* (New York, Walker, 1977); R. Cooke, *Improving on Nature: the Brave New World of Genetic Engineering* (New York, Quadrangle, 1977); M. Rogers, *Biohazard* (New York, Knopf, 1977); J. Goodfield, *Playing God* (London, Hutchinson, 1977).

8. For some more analytic work see S. Wright, 'A case study in the making of science policy', in R.E. Monro (ed.), *The Politics of the Life Sciences* (in press); J. Ravetz, 'Genetic manipulation as a problem in the control of environmental hazards', *International Journal of Environmental Studies* (forthcoming); J. Turney, *Recombinant DNA: Influences on Public Attitudes* (unpublished MSc thesis, University of Manchester, 1977). I am very grateful to Drs Wright and Ravetz, and Jon Turney, for helpful discussions and for bringing material to my attention. See also S. Cohen, 'The manipulation of genes', *Scientific American*, vol.233 (July 1975), pp.25-33; C. Grobstein, 'The Recombinant DNA Debate', *Scientific American*, vol.237 (July 1977), pp.22-32.

9. See T. Friedmann and R. Roblin, 'Gene Therapy for Human Genetic Disease?', *Science*, 175 (3 March 1972), pp.949-55; E. Loechler *et al.*, 'Social and political issues in genetic engineering', draft chapter of a book edited by A.M. Chakrabarty (in press), available from Science for the People, Cambridge, Mass.

10. E. Ziff, 'Benefits and hazards of manipulating DNA', *New Scientist*, vol.60 (25 October 1973), pp.274-5.

11. This is an interpretation of the speech by Sir John Kendrew to the British Association in September 1974; see Anon., 'B.A. – first the bad news', *Nature*, vol.251 (6 September 1974), p.5.

12. B. Dixon, 'Scientists back down on recombinant DNA research', *New Scientist*, vol.78 (6 April 1978), p.3.

13. This point is made by Ravetz, 'Genetic Manipulation' (see note 8); it was also made at the Asilomar conference (see text below) by Sydney Brenner of the Cambridge MRC Laboratory of Molecular Biology; see N. Wade, 'Genetics: Conference sets strict controls to replace moratorium', *Science*, 187 (14 March 1975), pp.931-4. It is open to discussion whether the regulatory system is controlled by molecular biologists or by an 'external' group or agency. In my view it is the former (see note 27).

14. B.J. Culliton, 'Recombinant DNA bills de-railed', *Science*, vol.199 (20 January 1978), pp.275-7; N. Wade, 'Congress set to grapple again with gene splicing', *Science*, vol.199 (24 March 1978), pp.1319-21; D. Dickson, 'Friends of DNA fight back', *Nature*, vol.272 (20 April 1978), p.664.

15. *Report of the Working Party on the Experimental Manipulation of the Genetic Composition of Micro-organisms* (London, HMSO, 1975; Cmnd.5880), p.iv (Ashby report).

16. Ibid.

17. Wright, 'Science policy' (see note 8); J. King, 'A science for the people', *New Scientist*, vol.74 (16 June 1977), pp.631-3.

18. Wright, 'Science policy' (see note 8); see also S. Wright, 'Doubts over genetic engineering controls', *New Scientist*, vol.72 (2 December 1976), pp.520-1.

19. D. Fishlock, 'ICI launches £40,000 project on genetic engineering', *Financial Times* (3 October 1974).

20. J. King, 'A science for the people' (see note 17).

21. M. Rogers, 'The Pandora's Box Congress', *Rolling Stone* (19 June 1975), pp.15-19, 37-8; see also Rogers, *Biohazard* (see note 7).

22. See for example the statement by P. Handler, to the Senate Hearings on Recombinant DNA, 2 November 1977, at p.21 of the typescript of his address; this is quoted in Ravetz, 'Genetic manipulation' (see note 8).

23. See Ravetz, 'Genetic manipulation', and Turney, 'Recombinant DNA' (see note 8).

24. D. Nelkin, 'Threats and Promises: Negotiating the control of Research', *Daedalus*, vol.107 (March 1978); S. Park and R. Thatcher, 'Dealing with experts: the recombinant DNA debate', *Science for the People*, vol.9 (September-October

1977), pp.28-35.

25. *Report of the Working Party on the Practice of Genetic Manipulation* (London, HMSO, 1976; Cmnd.6600), para.1.1(a), p.3. The next clause draws a connection between the Williams committee and the Working Party on the Laboratory Use of Dangerous Pathogens, the Godber committee, which was sitting at the same time, which recommended the creation of a Dangerous Pathogens Advisory Group.

26. It did not include any laboratory technicians, who are more likely to know how laboratories actually run than those who direct them. In May 1976, a porter died of typhoid at the Enteric Reference Laboratory at Colindale because no one believed he would come in contact with dangerous materials.

27. See, for example, the correspondence between M. Ashburner of Cambridge University and J. Locke of the HSE in *Nature*, vol.264 (4 November 1976), pp.2-3. It is important to note that in effect the scientific lobby won this contest, since GMAG is formally controlled by the DES, and not by the HSE.

28. E. Splicer, 'Political Biology', *The Leveller* (14 April 1978), pp.12-13.

29. J. Maddox, 'A way to safety without brakes', *Financial Times* (23 May 1978).

30. *First Report of the Genetic Manipulation Advisory Group* (London, HMSO, 1978; Cmnd.7215) (hereinafter GMAG report).

31. Ibid., p.25; see also G.S.A. Szabo, 'Patents and Recombinant DNA', *Trends in Biochemical Sciences*, vol.2 (11 November 1977), p.N246.

32. For details see GMAG report, para.9.3, p.25.

33. For details see the annual reports of the respective Councils.

34. Anon., 'Interfering with genes to make interferon', *New Scientist*, vol.76 (22-29 December 1977), p.751.

35. Splicer, 'Political Biology' (see note 28).

36. Campbell, 'Gene machine' (see note 4); Anon., 'Genetic engineering nears the factory floor', *New Scientist*, vol.76 (17 November 1977), p.432; Anon., 'Will Britain cash in?', *The Economist* (31 December 1977), pp.71-2; R. Casement, 'A new industry goes back to nature', ibid. (6 May 1978), pp.91-2; F.R. Simring, 'Technological innovation vs. environmental protection' (mimeo.); paper given at Session 2, 'Recombinant DNA, Public Health and Biomedical Research Policy', annual meeting, AAAS, Washington, 15 February 1978.

37. Berg *et al.*, 'Biohazards' (see note 1).

38. Ashby report, 'Genetic manipulation' (see note 15), para.6.4, p.13.

39. Ibid., para.6.5(d), p.14.

40. T. Vickers, 'Flexible DNA Regulation: The British Model', *Bulletin of the Atomic Scientists*, vol.34 (January 1978), pp.4-5. Dr Vickers assisted both the Ashby and Williams committees, and was until recently secretary to the GMAG.

41. Williams report (Genetic manipulation) (see note 25), paras.2.2-2.9, pp.6-8.

42. A. Mottershead *et al.*, 'Hazard Study of proposed molecular genetics research programme at the Corporate Laboratory', ICI Report No.MD 16,927 (October 1975).

43. A. Schwartz, 'Analysis of the probability estimates used in establishing the effectiveness of disarming *E. coli* by gene deletion' (mimeo.), document submitted to the Regents of the University of Michigan, 1976.

44. Dr Brenner has recently produced a 'hazards tree', organised around a canonical experiment with a high probability of serious hazards, which challenges these current assumptions.

45. For details, see GMAG report, paras. 2.11-2.13, pp.6-7. See also R. Lewin, 'Conflicts marked GMAG's first year', *New Scientist*, vol.78 (18 May 1978), p.427.

46. In Britain there are examples in this field at Imperial College, London, and Edinburgh University.

47. Minutes of the meeting of the Academic Board, University of Manchester Institute of Science and Technology (20 March 1978), p.18.

48. Anon., 'Genetic engineers plug brain gene into bacteria', *New Scientist*, vol.76 (10 November 1977), p.33.

49. Although it is a private foundation attempting to evade state support, a similar programme has been established at the Institut Pasteur in Paris; it led to severe problems: see Anon., 'Monod's answer to the Pasteur problems', *Nature*, vol.252 (8 November 1974), p.88.

50. V. Coleman, *The Medicine Men: Drug Makers, Doctors and Patients* (London, Temple Smith, 1975).

51. A similar idea is to be found in Wright, 'Science policy' (see note 8).

52. Grobstein, 'Recombinant DNA' (see note 8), p.32.

53. See Kamely, Curtin, 'Recombinant DNA Research' (see note 3).

54. H.M. Schmeck, 'Group urges new delays on gene-splicing', *New York Times* (8 March 1977), p.10.

55. Neither his speech to the British Association in 1974 (see note 11), nor his speech to the European Science Foundation in November 1977 (available from the Secretariat to the ESF) can be realistically considered contributions to a *public* debate.

56. Anon., 'Strategies for the Genetic Engineering Group', *BSSRS Internal Bulletin*, no.11 (June 1978).

57. C. Jenkins and B. Sherman, *Computers and the Unions* (London, Longmans, 1978).

13 POLITICAL FRAMEWORKS FOR THE CONTROL OF TECHNOLOGY: AN ASSESSMENT

Geoffrey Price

What is involved in existing processes of decision making for the 'control of technology'? What tacitly accepted social and political goals are involved, and how are they transmitted to the detailed operational level of technical management? Such questions are being forcefully raised in contemporary literature on the regulation of technology. Thus Wynne[1] has argued that prevailing approaches to technology assessment embody the strategies of centralising managerial elites for minimising societal hindrances to efficient technical change. Elliott and Elliott[2] have undertaken an extended analysis of differing political contexts for decision making, reviewing the expert-dominated 'technocratic' approaches, the democratic responses in theories of accountability, representation and participation, and the range of communitarian alternatives which seek full self-management of the goals of a society and the resultant patterns of technical innovation and resource-use. The value of comparative studies of this type is that they make it quite clear that differing approaches to the control of technology are themselves an expression of the basic assumptions made within different political traditions about the co-ordination of general social goals with the detailed activities needed to attain them. In short, approaches to the 'regulation of technology' are themselves particular instances of the political assumptions which articulate a given society — whether they be those of centralised planning, Burkean conservative liberalism, or radical communitarianism.

However, this insight may be reversed: in so far as social processes for the control of technology operate within the assumptions of a particular political settlement, then the strengths and weaknesses of those processes will be particular instances of the ability or failure of the society in question to achieve purposeful guidance of any of its own internal activities. Indeed, the growth of discontent over the handling of a particular technical issue frequently has the effect of reopening old debates over representation and participation in the political processes of the state. It would seem, therefore, that to understand and assess the existing range of decision-styles for the management of technology, we must enquire into the assumptions and

246 Political Frameworks for the Control of Technology

integrity of the general approaches to social and political order of which tney are a special case.

This task may be clarified by considering three contexts, of progressively widening scope, within which actions and choices may be considered.[3] The first is *regulatory*: it is the detailed level of operational action which seeks to manipulate resources and instruments in the most effective way, given a settled pattern of decisions concerning what needs to be done. In a bureaucracy, it is the level of routine procedures for papers, finance and records; in a production organisation it is systematised in the rules of operation, maintenance and accident prevention. The regulatory level acts within, and 'takes as read', a settled pattern of decisions concerning what needs to be done. This pattern constitutes the next, wider, context: that of *instrumental* choices, where strategies are set to co-ordinate a whole range of technical actions. In the factory, this is the sphere of the production planner, whether in the design of assembly lines or the design of work organisation for a particular plant; in the bureaucracy, it is the sphere of the administrator, the economist and the research manager; in education systems it is the sphere of the curriculum planner, the school architect, the headmaster or the professor. In each case, strategic planning is concerned to determine the most effective allocation of resources and the best pathways among future alternatives, in order to realise general social goals. Those general goals embody the influence of the third, *political* context, in which the overall ethical commitments of a society are made, and from which particular lines of activity are selected as fulfilling its basic intentions. This is — however occasionally — the sphere of the party-political conference, as well as that of the study of the moral philosopher, of the Cabinet committee as well as of the pulpit.

If we return to the particular problem of the 'control of technology' we may envisage a variety of ways in which, within a given society, the sense may grow that existing patterns of resource use and technical innovation do not fulfil the intentions of individuals or groups within it. Actions at the *regulatory* level may be out of order: inattention or incompetence, lack of knowledge or poor maintenance may be frustrating what is otherwise a well-designed and generally valued system of control. Strategies at the *instrumental* level may be incorrectly chosen: even though there is no lack of general agreement on the ends of society, and no lack of ability to implement them at the technical level, faults may exist in medium-range plans: the economic assessment of a particular technical innovation, or the plans for new production routines and administrative reform needed to implement it, may be mistaken or inadequate. Or it may be that choices at the *political* level are unresolved, short-circuited or ignored, so that society lacks an overall orientation for its activities and strategies, and these are increasingly experienced as purposeless and alienating. In general, then, failures in the 'control of technology' are a special case of failures in the internal co-ordination achieved by a society. By distinguishing the three contexts of regulatory, instrumental and political control, we can see that such failures may arise from breakdowns in any one of these contexts singly, or indeed from any combination of breakdown. If, as we have argued, 'technology control' activities are themselves an embodiment of the accepted decision-making and goal-setting patterns of a society, then in order to understand the strengths and weaknesses of those activities, we must ask what are the strengths and weaknesses of the socio-political process in the three contexts of *regulatory, instrumental* and *political* choice? Are any of these contexts overlooked, or tacitly merged with each other, in prevailing conceptions of the political order? If so, what are the consequences for the regulation of technology?

Within the limited scope of this review, we intend to concentrate on the area of the adequacy of choices in the *political* context within contemporary industrial societies, and in order to do so we must first enquire how far the prevailing social articulation of such societies recognises and allows for the making of such choices.

Following Wolin,[4] we may consider contemporary social thought as operating within the assumptions either of liberalism, or of the group-oriented 'organisational' and 'communitarian' paradigms whose critique of liberalism has been so widely accepted. What, first are the operative principles of liberalism? Wolin finds that central to this tradition is the view that man affirms his existence through economic activity, with the consequent tendency to treat economic phenomena as identical and coextensive with social phenomena. This tendency was greatly strengthened by the investigations of the classical economists into the causal connections between wealth, population and resources, which resulted in a body of economic knowledge coextensive with the whole of organised social life. The step of assuming that the diverse relationships and activities of a society could be summarised in a single comprehensive viewpoint through economic categories, could then be taken with apparent ease. But the result was to make the category of the economic primary, and the function of distributing goods according to some principle of justice was transferred to the market mechanism.

In consequence, what little remained of the concept of justice consisted of a Hobbesian principle of fairness. The characteristic liberal assumption was that economics provided the necessary assumptions for the handling of the common affairs of society; economic theory thus began to shoulder the burden of pronouncing on the good of the whole society.[5]

Contemporary liberal economic thought provides frequent examples of the continuing strength of this movement of thought, not least as applied to the 'control of technology' problem. The movement to assess the impact of technical change through 'social indices' seeks to include in a common accounting scheme measurements of, for example, changes in residential, educational and travel patterns, the impact of environment pollutants and the gains and losses of valued natural resources to different social groups consequent on a projected technological innovation.[6] By its very determination to leave no aspect of society activity unaccounted for in its audit, this movement embodies the primacy of economic thought discernible in liberalism. To the question, in what does the assessment and control of technology consist, it responds: in widening the scope of economic thought. But this defines the problem as lying within the second of the three circles defined above — the *instrumental* context. What then becomes of the *political* context?

Wolin's analysis makes it clear that the liberal tradition constitutes an attempt to order society with reference only to the *regulative* and *instrumental* contexts of activity. The 'common good' of liberal society is rooted solely in the desires of its members, and its economic wellbeing occurs not by actions intended to bring about a shared conception of the good of society, but by its members' success in satisfying their wants. Indeed, the sceptical element within liberalism discounted the possibility of a shared common good. Seeing no basis for a thought world common to all men, it founded an alternative world, where men, unable to communicate on the basis of a shared moral outlook, were reduced to knowing each other from externally-perceived, socially-acquired responses and values. The liberal argument against government intervention into economic activities followed directly. If no individual could truly understand another, then each was the best judge of his own interests, and no other agent could determine the best course of action to secure his happiness. Hence no governing group has any secure basis of judgement to act for the best interests of society. The 'political' is therefore reduced to that set of protective arrangements which leave men free to 'acquire what they

further want'.[7] This outlook has been succinctly translated into the
field of technology policy by John Jewkes, whose minimalist
conception of the function of government — defence, law and order,
justice, central standards, prevention of misrepresentation — is typical.
Although he is prepared to concede that governments have a function
in the field of science and technology to provide services which would
not otherwise be carried out because a market price cannot be paid
for them in the normal way, he exemplifies the liberal recourse to
private judgement by arguing that governments

> are not justified to support technology to an extent greater than
> that which would emerge through the activities of companies
> working with their own capital and operating independently or in
> collaboration with other companies here or abroad.[8]

So far is the liberal tradition from seeking to articulate society around
a rationally agreed common good, that activity within the regulative
context becomes its central preoccupation. What, asks Wolin, moves
liberal man to action, and once he is in action, provides him with an
unceasing stimulus? Given the central premiss of political economy,
that labour and production were the fundamental processes by which
society maintained its existence, liberal man was driven to unrelenting
activity by anxiety: the anxiety of needing to produce the means of
existence in the face of a hostile nature, the anxiety of possessions,
and the anxiety to meet appetites themselves instilled by society.
Liberalism effectively erected production into a way of life, on the
assumption that nature was infinitely adaptable to the satisfaction of
felt needs. But its most persistent anxiety has been, and remains, that
nature will exact a fatal toll from man in return. In the nineteenth
century Malthus forecast the determinate interaction of economic and
social laws to bring catastrophes in food supply. The 'assault on nature'
had been launched without enquiring into her capabilities; now, the
impending crisis in the means of subsistence was nature's reply to man's
presumption.[9] In the last decade, precisely this anxiety has become
focused on the whole range of 'natural resources'. Epitomised in
Meadows' *The Limits to Growth*,[10] it has made profound inroads in
the common imagination and in political rhetoric, academic disputants
notwithstanding. The structure of the dilemma remains the same
(though its scale appears increasingly apocalyptic). In the absence of
agreement in the political context concerning the *ends* of instrumental
action, that action will be centrifugal; the resulting plunder of nature

can at first be neglected, but it eventually encircles man with evidence of his own political failing.

In some senses the critique of liberalism has become a commonplace: but the dominant critique, as Wolin shows,[11] itself defines the new 'certainties' of a group-centred outlook which was widely supplanted liberalism. In that revival of the notion of social solidarity which has characterised both managerial theorists and the Marxist critique of liberal capitalism, the consensus has been that the individual's primary need is for integration with his fellows. There is a reaction against the liberal 'politics of interest' which had centred around the system of private property; human achievements are conceived as primarily collective in quality: each does not pursue his ends against another's, but finds fulfilment of his needs by co-operating in the common task. Economic rationalism is attacked in the name of social solidarity; acquisitiveness is condemned for its destructive effects on the 'traditional' moral and social bonds of communities; liberal rationalism is seen as reducing society to a mass of isolated individuals, and those individuals other than those of self-interest. Correspondingly, it is only in community with others that each individual is believed to be able to fulfil his potential. For Marx, labouring man, united with his class-fellows, has the chance to overturn the relations of production which oppress him and realise his true nature. For Saint-Simon, a whole society organised and united in the pursuit of industrial production could conquer happiness by fashioning the goods needed to fulfil its desires. It is to these ideas — at least in their Saint-Simonian managerial form — that Western industrial societies have increasingly turned in the last decade when the dysfunctions of science and technology have returned so strongly to public awareness. The influential Brooks Report, *Science, Growth and Society*, is a prime example:

> The problems faced in government decisions are characterised by increasing interconnectedness of the various sectors of policy. . . This interconnectedness. . .is incompatible with the purely vertical bureaucratic structures characteristic of most government organisations. Horizontal connections between these vertical structures at several different levels become necessary.
>
> These considerations are especially relevant for science policy for two reasons. First, science and technology are inherently future-oriented and long-range activities and they cannot respond very effectively to goals that constantly change with political fashions or with shifts in public attention. Second, long-range

planning for all the many interacting sectors of government
responsibility demands a base of knowledge and data that can be
acquired and interpreted only through science, including the social
sciences. The acquisition of this knowledge itself requires planning
beyond the time-horizons of traditional political thinking. Thus
science policy and general long-range social and economic planning
are closely bound up with each other and require the same types of
thinking and perspective. Policies for science, technology, education,
public health, economic development, social welfare and public
services must be closely co-ordinated.[12]

What is the effect of this 'organisational' outlook in so much
contemporary political life on conceptions of the 'control of
technology' problem? The problem of political order is redefined as a
problem in management: so that technocratic programmes, whether of
the benevolent, self-interested, executive or autonomous varieties as
Elliott and Elliott categorise them,[13] assume that only by conceiving
human institutions as a complex problem for rationality can solutions
be found to endemic ills. The recurrent debate concerning the
possibility that managerial groups are themselves in process of
establishing a dominant authority and a new conception of 'politics',
which has been focused successively by the work of Burnham,[14] Bell[15]
and Galbraith,[16] is couched in terms which confirm Wolin's analysis:

> During the past two centuries the vision of political theory has been
> a disintegrating one, consistently working to destroy the idea that
> society ought properly to be considered as a whole, and that its
> general life was best expressed through political forms. One result
> of this kind of theorising has been to flatten the traditional *majestas*
> of the political order. This has been achieved by reducing the
> political association to the level of other associations, at the same
> time that the latter have been elevated to the level of the political
> order and endowed with many of its characteristics and values.[17]

The very notion that the 'government of men' could be replaced by a
scientific view of society enabling it to be treated as an administrative
problem in correct manipulation, so characteristic of the technocratic
outlook, is not only an eclipse of the political, it is blind to the
possibility that a political context for human decisions may even exist.

Reality is conceived as *socioeconomic* in nature, and so social as well
as material technologies are sought to order it. It is not necessary to

belittle the enormous technical advances that have been made at the
analytical level of operations research, planning programming and
budgeting, or general systems analysis, in order to argue that the
context within which they conceive the problems both of the planning
and the control of technology is one that neglects the possibility of a
political context for affirming the central intentions of activity. Indeed,
the emergency development of the foundations of such techniques in
the exigencies of the last war, from which scientists gained so much
prestige, has probably itself contributed to a further collapse of residual
notions of the 'political'. That war was fought against the military
might which was the effect of a formal rationality in the service of a
pathological *ressentiment.* Lamb quotes Weisskopf:[18]

> If formal, maximising rationality is 'good' regardless of its context,
> and if rationality exhausts itself in the efficient pursuit of any goal
> regardless of its origin and content, there is no principle from which
> one could deduce the duty to examine the goal itself.

in order to make a judgement which, though harsh, may grasp the
significance of the rise of managerialism in postwar politics:[19]

> Unfortunately neither governments nor scientists nor business
> learned their lesson from the war. In the very act of gearing
> productivity to defeat the horrendous symptoms of formalised
> technocratic rationality in Nazism, they became all the more
> infected with the disease itself.[20]

Again, there is a limited sense in which the critique of technocratic
programmes is a commonplace. Indeed, at first sight it would appear
that the differing contemporary movements for the 'social' control of
technology constitute an attempt to reassert a *political* context for
decisions against their reduction to a managerial problem. The different
degrees of diffusion of choice and influence implied in theories of
accountability, representation and participation, embodied in
movements for consumer or trade union influence in technical decision
making, appear to seek a measure of common agreement on the purpose
to which technical actions and plans can be directed. But what are the
aims of such movements? Elliott and Elliott are not atypical when they
speak in terms of 'enlarging the democratic and self-determining powers
of the individual or group', and of a need for 'organisation which will
positively *emphasise* the values, goals and priorities of under-represented

sections of society'.[21]

The implied expectation, which has the best of intentions, is that a devolution of power to under-represented groups will bring about a more adequate pattern of determining choices of technology. But this expectation depends on a belief that those groups are themselves capable of self-actualisation. Thus the notion of supporting local citizen, trade union, residential or educational groups to present their own assessment of technology assumes that such groups can act as forms of political association in their own right. On this basis, the problem of the control of technology becomes a problem in ensuring adequate access of the whole spectrum of communities and individuals affected by a decision to the debate preceding it, and seeking their agreement on a compromise between their interests. But to think in these terms only brings to the fore the tendency which Wolin identifies as the apparent elevation of non-political forms of association to the level of the political order. By contrast, Western political thought has (Wolin reminds us) identified the political with what is *general* to a society; the status of 'citizen' has been conceived in terms of a role which defined the individual's duties and expectations in matters of general concern. The characteristic that makes responsibility political is then its *general* quality, deriving from commitments.[22] By contrast, the contemporary versions of the social control of technology which Elliott and Elliott review, do not depend on such a shared constitutive framework. In their preoccupation with maintaining *access* to decision making, they leave aside the possibility that the political process it constitutes will degenerate to power bargaining among articulate and powerful groups in the absence of a 'political' order which symbolises and constitutes the ends of social activity. Indeed, the effect of such assumptions that, in their fragmented capacities as members of residential, occupational, resource-utilising, travelling or other groups, men can adequately participate in the 'social control of technology', is to reinforce

> a picture of society as a series of tight little islands, each evolving towards political self-sufficiency, each striving to absorb the individual members, each without any natural affiliation with a more comprehensive unity. . .Thus the contemporary vision of the social universe is one where political society, in its *general* sense, has disappeared.[23]

The notion of the 'social control' of technology is thus itself representative of a widespread reaction against the general nature of

political theory, and along with this, against the claims of the political
to a scope as wide as society itself. The 'communitarian' and 'self-
management' alternatives which Elliott and Elliott review are still
more radical steps along this road. Perhaps their ultimate hopes can be
summed up as repetitions of the demand implicit in Rousseau, that
'society' should provide

> something more than the conditions for a moral life, more than the
> opportunity for self-development, more than material necessities.
> The community must be designed to satisfy man's feelings, to fulfil
> his emotional needs.[24]

The idealisation of small community life, of economic organisation
independent of private or state monopolies in which face-to-face human
relationships can be valued and experienced, of the possibility of
harmony between man and nature, which recurs so frequently in the
contemporary alternative technology movement, suggests that
Rousseau's conception is indeed 'a spectre haunting the age of large
organisation, a continuing critic of the sort of life lived within
large-scale depersonalised units'.[25] It may be as unlikely that such ideals
will have any marked effect on the economic organisation of Western
society as it is the equivalent critique at the detailed level of work
organisation will go any further than softening the edges of worker
alienation. What is significant is the evident attachment to the
continuing ideal in the pursuit of communitarian solutions to the
problem of the 'control of technology'.

The 'revival of solidarity' whose outworkings we have considered,
leads therefore not so much to neglect of the *political* context as we
defined it earlier, as to its misunderstanding. Classically, a lesser
group – family, trade association, town – was understood as serving
only a limited end, which could therefore justify only a partial loyalty.
The truly political aspect of man was revealed only in the general
public arena whose invention marks the achievement of the Greek
city-state. Into it, men entered, leaving aside the 'household' and 'group'
management problems or 'economy' of their private associations, in
order to debate the issues concerning the good of all. Only to the
general community, for which men made such decisions, did they owe
their full allegiance.[26]

It will be apparent that the present reviewer judges that the
predominant contemporary approaches to the 'control of technology'
are flawed by – in the liberal tradition, a turning away from, in the

'organisational' tradition a false sublimation of – this central *political* experience, capacity and responsibility of determining the best attainable good of the community. Given the experiences of the present century, it is well, however, to be doubly cautious concerning the possibilities of 'reinstating' the sphere of the political. The political theories both of liberalism and of revived social solidarism have embodied defences against autocratic state power. Liberal political theories have bent much ingenuity to devices of constitutional checks and balances, while the 'organisationalists' have agreed that the isolation of the individual was the root cause of statism, and that only by re-encircling him with self-sufficient autonomy associations could he be protected from unbridled central power.[27] A perspective such as the present one, which assigns only a derivative role to such associations, may arouse understandable anxieties that it will remove well-established defences against statism. A still more salutary objection can be made,[28] that the attempt to revitalise the political dimension of existence may open the way to totalitarian theories of the community. There can be no doubt that the mass totalitarian movements of the present century achieved their success by filling the vacuum left by the decline of the 'political' with a substitute sense of order, shared status and commitment. It does not thereby follow that those movements embodied the concept of man as open to the sphere of the general good; indeed, substantial arguments can be presented that they represented a still more extreme step *away* from the classic conception of man as a 'political animal'.[29] Nevertheless, the very ability of such movements to exploit felt absences of a shared identity or purpose is a warning when we come to assess any movement for reintegration.

Although the present essay ultimately ascribes the failure of contemporary decision making about technology to the absence of a 'political' context, it must be said that a recovery from this situation cannot but be prolonged. Wolin's prescription is that

> efforts must be made to restore the political art as that art which strives for an integrative form of direction, one that is broader than that supplied by any group of organisation. It means finally that political theory must once again be viewed as that form of knowledge which deals with what is general and integrative to men, a life of common involvements.[30]

But it is precisely such integrative forms of knowledge which demand so much time and application – by individuals in their reflection on

social and moral experience, through educational institutions in
reflection on history, politics and language, and in the diverse
experiences of community and national life — before they can be
handled. Those who are pessimistic about the capacity of modern
societies to sustain a sense of internal direction under the conditions
of industrialism, have often focused their concern at precisely this
point. D.H. Lawrence, despairing over the dismal scene of a coal town
and the mechanical character of its children's education, wrote

> What could possibly become of such people; a people in whom the
> living, intuitive faculty was dead as nails, and only queer mechanical
> yells and uncanny will-power remained?[31]

Similarly, Hannah Arendt believes that to be immersed in the process
of labouring to sustain existence, and/or in the process of consuming
the fruits of that labour is to be in oblivion: to be a nobody. For we
are then confined in the circle of our own needs and wants, and have
missed the possibility of attaining that freedom which for Arendt is the
mark of human stature.[32] Plainly, if human experience *is* contracted to
these dimensions, then the corresponding symbolisation of that
experience in political frameworks will be diminished to the regulatory
and instrumental contexts. Again the pessimists remind us that such
'contracted' political systems will build up their own hegemony, and in
the process allow or require human education to be permanently
narrowed.[33] If then there is to be a renewal of meaning in the 'political'
context, a capacity of human beings to develop and assert their freedom
in relation to the control of technology or any other instrumental
activity, then the crucial issues lie in the restriction or expansion of
each individual's horizons. As Sebba says:

> This is today's battlefield. On the one hand, technocracy *must*
> restrict reality to the order in which human action is effective. On
> the other hand, the full dimension of reality in all its reaches *must*
> be understood if we are to find our own answer to the inescapable
> questions which confront a being endowed with consciousness. And
> this answer must be rational, scientific, in the Greek sense.[34]

Can this 'drive to understand' the successive realm of human meaning
be the anchor-point for a constructive approach to the problems of the
'control of technology'? Can we attempt to provide, in the educational
experience of the individual, opportunities for strengthening a grasp on

a sense of the ethical? — for allowing reflection to develop on the meaning of responsible action?

Developmental approaches to the growth of moral judgement have drawn attention to the existence of discontinuous but genetically-related stages in the process, and have thereby highlighted both the possibilities for maturation and for its avoidance. Thus Kohlberg, adopting a Piagetian approach, has presented people with hypothetical moral dilemmas and then sought to analyse the types of reasoning they use to reach conclusions.[35] He claims evidence for a sequence of development in general forms of moral reasoning, falling into three levels, each with subdivisions. Briefly, Level I is described as *premoral or preconventional* — the individual is concerned only for concrete consequences for the self, and responds to cultural rules and values only on those terms. Level II is that of conventional role — conformity — the individual is concerned to preserve the expectations others make of him or herself: the views of family, group or nation are valued irrespective of immediate consequences to self. At Level III we may pay fuller attention to the subdivisions of Kohlberg's scheme. This is the *post-conventional, autonomous or principled* level. Here there is a definite attempt to define moral principles or values which are valid independent of authority or group expectations. The first stage consists of a morality which recognises the relativism of personal values, and lays corresponding emphasis on procedures for reaching consensus and for changing laws on the basis of rational considerations. In the most mature, final stages of moral development, Kohlberg speaks of a universal ethical-principle orientation where right is held to be defined by conscience, appealing to conclusions which are comprehensive, universal and self-consistent. Kohlberg argues that this sequence of levels is cumulative, so that at each new stage the individual incorporates the principles of earlier ones but achieves a higher viewpoint from which to address problem situations unresolved or even unrecognised by lower stages. On the other hand, while one is 'confined' at a particular stage, one operates with a conception of 'justice' — a 'justice structure' as Kohlberg puts it — which organises recurrent patterns of role-taking in moral conflict situations.

Here we have a systematic attempt to understand patterns of moral responses. Now the argument of this paper has sought to draw out the parallels between the failure of the 'control of technology' debates to grasp the *political* context for symbolising and understanding the problem, and the contraction or restriction of the individual's range of political and ethical reflection. Under what circumstances then may individuals achieve a fuller maturity of judgement — in Kohlberg's terms, make a stage-transition between 'justice-structures'? We may ask this question not with manipulative or even indoctrinating intentions, but rather in order to understand the circumstances under which the individual may grasp the possibility of a more comprehensive and authentic approach to ethical decisions. In his account of maturation, Kohlberg, like Piaget, places central emphasis on the individual's active interaction with his or her environment, in which he or she can apply and check the use of various schemes of action and representation rather than just passively accepting 'given' definitions of the social world. This process throws up discrepancies between expectations and results, which in turn lead to attempts at cognitive reconciliation.

This account is necessarily brief, but it serves to bring us to the point of recognising that an educational- (or indeed, life-) experience which offers the opportunity of individual maturation, will be one which includes socio-moral conflicts in role-playing (or real-life) situations whose meaning can only be integrated by 'justice structures' at or above a person's own level. Plainly, there are many different responses: the individual may temporise, hesitating to accept the implications of a possible new viewpoint; he or she may return to a previously held, simpler position.[36] At all costs, the analysis and observation of individual maturation must not be allowed to degenerate into attempts at forced development that obscure or deny just that integrity in the student whose development the process seeks to facilitate. Nevertheless, there are challenging possibilities which do not appear to have been considered in the special field of the human control of technology with which we are concerned. Ethical conflicts in the application of science and technology, both historical and current, frequently provide situations to which responses in premoral (Level I), relational (Level II) or reflective (Level III) responses are possible: one only has to recall the examples of the medical prolongation of life, of semi-artificial reproduction, of vaccination campaigns, of research in scientific subjects with sensitive military, forensic or commercial implications, of the relations of science to industrial productivity as they bear upon labour relations. If the experience of higher education at least, included for students of *all* disciplines, the opportunity for role-playing, debate-, seminar-, and study-programme-encounter with moral dilemmas which included some examples drawn from the problems of the control of science and technology, then situations could arise in which the individual could grasp the possibility of a range of responses wider than in his or her current 'justice structure'. In relation to the scale of

national effort in the field of developing cognitive capacities for the
manipulation of science and technology, the attention given to the
'hidden curriculum' in which moral and political patterns of behaviour,
and technology, is at precisely that low level that one would expect on
the earlier argument that identified the absence of political context for
the 'control of technology' problem.[37]

These suggestions could readily, and understandably, be mistaken
for a call for a reimposition of a classical moralistic framework within
which the control of science and technology might take its due place.
Ethics itself has so often been confined in a regulatory horizon that
such suspicions arise readily. The context in which these proposals are
made is, however, that of the historical ambiguity which will always
pervade the problem of the 'control of technology'. The education of
the individual will always be a search for meaning in the context of the
issues of the day, and meaning will always have to be translated into
working axioms for everyday situations. The possibility of grasping
meaning will always threaten to slip away, and the fragile achievements
of values, pruposes and understanding in our use of technical artefacts
will all too readily collapse.[38] Equally, as a community, we are situated
in ambiguous historical circumstances – yet, as Gibson Winter writes:

> The solution to historical ambiguity is risk, commitment, and
> answerability. This is what history is about; it is what man is about
> in making history. When we develop the notion of the responsible
> society, we are addressing ourselves to this human search for
> temporal integrity in which the past becomes the material for
> fashioning a future through human decision.[39]

This 'search for temporal integrity' is, I suggest, the historical
significance of debates over the 'control of technology', and is the
proper concern of politics. And if we believe that the best defence of
freedom is in the hearts of free men, then our concern for the problem
of technology will merge with our concern for the capacity of
individuals to understand and act on historical realms of meaning; for
as Winter says:

> Man is lured constantly beyond the versions of justice, order and
> harmony which he has achieved: he presses constantly towards more
> ultimate and inclusive horizons of meaning; in coming to terms with
> his future and the problem of fulfilment or defeat, he wrestles with
> ultimacy from first to last, and the more so as he becomes immersed

260   *Political Frameworks for the Control of Technology*

in his historicity.[40]

Notes

1. Brian Wynne, 'The Rhetoric of Consensus Politics: A Critical Review of Technology Assessment', *Research Policy*, vol.4 (1975), pp.108-58.
2. David A. Elliott and Ruth H. Elliott, *The Control of Technology* (London, Wykeham Publications, 1976).
3. These 'contexts' are suggested by the work of Sir Geoffrey Vickers: see his *Freedom in a Rocking Boat* (Harmondsworth, Penguin, 1972) and *Value Systems and Social Process* (London, Tavistock, 1968).
4. Sheldon S. Wolin, *Politics and Vision: Continuity and Innovation in Western Political Thought* (London, Allen and Unwin, 1961), chs.9 and 10.
5. Wolin. *Politics and Vision*, pp.300-1.
6. Elliott and Elliott, *Control of Technology*, pp.154-8.
7. Wolin, *Politics and Vision*, pp.331-4, 338-41.
8. John Jewkes, *Government and High Technology* (London, Institute of Economic Affairs, Occasional Paper 37, 1972), p.14.
9. Wolin, *Politics and Vision*, pp.314-21.
10. Dennis L. Meadows, *The Limits to Growth* (London, Earth Island, 1972).
11. Wolin, *Politics and Vision*, pp.1353-68.
12. OECD: Secretary-General's Ad Hoc Group on New Concepts of Science Policy, *Science, Growth and Society* (Brussels, OECD, 1971).
13. Elliott and Elliott, *Control of Technology*, pp.51-101.
14. James Burnham, *The Managerial Revolution* (London, Putnam, 1942).
15. Daniel T. Bell, *The Coming of Post-Industrial Society* (New York, Basic Books, 1975).
16. John K. Galbraith, *The New Industrial State* (London, Hamish Hamilton, 1968).
17. Wolin, *Politics and Vision*, pp.430-1.
18. Victor L. Weisskopf, *Alienation and Economics* (New York, Dutton, 1971), p.81.
19. See, for example, Norman J. Vig, *Science and Technology in British Politics* (London, Pergamon, 1969).
20. Matthew L. Lamb, 'The Production Process and Economic Growth', mimeo, Marquette University, Wisconsin, 1976, p.35.
21. Elliott and Elliott, *Control of Technology*, pp.139-51.
22. Wolin, *Politics and Vision*, p.429.
23. Ibid., p.432.
24. Ibid., p.371.
25. Ibid., p.325.
26. Hannah Arendt, *The Human Condition* (Chicago, University of Chicago Press, 1958).
27. Wolin, *Politics and Vision*, p.417.
28. Compare Wolin, ibid., pp.433-4.
29. Eric Voegelin, *The New Science of Politics* (Chicago, Chicago University Press, 1960).
30. Wolin, *Politics and Vision*, p.434.
31. D.H. Lawrence, *Lady Chatterley's Lover*, quoted in F.R. Leavis, *The Living Principle* (London, Chatto and Windus, 1975).
32. Margaret Canovan, *The Political Thought of Hannah Arendt* (New York and London, Harcourt Brace and Jovanovich, 1974).

33. See, for example, Herbert Marcuse, *One Dimensional Man: Studies in the Ideology of Advanced Industrial Society* (London, Routledge and Kegan Paul, 1968). For a review of the pessimistic and optimistic positions, see Roger Williams, *Politics and Technology* (London, Macmillan, 1971).

34. Gregor Sebba, 'Prelude and Variations on the Theme of Eric Voegelin', *Southern Review* (Louisiana), vol.13 (1977), p.657.

35. The following account draws on Peter Tomlinson, 'Perspectives from Academic Psychology', in Kenneth G. Collier, John B. Wilson and Peter D. Tomlinson (eds), *Values and Moral Development in Higher Education* (London, Croom Helm, 1974). For an account of Kohlberg and Piaget and for primary references see Ronald Duska and Mariellen Whelan, *Moral Development: A Guide to Piaget and Kohlberg* (Dublin, Gill and Macmillan, 1977).

36. William G. Perry Jr., *Forms of Intellectual and Ethical Development in the College Years: A Scheme* (New York, Holt, Rinehart and Winston, 1968).

37. For an educational perspective see Philip H. Phenix, *Realms of Meaning* (New York and London, McGraw-Hill, 1964).

38. Ibid.

39. Gibson Winter, *Elements for a Social Ethic: Scientific and Ethical Perspectives on Social Process* (London, Collier Macmillan, 1966), p.257.

40. Ibid., p.256.

CONTRIBUTORS

Ian Chapman, Associate Professor of Chemistry, Trent University, Peterborough, Ontario.

Dave Eva, Tutor, Workers' Education Association, Wirral, Cheshire.

Michael Gibbons, Professor of Liberal Studies in Science, University of Manchester.

Brendan Gillespie, Research Fellow, Program on Science, Technology and Society, Cornell University.

Philip Gummett, Lecturer, Liberal Studies in Science, University of Manchester.

John Hartland, Deputy Secretary, Committee on Science and Technology, Parliamentary Assembly of the Council of Europe.

Ron Johnston, Senior Lecturer, Liberal Studies in Science, University of Manchester.

Keith Pavitt, Senior Fellow, Science Policy Research Unit, University of Sussex.

Geoffrey Price, Lecturer, Liberal Studies in Science, University of Manchester.

Judith Reppy, Senior Fellow, Center for International Studies, Cornell University.

Harry Rothman, Lecturer, Liberal Studies in Science, University of Manchester.

Peter Stubbs, Senior Lecturer in Economics, University of Manchester.

Roger Williams, Professor of Government and Science Policy, University of Manchester.

Edward Yoxen, Lecturer, Liberal Studies in Science, University of Manchester.

INDEX

Adams, B. 149, 150, 155
Adelman, L. 173
Agricultural Chemicals Approval
    Scheme (UK) 208, 210, 211
Agricultural Development Advisory
    Service (UK) 210, 212
Agricultural Research Council (UK)
    228, 232
Agriculture, Department of (USA)
    169
Agriculture, Fisheries and Food,
    Ministry of (UK) 85, 204, 206,
    210-12, 216
Agriculture (Poisonous Substances)
    Act (UK) 208
AIF (Germany) 29
Air Quality Act (USA) 144
Air Registration Board (UK) 92,
    94, 103, 104
Alkali Inspectorate (UK) 135, 172,
    215
Allardice, C. 74
Anticipatory Control 16, 164
ANVAR (France) 30
Applied Research and Development,
    Advisory Council for (UK) 239
Arendt, H. 256, 260
Ash Report 142
Ashby Committee 228-9, 234, 239
Ashby, Lord 228
Ashburner, M. 243
Asilomar Conference 229
ASTMS 241
Atomic Energy Authority (UK)
    see UKAEA
Atomic Energy of Canada Ltd
    43, 44, 55
Atomic Energy Commission (USA)
    13, 60, 77, 78
Aucoin, P. 57
Auerbach, L.E. 186, 187, 190
Automotive Engineers, Society
    of 147
Auto Pact (USA-Canada) 46-7
Auto Pilot (SEP 2) 99
Aviation, Ministry of, (UK) 80
Avro Arrow 53

Baier, K.E.M. 107
Baker, M. 131
Barker, A. 88
Bartocha, B. 190
barriers, to new entry into
    industry, 116, 130
Bartlett, D. 172
Bates, J.A.R. 222
Beck, E.C. 154
Beckler, D. 197-8
Beechams Ltd 233
Belfast Strategic Freighter 97,
    101, 103, 104, 105, 106
Bell, D. 251, 260
Bendix Corporation 98, 99, 100
Benn, Rt Hon. Anthony Wedgwood
    89
Benstock, Y. 172
Berg, P. 226, 227, 234, 241
Bernstein, M. 154
Bingham, D.A. 224
Blackett, Lord Patrick 81, 87, 89
Blind Landing Experimental Unit
    (UK) 101, 102, 103, 106
Blodgett, J. 223
Blood, F.R. 171
Bly, P.H. 131
Board of Trade (UK) 92, 94, 102
Boeing Corporation 100
Boulding, K. 92, 107
Boulloche, R. 201
Bowers, R. 184, 190
Boxall, D.G. 57
branch plant 43, 45, 55
Brenner, S. 230, 242
British Agrochemicals Association,
    211-12, 213, 223
British Association for the
    Advancement of Science 240
British European Airways 93, 96,
    97, 102, 103, 104
British Leyland 112, 123, 125,
    127, 129
British Overseas Airways Corporation
    100, 106
British Petroleum 233
British Research and Development

263

Edmonds, M. 88
education, moral 257-9; political 258-9
Education and Science, Department of (UK) 231
effluent tax 139
Egler, F. 158, 159, 172
Electricity Council (UK) 128
Elliott Automation 97, 98, 99, 100, 106
Elliott, D. and Elliott, R. 10, 17, 245, 251-4, 260
Employment, Department of (UK) 13
energy 24, 34, 36-7, 71, 72, 73
Energy, Department of (UK) 13
Energy Policy and Conservation Act (USA) 144, 149
Energy Research and Development Agency (USA) 13, 72
enforcement of regulations 165
engineers, status of 28
Enloe, C.H. 154, 217, 221
Enterprise Development Programme (Canada) 51, 56
Environment, Department of the (UK) 13, 85
environment, standards for protection of 163
Environmental Defense Fund (USA) 158
Environmental Impact Statement 164-5
Environmental Pollution, Royal Commission on, (UK) 75, 216, 221
Environmental Protection Act (Sweden) 162, 163, 164
Environmental Protection Agency (USA) 144, 145, 151, 164, 169
Environmental Protection Board (Sweden) 163
environmentalism 158-60
Enzer, S. 190
Eposito, J. 172
Epstein, S.S. 172, 223
Erskine, H. 172
Etzioni, A. 182, 183, 186, 190
Euratom 33, 40
European Air-Bus 103
European Economic Community 27, 38, 166, 198; Commission of 239

European Molecular Biology Organisation 226, 239
European Parliament 198
European Science Foundation 226, 239
Europe, Council of, Parliamentary Assembly's Committee on Science and Technology 199; Parliamentary Hearings, Exercise in Scientific Co-operation 192, 198-201; future of 38
'Europe plus Thirty' project 198
Eva, D. 224
Evans, W.G. 107

fast reactor 24, 37, 39, 61, 73, 200
Feckhauser, R. 153
Federal Aviation Administration (USA) 144
Federal Communications Commission (USA) 135
Federal Highway Administrator (USA) 144
Federal Water Pollution Control Act (USA) 144; Administration 144
federalism by contract 77
Fels, G. 39
Fiat Company 112
Fisher, A.C. 153
Fishlock, D. 242
Food and Agriculture Organisation (UN) 166
Food and Drug Administration (USA) 141, 143
Ford, President G. 143, 145, 154
Ford, H. 114
Ford Motor Company 112, 119, 120, 128, 145
Forrest, J.S. 75
Fox, Mr Justice Russell 75
Frankel, M. 172
Freedom of Information Act (USA) 167, 168, 170, 215
Freeman, C. 12, 17, 39, 57, 78, 88, 119, 120, 131, 174
French, R. 57
Friedmann, T. 242
Friends of the Earth, 65, 159
Frey, J. 190
fuel reprocessing 62

JUL 1 6 1980